BUSH WIVES AND GIRL SOLDIERS

Bush Wives and Girl Soldiers

*Women's Lives through War and Peace
in Sierra Leone*

Chris Coulter

Cornell University Press
Ithaca and London

First published 2009 by Cornell University Press
First printing, Cornell Paperbacks, 2009
Printed in the United States of America

Library of Congress Cataloging-in-Publication Data
Coulter, Chris, 1969–
    Bush wives and girl soldiers : women's lives through war and peace in Sierra Leone / Chris Coulter.
        p. cm.
    Includes bibliographical references and index.
    ISBN 978-0-8014-4782-2 (cloth : alk. paper) — ISBN 978-0-8014-7512-2 (pbk. : alk. paper)
    1. Sierra Leone—History—Civil War, 1991–2002—Women.
    2. Sierra Leone—History—Civil War, 1991–2002—Participation, Female.   3. Women and war—Sierra Leone.   4. Women—Crimes against—Sierra Leone.   5. Rural women—Sierra Leone—Social conditions.   I. Title.
    DT516.826.C68 2009
    966.404—dc22   2009010909

Cornell University Press strives to use environmentally responsible suppliers and materials to the fullest extent possible in the publishing of its books. Such materials include vegetable-based, low-VOC inks and acid-free papers that are recycled, totally chlorine-free, or partly composed of nonwood fibers. For further information, visit our website at www.cornellpress.cornell.edu.

Cloth printing   10   9   8   7   6   5   4   3   2   1
Paperback printing   10   9   8   7   6   5   4   3   2   1

To Stella Loyce, Martha Brae, and Mary

Contents

Acknowledgments

A work of anthropology is not only the result of a process of reading, thinking, and writing, but as much, if not more, of being in "the field." Leaving my home to live in rural Sierra Leone with two young children could have entailed some practical difficulties had it not been for the enormous help and assistance of many kind and generous people. The people in Koinadugu District made me a welcome "stranger" to their lives and I thank them all, especially Joseph, Kumba, Theresa, Paul and Mary Kortenhoven, and Pa Morowa and his family. Although I am not at liberty to share their names, all the women, and the few men, with whom I worked in Sierra Leone made this research possible through the trust they granted me by sharing some of the worst experiences of their lives, sometimes at great emotional cost. When they asked me how my research would help them, I always answered that I did not know, but that I hoped that by talking to me I could share with my readers their strength and resilience in the face of hardship. This work would have been inconceivable without the tireless and unwavering support of my research assistant/interpreter Mary

Korsarow Jalloh Kowa. In Freetown we were always welcomed to rest and reconvene at the house of our dear friends the Kabba family. We cannot thank them enough for their great hospitality, for the love they showed us and in particular our children. It was in the Kabba household I learnt *Krio,—una tenki!* Other invaluable friendships in Freetown include O'Bai Kamara, Unisa Bangura, Petra Lindberg, and many others. Cecilia Utas and Tommy Garnett require a very special thanks, as do Mats and Umu Utas. I wish to thank all my colleagues for their support and encouragement, and for reading and commenting on various papers and chapters over the years, especially Staffan Löfving, Becky Popenoe, Lars Hagborg, and Eva Evers Rosander. I want to thank all the members of the Living Beyond Conflict (LBC) Seminar, and many of our inspiring guest lecturers, Michael Jackson, Paul Richards, Begoña Aretxaga, Harri Englund, Carolyn Nordstrom, and Don Handelman, among others. Other avid scholars on Sierra Leone with whom I have shared many common interests are Mariam Persson, Danny Hoffman, Rosalind Shaw, and Susan Shepler. No acknowledgment is complete without thanking those institutions who made this work possible. For funding my dissertation work I thank Sida/SAREC, and for generously funding my fieldwork I thank the Swedish Research Council, Olof Palme's Memorial Fund, Lars Hierta's Memorial Fund, the Nordic Africa Institute, the Swedish Royal Academy of Letters, and the Wallenberg Foundation. A book is not written on its own. It is the result of a long and sometimes cumbersome process. As the process of writing stretched over years, family and friends have also played a big part in why I came to be where I am. I dedicate this dissertation to my wonderful children who have endured malaria, typhoid, conjunctivitis, and so many other things while accompanying me to Sierra Leone. I hope, and know, that your lives too will have been enriched by living in Sierra Leone, *Sweet Salone,* and hope you will carry with you those memories always. I also dedicate this dissertation to the most important person in my life, my husband Mike Barrett. You are my favorite anthropologist, thank you for intellectual challenges, a sharp eye for proof reading, and our continual conversations. Your love and support throughout this process belong to a realm of experience that does not easily translate into words, but I think you know what I mean. This is for you.

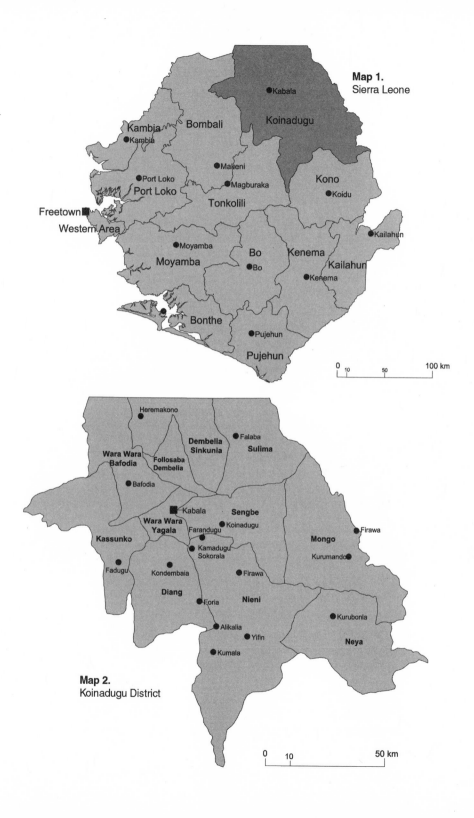

Map 1.
Sierra Leone

Kabala

Kambia
Kambia

Bombali

Koinadugu

Makeni

Kono

Port Loko
Port Loko

Magburaka

Koidu

Tonkolili

Freetown
Western Area

Kailahun

Moyamba

Bo

Kenema

Moyamba

Bo

Kailahun

Kenema

Bonthe

Pujehun

Pujehun

0 10   50   100 km

Heremakono

Falaba

Dembella
Sinkunia

Sulima

Wara Wara
Bafodia

Follosaba
Dembelia

Bafodia

Kabala

Sengbe

Wara Wara
Yagala

Farandugu

Koinadugu

Firawa

Kassunko

Kamadugu
Sokorala

Mongo

Kurumando

Fadugu

Kondembaia

Firawa

Diang

Foria

Nieni

Kurubonla

Alikalia

Yifin

Neya

Kumala

Map 2.
Koinadugu District

0 10   50 km

Bush Wives and Girl Soldiers

Introduction

After the war, Aminata stayed with her "bush husband" in Makeni and gave birth to their second child. Her parents had fled to Guinea during the war, and as she did not know where they were, she had nowhere else to go. One day she met an old neighbor from her hometown. At the sight of him she became happy and thought he might have news of her family's whereabouts, but when she greeted him she noticed he was afraid of her. "Don't be afraid," she told him, "we are all human beings." When she asked after her family, the neighbor told her that they had returned home but that he had heard them say that she was not alive, and even if she were, they would not accept her. Aminata asked him why, and he said that it was because she had been with the rebels for a long time. Saddened, Aminata went back to her bush husband to tell him the distressing news. He nevertheless encouraged her and suggested that they both go together to see her parents. When they arrived, Aminata was too scared to go directly to her parents and instead went to her father's sister, who tried to negotiate with her family. Her older brother wanted to see her, but her mother initially refused.

Still they went. Her bush husband wanted to formalize the marriage with Aminata and offered the traditional kola nut and a small amount of money as bridewealth. But Aminata's parents refused, saying that they did not want to see him or have anything to do with him. Eventually they agreed to let Aminata and her children stay, but the bush husband had to leave.[1]

Aminata was lonely in her family's house. Only her older brother showed her love and support; the others were wary and cautious around her. Aminata believed they hated her. She felt that people were afraid of her and many did not even speak to her. Whenever she sat down next to her mother, her mother just got up and left. The mother said she wanted Aminata to leave the house as she feared Aminata would kill the other children; she believed that Aminata was still under the influence of the drugs she took throughout the war. Aminata felt she was blamed for everything, and if she quarreled with someone everyone turned against her. Her father tried to get her married to another man, but when the man found out that Aminata had been a rebel, he rejected her. She became worried that no man would ever want to marry her. Aminata thought that the reason her father wanted her to get married as soon as possible was so he would be rid of her. What Aminata really wanted was to formalize the marriage with her bush husband. Even if he did not have money, she felt life would be better with him, but her parents adamantly refused. After some time she started to stay away from home. She left early in the morning, moved from one place to another, and returned home only to sleep. She was maltreated by her father, and she was physically and verbally abused and often denied food. She had a few lovers who gave her some money and food for herself and the children, but no one who wanted to commit. She also became worried about having sex with many men, as she had heard about HIV/Aids. "How can I live only on loving?" she said. The men also used her, she said, and only gave her scraps of money for sex. She became ashamed of her rebel past and afraid of the people whom she used to know, her family, friends, and neighbors. They too were scared of her, she said, even her closest friends. She said that when she came back home, she had hoped her parents would be happy that she was alive, but instead they did everything to drive her away. She could not understand why they did not let her marry the only man who wanted to marry her. Instead, she had to face rejection after rejection from other men. All of her lovers eventually left her. She felt she was a hostage in her own home.

During the course of the Sierra Leonean war, many thousands of girls and women, just like Aminata, were abducted from their home areas when rebels or other fighters attacked and looted. An overwhelming majority of these girls and women also suffered physical abuse, frequent rapes, and pregnancy as a result. Some were used as forced labor, and some were forced to witness or to participate in the killing of relatives. A majority of abducted girls and women were also subjected to forced marriage, becoming so-called bush wives, and some also became rebel fighters. Most of the women I have worked with have seen or experienced all of the above. During the decade-long war, most of them had also fallen in love, some had married, others had divorced, and most had had children. Whatever their personal circumstances, they grew from girls to young women during a period of intense and sometimes extreme social change. Some girls and women managed to escape within days or months after their capture, but others stayed with their captors for up to ten years, and some still live today with their bush husbands. Some fled from war zones, but many also took the opportunity to loot and fight in the destructive trail of rebels or other fighters. These young women also have varied experiences of postwar society; some had been welcomed back to their families and communities while others were ostracized and expelled. The way they communicated their war and postwar experiences also varied, according to factors such as context, arena, personality, and position in household, to name but a few.

A number of questions emerge from Aminata's story. What had happened to Aminata during the war? Why were people afraid of her? Why did her parents initially reject her, even though she had survived the war? Was this perhaps the reaction that any rebel, or person associated with the rebels, would expect, or was it because she was an unmarried mother? It was obvious that her father wanted her married, if only to get rid of her, but if that was the sole reason for her to get married, why did he not accept the bush husband? And why did Aminata accept this? Could she not just leave her unsupportive family and go to live with her bush husband? Why did she say that she had "shamed" her parents? The way she was treated by her family forced Aminata to seek other means of material and social survival. What were some of the conditions of these other means? In order to answer these and other questions that will emerge throughout this book, we will have to understand the roles local morality and notions of gender and kinship relations played in the lives of these young women, and we also need to know more about the social dynamics of the Sierra Leonean war.

The overall purpose of this book is to examine the war and postwar experiences of young women in northern Sierra Leone who were abducted by the rebels. These young women had strategies and options, but their choices were circumscribed in ways different than for men. As part of my underlying aim to analyze gender and war, I will deal with phenomena such as abduction, rape, and female fighters, as well as postwar issues such as demobilization, impoverishment, stigma, and healing. My intention is to engage in a critical discussion of these in relation to larger processes of humanitarianism and to their local social context.

I have been interested in examining how war and postwar experiences were shaped by and given meaning by the women themselves, their communities, but also by those humanitarian institutions that populate and to some extent dominate many postwar societies. I examine what informed women's choices in becoming rebel fighters and focus among other things on what postwar processes such as demobilization, reintegration, and reconciliation can signify if we direct our analytical gaze at young women and the relationships they are immersed in rather than at large-scale international postwar planning. I also examine what happened when these young women returned home after war, how they were treated, and how their circumstances were particular but also general, given the fact that they were women and as such positioned in a hierarchy of gender relations in Sierra Leonean society.

The focus of this book is almost exclusively on young women. It has been said that a narrow focus on "women" often tends to obscure their relations with men and can also be blind to differences that exist between women (Leach 1994, 28). Even if I have not researched particular men's lives, I do focus on how women's experiences were articulated *in relation to* their social environment, with an emphasis on gender, age, kinship, and socioeconomic position, and on the social aspects of being a woman. My focus is warranted, as I believe that to analyze women's position in and experience of a war-torn society provides new perspectives, new angles, and produces new knowledge in an area that heretofore has been characterized by its male bias. However, since previous research has shown that there is no univocal position of women in relation to war (Schott 1996, 20),

I also argue that one must go beyond the universalistic narrative of *women's* experience of war (cf. Sørensen 1998, 5).

To understand women's very diverse war and postwar experiences, one must be alert to the factors that shape them, and how, to whom, and when they are expressed. Therefore, I will focus on the specificity and diversity of young Sierra Leonean women's wartime and postwar experiences, as well as on the social processes involved in shaping both experience and stories of experience. As this suggests, gender alone does not suffice as a factor for examining young women's position in wartime and postwar society. In the context of Sierra Leone, generation, kinship, and morality are equally relevant dimensions of exploration. It is by examining the experiential intersection of norms of gender, age, and kinship that we will reach an understanding of the complex reality of young Sierra Leonean women's everyday lives in this war-torn society.

Researchers and journalists have written about women and war before, both thematically and regionally, many of them commendably, but no one has yet undertaken a comprehensive analysis of what happened to rebel women during and after the war in Sierra Leone. My contribution is to analyze how women articulated their experiences of war, specifically in relation to how they were seen by their families, their communities, and by the international humanitarian community. I also focus on how war and postwar experiences may have changed social and kinship relations, marriage practices, initiation, and the gendered division of labor. In this vein I examine how and to what extent cultural idioms have provided solidarity and solutions, or stigma and crisis, for women like Aminata who returned home after spending years with rebel fighters. My ambition has been to focus on what type of strategies young women used in their everyday lives to cope in war and postwar society, and on how those strategies were informed by the cultural space in which they occurred.

The Sierra Leonean war began on 23 March 1991, when a small rebel group, the Revolutionary United Front (RUF), entered southeastern Sierra Leone from Liberia. The war went on in varying intensity throughout the 1990s, and peace was officially declared on 18 January 2002. The war has been described as one of the more brutal in the late twentieth century, its level of brutality compared to that of Rwanda or even Cambodia in the 1970s. The war was particularly destructive in the rural areas, in particular the diamond-rich east, but no part of the country was left unharmed. Approximately fifty thousand people were killed, and many more injured. In the late 1990s Sierra Leoneans constituted one of Africa's largest refugee populations, in which half of the country's population of almost 6 million was displaced. The RUF rebels have been accused of committing widespread atrocities such as cutting off people's limbs, rape, and creating mass destruction, but all fighting factions targeted civilians. Today, after three elections, six governments, four peace accords, four coups d'état, and the deployment of one of the largest peacekeeping operations ever mounted by the United Nations, the country enjoys a fragile stability.

The war brought about massive social change and caused ruptures in the social relations of both families and communities, from the clearly visible scars of war inscribed on the bodies of those mutilated to more subtle processes of how one becomes an adult in the absence of kin and community in times of great social stress. Even before the war, mass urbanization and mass unemployment had made visible the demographic category of youth, which had increased dramatically in Sierra Leone as in so many other countries in Sub-Saharan Africa. In the urban settings, new affiliations have sometimes become more important than those of ethnicity and kinship in the formation of a youth, and eventually adult, identity. Eleven years of civil war and the subsequent uncertainties of postwar society have exacerbated these new processes of identity formation, not to mention gender identities.

In Sierra Leone, gender opposition and differentiation have been very pronounced in official discourse. Sierra Leonean society has traditionally been based on the sexual division of labor, where gender analyses based on a sexual continuum have placed men and women at completely opposite ends in terms of roles, responsibilities, and also opportunities. However, it is also apparent when consulting ethnographic literature from decades back (e.g. Bledsoe 1980; Jackson 1977; Little 1951), and when interviewing elders, that much is changing in Sierra Leonean society, especially relating to gender relations and women's and children's rights. To some, these changes are perceived as having become more pronounced due to the war; internationally funded postwar rehabilitation; increases in levels of education; and national and international migration, the spread of telecommunications, and so forth. Only a decade ago in the small village of Kamadugu Sokorala in northern Sierra Leone, it was inconceivable that women could become politicians, or for that matter, wear trousers. Last year my former assistant ran for political office and won; however, a woman in trousers is still a contested issue.

In most of Sierra Leonean society, the distinction between the categories of male and female is fundamental and all-pervasive. For the Kuranko of northern Sierra Leone, Michael Jackson wrote that this male-female dichotomy "serves as one of the basic armatures for structuring all social relations" (1977, 81). In "traditional" society, women and men had different and exclusive rights and obligations, occupied different spaces in the village and in the house, and had different emotional and intellectual dispositions. Men and women were in a dichotomous yet complementary relationship. This sexual division of society has changed somewhat in the past decades. The roles of men and women have changed, job opportunities and educational possibilities are open to both sexes, women have political representation, and gendered spaces in villages have changed or been eroded. Still, notions of what constitutes men and women to some extent remain. This had consequences, I argue, for how men and women's active participation in the war was interpreted locally.

Despite the often brutal reality of the Sierra Leonean war, my aim is not principally about making something so seemingly unintelligible comprehensible, nor is it about explaining how or why it came to be. Rather, this is an examination of social relations from the perspective of young women in a particular context of war and postconflict society. Nevertheless, considering the recent debate on greed/grievance, "new wars," and primordialism (see e.g. Besteman and Gusterson 2005; Moran 2006; Richards 2005c), it is important to emphasize that there are many who feel that these perspectives are inadequate in explaining the reality of the Sierra Leonean war. The notion of war as a *thing in itself* that is inherently bad conceals that war is socially situated and "but one among many different phases or aspects of social reality. War, like peace, is organised by social agents" (Richards 2005c, 3). Or as Staffan Löfving writes, "However chaotic war may be to some, wars are designed both locally and globally, and though they are incomprehensible to some, they have purpose for others" (2002, 19). I am critical of the view that war and peace are two mutually exclusive, compartmentalized, and discrete parts, and have instead emphasized the social and cultural continuities in war, whether in structural violence or in systems of marriage. The transition from war to peace can be a slow process, because, as I am not the first to point out, peace is more than just the absence of war. What are the beginning(s) and end(s) of war? Where does war end and peace begin? "Peace and war are not so much two opposed states of being as they are multifaceted, ambiguous, mutually imbricated arenas of struggle. Peace does not necessarily entail the end of violent conflict," wrote Begoña Aretxaga (1997, 4–5).

In the introduction to the book *The Postwar Moment* (Cockburn and Zarkov 2002, 10), the editors warn against this compartmentalizing of war and peace as two discrete parts and instead emphasize the continuum of violence that runs through the social, political, and economic spheres, a continuum that, they argue, becomes apparent when a gendered analysis is applied. In such an analysis the significance of structural violence, long-term oppression, and impoverishment is not concealed by a focus only on the outbreaks of armed conflict. To Aminata and many of my Sierra Leonean informants, the signing of the peace accord on 7 July 1999 did not immediately affect their lives, especially in view of continued sporadic fighting. For many abducted women, the period immediately following the cease-fire instead presented new challenges and hardships, and a continuation of the structural violence that is largely ignored in an analysis with a peace/war dichotomy.

Within anthropology, much space has been devoted to the critique of humanitarianism (see, e.g., Cowan, Dembour, and Wilson 2001; Englund 2000a, 2006). Most UN and NGO studies work from a human rights framework, and it is not their aim or purpose to describe cultural systems of meaning or social relations; they are instead geared toward policymaking and are also often framed in legalistic language. However, these organizations are among the most important actors in the production of knowledge about war-torn and postwar societies and are not easily dismissed. But, explaining social relations, issues of agency, notions of self, culture, and cosmology is a project better suited to anthropology. Anthropology, and its method of ethnography, has much to contribute in the production of knowledge of war-torn societies, as it is an approach that has as its focus the complexity of social processes, and at the heart of these processes is the construction of the meaning of individual experiences of violence. "Ethnography," wrote Richards (2005c, 18), "is a tool to probe the social content of war."

Because most studies of war and conflict do not give much attention to women, this book will help balance the uneven record of war presented in much scholarship. Some studies of women and war focus on women either as inherently more peaceful or merely as victims; in this book, I engage in a critique of such theorizing by demonstrating instead the diversity and context specificity of women's war and postwar experiences in Sierra Leone. War is not exempt from the social but creates its own social orders. Sometimes social actors reject past traditions, while at other times the former social order is reproduced. For this reason, I emphasize not only the ruptures and discontinuities of the social order but also the continuities. In this vein, I attempt to examine how the very discourse of war is gendered. Therefore this book can also be said to contribute to a growing body of anthropological literature on war-torn countries, much of which tries to understand war and violent conflict by paying attention to social context and social action, contesting the idea that seems to be proliferating in much of the work on war and conflicts today, that war is that "other" inexplicable something, somehow *exempted* from the world of the social (cf. Richards 2005c, 4).

Women and War

"What people tolerate in peace shapes what they will tolerate in war," argued anthropologist Carolyn Nordstrom (1997b, 1). Part of my aim with this book has been to explore local structural conditions and predicaments that had bearing on women's wartime and postwar experiences and on how they were articulated. Because, although the war is over, women and girls are still facing structural constraints that are seldom addressed, and as focus has generally been on the universal "women in war," there has been less focus on the local continuities and cultural context that were involved in shaping Sierra Leonean women's war experiences.

My female informants told of different experiences of war. As I will show, almost all were raped and abducted, and many have been both bush wives and fighters, some by force, some for survival, and others by choice. To fully comprehend what women really do in war-torn societies, it has to be acknowledged that women not only have their own agenda but that "women" is a highly differentiated social category (see e.g. Sørensen 1998, 6). Women can be active participants in war, supporters and advocates of continued armed struggle; they can be spies, soldiers, and rebels.

But still—and this is an important distinction to make—more often than not, women's choices in times of conflict and war are at best circumscribed, at worst nonexistent. Statistically speaking, men are still overwhelmingly the perpetrators of violence, not women. And both men *and* women are victims. But by focusing on women *only* as victims we conceal their full range as political and social actors. Still, in discussions about women and war, it is mainly as passive victims that we meet them. Literature from the perspectives of development and humanitarian discourses on women's situation in war and conflict abound, but they concern mostly the parts women have played in refugee situations, as rape victims, abandoned mothers, or mourning widows (cf. Malkki 1995). The notion of *victim* has become a socially constructed identity that often reifies *women's* experiences of war.

In view of recent research (see, e.g., Aretxaga 1997; Denov and Maclure 2007; Enloe 1991; Mazurana et. al 2002; McKay 2007; Specht 2006; and Turshen and Twagiramariya 1998), it is impossible to view *all* women in war as victims *all* the time. It has become necessary to expand the inquiries into what women do in war and to critically analyze women's roles as perpetuators of and perpetrators in war and conflict, while still acknowledging that even in situations where one can talk about the violence *of* women, as in the example of female combatants, one often finds violence *against* women as well. And as in peacetime, in war women must also cope with menstruation, pregnancy, childbirth, and childcare, further gendering their actions and position. Most women fighting in the war have thus had multiple experiences of having been at one time or another fighters, rape victims, looters, mothers, or lovers. In spite of women's active participation in the war, they were clearly more vulnerable to sexual abuse and forced labor because they were women. Although there is ample evidence of the participation of women in armed combat, the perception of rebels and soldiers as male remains, signifying the endurance of gendered ideas of war and peace. The "experience of being a woman...can never be a singular one," writes Henrietta Moore, "and will always be dependent on a multiplicity of locations and positions that are constructed socially, that is, intersubjectively" (1994, 3).

Through the mass of UN and NGO reports and media coverage, we have become acquainted with wars all over the world and of how these have affected the female population. We are presented with comparisons of war rapes in Bosnia and Rwanda, we hear about female fighters in

Sierra Leone and Sri Lanka. War tribunals and war-crimes courts catch our attention. What happened in the Hague and in Arusha affected the war-crimes trials in Sierra Leone, and the outcome of these may in turn affect proposed trials in Uganda, if that war ever ceases. Research suggests that increased militarization of women's lives intensifies sexism and misogyny, and that rape in war is widespread and mostly goes unpunished. Although probably true, frequently, however, such accounts are ahistorical and lack cultural context.

Women's positions in various wars are often described in similar ways, where war rapes are a result of war's own logic. Most literature on the subject of women and the Sierra Leonean war is based on quantitative studies, NGO reports, and war correspondents' anecdotes. Susan Shepler, who has studied child soldiers in Sierra Leone, found that most studies of the war "almost always begin from a human rights framework, and focus mainly on estimating numbers involved, recounting individual horror stories, describing the legal instruments against the use of child soldiers and evaluating reintegration programming" (2005, 4). From an anthropological perspective, such data records and illustrates but does little in the way of providing a deeper understanding of the war and the people in it, but, to be fair, this is not the objective of such data. But are there differences, for example, in women's experiences of war and war rapes in Sierra Leone and Bosnia? I would have to say yes. Although the act of rape is similar everywhere and involves the body, the ways in which the body, and the violence enacted on it, is experienced may be different. The ways these experiences may or may not be communicated are also different. These are issues that have to do with personhood and the moral economy of sex and violence, kinship, ethnicity, and religion.[2] I will discuss these issues further below and in the succeeding chapters.

There are few anthropological works dealing explicitly with women and war, and even fewer on women and war in Africa. Nonetheless, in the last two decades a number of books, reports, and articles across a range of disciplines have been published concerning women, war, and armed conflict. The war in Sierra Leone, and hence the experiences of people in it, did not occur in a cultural void. I wish therefore to explore not only the contemporary sites of debate on women and war and what these have to say about the Sierra Leonean context but also to address the complexity of Sierra Leonean history and culture in framing these experiences.

Anthropological research in the past decades has made it clear that it is not relevant to speak of a front line in wars (see, e.g., Aretxaga 1997; Nordstrom 1997a, 2004; Richards 2005c). Increasingly, wars take place not on the front line but in the middle of communities, including soldiers and civilians alike. However, the idea of a front line around which war is enacted persists, and this is to some extent apparent in the overly generalized and stereotypical way in which men and women in war often are portrayed. This polarization of men and women as analogous with war and peace has been quite a popular perception, but to quote Valentine Daniel, "Popular perceptions are popular precisely because they do not entertain complexity" (1996, 20). For example, in Sierra Leone, the number of women fighting in the various armed forces has been estimated at up to 30 percent, and the number of child fighters 37 percent, almost half of them girls (Mazurana and Carlson 2004). Another example is that of the Sendero Luminoso in Peru, where women were among the core of *senderista* militants, and where they were predominant in both the ranks and leadership of the organization; even so, their existence was largely ignored by foreign scholars and journalists (Andreas 1990–91). This alone changes the way we conceive of war's gender. War can no longer be said to be only men's business, if it ever could.

It is often as mothers that women are positioned in discourses on war, and this is problematic. For in contexts of war and violent conflict, it is precisely as mothers, real or metaphorical, that women are made the targets of enemy male violence. If women as mothers are metaphorically associated with the nation in a conflict situation, as, for example, in *Mother Yugoslavia* or *Mother Ireland,* men in power and male soldiers often use this as a reason to circumscribe women's freedom of movement. In nationalist discourses, women as mothers in situations of war and conflict have often been persuaded to reproduce and have been "encouraged to see their maternal duty as a public duty" (Enloe 2000, 11). Women are seen as providers of young men to fight in armies, and it is also as mothers that women are recruited into the rhetoric of the nation-state and of *patriotic mothering.* In Cuba, mothers of war heroes were given medals.[3] In the aftermath of the U.S.–Vietnam war, Vietnamese mothers of killed soldiers, not their wives, were the beneficiaries of war commemorations.[4] In Sierra Leone no such maternal emphasis was laid on the nation-state, but it was also a war exempt from an overtly nationalist discourse.

Women as mothers are also often associated with peace, but Sierra Leonean researcher Binta Mansaray, an advocate for women's peace work, has warned against "the caricature of 'naturally peace-loving' women. Trite expressions like 'women love peace and men make war' are misleading.... Women represent the best bet for peace, not because they are 'naturally' or 'inherently' peace-loving human beings...but because women are usually excluded from the male-dominated political groups which take war-like decisions" (Mansaray 2000, 144).

Just as stifling as the image of women as helpless victims may be, so also is the ultimate male stereotype of the soldier. Although gender dichotomies and gender generalizations are as prevalent in Sierra Leone as in "the West," the local context of the Sierra Leonean war deconstructed any notion of a combat-clad, crew-cut, clean-shaven soldier, as hardly any of the irregular armed combatants conformed to this soldier image. Here, fighters ranged from traditional hunters, naked or dressed in beads and charms, rebels sometimes wearing wigs and women's clothes, to female and child combatants.[5] This wartime transvestism did not go unnoticed in Western media, where it was considered bizarre and inexplicable, as it "seemed to contradict every taken for granted notion of the unambiguous masculinity of war" (Moran 1995, 75). For much Western media and many Western militaries it was difficult to comprehend the warrior, as this was not a familiar type of militarized masculinity. The Western soldier has been based on an ideal of masculinity that is often defined in exclusive terms. It is a masculinity that is antifeminine; to be a soldier-man is by definition not to be woman. It is a masculinity shed of anything remotely feminine; a "real" man must not possess any so-called female characteristics. Western gender categories were unsuited to explaining and situating the warrior in Sierra Leone as well as in Liberia. What was shocking to a Western audience, the male transvestite warriors, did not provoke local observers in the same way. As I will discuss in chapter 4, it was rather female combatants in army fatigues who disrupted expected gender norms, as Mary Moran has argued (1995, 84).

Linked to a militarized masculinity has been the *feminization* of the enemy, which has been a well-documented phenomenon in many wars (see, e.g., Adams 1993; Cohn 1993; Ruddick 1989, 1993). But caution must be exercised when making these generalizations, as they may vary over time and have different cultural connotations in different contexts. This notion of the feminized enemy, as Henrietta Moore (1994, 63) among others has pointed out, rests on a Western discourse on hegemonic masculinity and otherness.[6] In Sierra Leone, for example, differences between forces loyal to the government and the rebels, the enemy, were phrased not so much in terms of a genderized difference, male/female or strong/weak, as in the binary opposition of human/nonhuman. The state enemy, the rebels, were frequently demonized and dehumanized, but they were not feminized. The concept of the *dehumanized* enemy is a common topic in many analyses of violence. It is perceiving and experiencing the enemy as having *no human* qualities that makes committing atrocities possible for the perpetrator, an ideological dehumanization of sorts (cf. McC. Lewin 1993, 296). Many people in Sierra Leone spoke of the rebels, both male and female, not only as "coming from the bush" but as *animals* or *demons.*

While it may be something many people do not particularly want to acknowledge, the presence and participation of women in war is neither unusual nor new. But to deviate from acceptable feminine or masculine behavior in times of war and conflict can be costly. Men who refuse to fight might be ridiculed, jailed, or even killed for their cowardice or lack of manliness. And women who oppose female stereotypes in war will often be regarded as deviant or unnatural. Therefore, I argue, the notion of a militarized masculinity has consequences for how female combatants are interpreted. For example, in my own field in Sierra Leone as well as in Peru and Sri Lanka, female rebels were often regarded by the civilian population as monsters, barbarians, and frequently as more cold blooded than male rebels. Fighting women may also be susceptible to rape as a punishment for transgressing accepted female behavior. To describe female fighters as more terrifying than male fighters was not the prerogative only of the population in Sierra Leone, however. Western media also frequently engage in and reproduce such images, as in the cases of the female Chechnyan terrorists and suicide bombers in Russia.

Nevertheless, the notion of women as more peaceful, as innocent, and as passive victims has also been manipulated effectively by some rebel groups and other insurgents, as has been pointed out during the war in Rwanda, for example. Women can also, up to a point, exploit this label of innocence by becoming spies, smugglers, and also killers (African Rights 1995, 255). This was initially also the case in some of the Chechnyan suicide bombings, where veiled women could use the veil as protection from unwanted attention, since veiled women were not, at that time, seen as potential terrorists.[7] Also in Northern Ireland, the IRA used women to transport ammunition, and they thereby "turned the hegemonic discourse of gender identity that rendered women invisible in the political world into a subversive technique" (Aretxaga 1997, 66). In Sierra Leone, women were found smuggling weapons through military checkpoints in bags of women's underwear and hidden on their own or their children's bodies (Mansaray 2000, 148), and my informants told me that the rebels often sent the most beautiful girls to go and spy on the enemy.

An often-quoted reason for the increase in the numbers of female and child fighters in rebel insurgencies is the development and distribution of small arms and light weapons, which can be carried and used by almost anyone and which require little skill to operate (Mansaray 2000, 149). This argument has lately been challenged. David Rosen argues that, in the first place, there have been children, although more boys than girls, in wars for centuries; second, small arms are not that much lighter than weapons used during the American Civil War; and third, the phenomenon of the innocent child soldier has more to do with the development of a political agenda in civil society and the international humanitarian community (Rosen 2005).

Although women participate in insurgencies and rebel movements, they are also frequently employed in state-sanctioned violence. In some national armies, the number of women is increasing: in the United States 14 percent of active-duty personnel are women; women make up around one-fifth of the armed forces in Eritrea, and almost one-third of the fighters of the Tamil Tigers in Sri Lanka are women (Lindsey 2000). Still, although there is ample evidence of the participation of women in armed combat, the popular notion of the soldier remains male, signifying the endurance of gendered ideas of war and peace.

Moore reminds us that it is not "possible to analyze discourses on gender, wherever they occur, without recognizing the ways in which they are implicated in larger processes of economic and political change well beyond the control of local communities" (Moore 1994, 63). The culture of militarization became globalized during the twentieth century—the organization, the hierarchy, the fatigues, the training are now similar in most national armies.[8] In many societies the concept of an ideal masculinity has been intimately connected to the military. Armies have until quite recently been considered an exclusively male domain, and military service has often been interpreted as a rite of male initiation.[9] Not much research has been conducted on this phenomenon, however, and in existing research there is a dominant focus on the West, in particular the United States and Israel (Ben-Ari 1998; Clark 2000; Connell 1992; Dawson 1994). However, there is not only one masculinity or femininity, not only one way of being a man or a woman, for "cultures do not have a single model of gender or a single gender system, but rather a multiplicity of discourses on gender which can vary both contextually and biographically" (Moore 1994, 55–56).

To get an in-depth understanding of the thematic and regional focus I have used in this book, and to further examine the idea that wartime experiences are inevitably tied to history and social and cultural contexts, I have mainly used my informants' narratives of their war and postwar experiences. But narratives, especially narratives of pain and violence, are also problematical in a methodological sense and challenge many assumptions that are taken for granted about experience, violence, and social structure, as I will explain below.

Narrating Experiences of Violence and War

> How does an anthropologist write an ethnography—or to borrow
> a more apt term . . .—an anthropography of violence, without its
> becoming a pornography of violence?
>
> VALENTINE DANIEL, *Charred Lullabies*

Stories of war and conflict are often distinguished by the fact that many of them deal with violence and pain. There has been much debate in the social sciences about whether or how pain and violence can actually be articulated in language (see, e.g., Das 1996; Das et al. 2001; Good et al. 1992; Mattingly and Garro 2000; Scheper-Hughes 1992). Elaine Scarry's *The Body in Pain: The Making and Unmaking of the World* (1985) has inspired many anthropologists working with violence and the body to understand how language is inhibited or even destroyed by pain, how violence unmakes the world (see, e.g., Aretxaga 1997; Feldman 1991; Green 1999; Löfving 2002; Mǎek 2000). "Whatever pain achieves, it achieves in part through its unsharability, and it ensures this unsharability through its resistance to language," Scarry writes (1985, 4).[10] Much human rights work nevertheless operates on the basis of a need to *give voice* to pain as inflicted by violence on the body.

Scarry interprets this as resting on the assumption "that the act of verbally expressing pain is a necessary prelude to the collective task of diminishing pain" (1985, 9). Following Scarry's work, one can infer that narrating a violent experience, by necessity, is focused on tangible events rather than on the actual experience of pain and violence done to the body, as language is not only unable to communicate it, language is destroyed by it (Scarry 1985, 4).[11] Inspired by Wittgenstein and in contrast to Scarry, Veena Das argues that pain "is not that inexpressible something that destroys communication or marks an exit from one's existence in language" (1996, 70). Yet Das, too, in an earlier text, notes that "the person who has been visited by unfortunate events has no easy way of formulating how the conditions for her suffering were created" (1995, 22). Das argues that pain makes a claim for recognition, a claim which can be given or denied, and while interviewing women about their experiences of violent conflict, she found a zone of silence around the event, a silence that was "achieved either by the use of language that was general and metaphoric but that evaded specific description of any events so as to capture the particularity of their experience, or by describing the surrounding events but leaving the actual experience of abduction and rape unstated" (1996, 84).

This form of coping, through public silence, sometimes clashes with dominant forms of healing in war-torn societies in the world today—therapy, bearing witness, or giving testimony—as means of transforming and overcoming violent experiences. But silence, maintains Michael Jackson, is not a sign of resignation or indifference, but also of respect, silence as a way of healing and reconciliation. This is "not shocked silence...but silence as a deliberate choice" (Jackson 2004b, 56). In his book about the violence in the Sri Lankan conflict, Valentine Daniel noted that whereas "silence or speechlessness is one of the main and pervasive effects of violence, the juridical apparatus demands words (or other signs) so that justice may be done" (1996, 121).

Anthropologist Fiona Ross notes that the work of the South African Truth and Reconciliation Commission (TRC) relied on giving words to experience, and that the commission wrongly assumed that "the world is knowable only through words and that to have no voice is to be without language, unable to communicate" (2003, 50). Ross showed in her work on women's testimonies to the TRC how there is an ethical responsibility to recognize that silence in fact is a legitimate discourse on pain. In this respect, Ross sees silence as an act of conscious agency. However, recalling the quote by Daniel above, how do anthropologists tell stories of violence, and what do they tell of what people say "when the most poignant parts of their voices are their silences?" (1996, 121).

Not all interpret silence as a good thing, arguing instead that in societies emerging from intense periods of war and humiliation, "silence has powerful and violent consequences in its non-performance. Silence conceals knowledge, it can bring about a breach of sign and object, it refuses to be fully human and rejecting others' humanity" (Golden 2004, 75). For whom, then, is it valuable to narrate experiences of violence and pain? Is it for the victims or for the institutional bodies that want to bring justice? More specifically, does it help victims of violence to heal? Much anthropological research of late would say no, it does not unequivocally help healing to retell and relive past experiences of violence (see Argenti-Pillen 2003; Colvin 2004; Finnström 2003; Ross 2003; Sampson 2003; Shaw 2005).

In her work on how women contain violence in Sri Lanka, Alex Argenti-Pillen did extensive research on how humanitarian agencies attempt to "modernize discourses on suffering and violence by teaching people about trauma and trauma counselling" (2003, xii) and how this in turn excluded culture-specific strategies of narrating experiences of violence. Das has also argued that the suffering of victims acts as a narrative trope in certain discourses, that "it cuts off the experience of suffering from the victims and, instead, becomes a means of legitimizing the producers of the professional discourses" (1995, 18). This intellectualizing of violence, argues Jackson, "suggests that theoretical meaning may be just one of many consoling illusions for making our relationship with suffering bearable and endurable—taming and domesticating with words, in order to make it seem safe" (2004b, 50).

I encountered many narratives that were, I believe, influenced by the almost hegemonic humanitarian discourse on victimhood and suffering. By this I mean that they were to some degree standardized and collectivized. Although they were personal in that they were told by an individual and were based on her unique experiences, they were also standardized as they more or less told the same story or emphasized experiences shared by many (and also the same experiences emphasized by humanitarian agencies as being war traumas). In most "war narratives" it is the individual women's bodies and the violence done to them that occupy center stage. Yet these stories often divulged little about the women's own feelings or *how* they experienced violent events or long-lasting abduction, but were delivered in a very detached manner and included features common to many. There is also a difference between collective war narratives and personal narratives of war. Collective stories become part not only of individual recollection but of collective memory, which usually involves a standardization of the recounting of past events. In chapter 3 I will return to this distinction between standardized narratives and personal narratives of war. In studies of war and violence, this relationship between memories of past experience and the telling of them is also, as Harri Englund (2000b, 70) reminds us, a methodological problem.[12]

As the war had officially ended at the time of my latest fieldwork, the stories of abduction that I collected were in the form of narratives or stories of past events. Throughout this book I will use narrative and story interchangeably. As Shepler remarks, when doing fieldwork on war experiences after war, "it is impossible to conduct ethnographic interviews with girls except in *the register of memory*" (2002, 2 my emphasis). Few researchers actually do fieldwork with informants during actual war, and so most have to work with interviews about past experiences. It has been remarked that there is a discontinuity between life stories and life as lived, that narratives neither represent nor re-present experience. Therefore it is necessary to make a distinction between *experience* and *experience as expressed* (cf. Bruner 1986; Mattingly 2000). In this book I take particular notice of how experiences emerged and were given meaning in my informants' stories and have paid less attention to the structure or narrative patterning of the stories. As this ethnography will show, there were instances and situations in which my informants simply did not want to or could not share their experiences. Sometimes their experiences were not "storyable," or my informants lacked the performative and normative resources to tell them. There is also a risk of taking stories of war and violence at face value. I have tried not to take for granted the verisimilitude between my informants' experiences and their stories about their experiences (cf. Linden 1993, 138), but to be attentive to the fact that my informants' war narratives reconstructed the war and their experiences of it in light of the present. As I will show, the circumstances of their narration influenced in a significant way both content and style of the stories.

Stories about past experiences involve a re-presentation, a re-interpreting and sometimes a re-sequencing of the past. In this book I have been interested in lived experience but have had to acknowledge that, first, lived experiences are expressed, and second, that they are also fleeting. "They last only a moment, then disappear, leaving only traces—stories," writes Ruth Linden (1993, 90). The stories, or narratives, I have worked with, I contextualize against a backdrop of other ethnographical and historical material, all the while being aware that narratives involve selective remembering, are situational and context dependent, and also change over time. Still, just as Cheryl Mattingly and Linda Garro (2000, 8) argued that a story "foregrounds the human dramas surrounding illness," so I maintain that a story brings to the fore the human drama of violent experiences.

Where I write in this book about my informants' experiences of war and postwar life, it is to the experiences that emerged in their narratives that I refer. As such, the representations of abducted women's lives in a war-torn society are a result of a negotiation between my informants and their memories, but ultimately between my informants and myself, between them as narrators and myself as listener and producer of text and analysis. This is my reading of their narratives. I heed the advice of those before me and do not take narrated experience at face value, but I still believe that these stories do tell something about the women's experiences, as well as about the cultural, socioeconomic, and political situation of Sierra Leonean women during a particular time in history. Still, stories can never do justice to the experience of violence and terror.

Anthropologists Das and Arthur Kleinman has urged us to distinguish between collective and individual memory in dealing with social suffering and recovery, and to look for "alternate public spheres for articulating and recounting experience silenced by officially sanctioned narratives" (Das et al. 2001, 3). However, for women who fought with the rebels in Sierra Leone, there seemed to exist no alternate *public* spheres suited to recounting their experiences. It is not that "the World" does not want them to recount their sufferings—on the contrary, there is a huge demand to hear them—but many of the women do not want to, or do not feel safe to share their ordeals, and why should they? What the World thinks is often irrelevant to the choices they make. What matters to them is their intimate social relations. If the condition of social existence for human beings is the quest for balance and control, for ontological security, as Jackson suggests, for "the need to belong to and engage effectively in a world of others, having some say, some voice, some sense of making a difference" (1998, 16), how can this be related to and explain the modalities, the social processes underlying behavior, that are at work during years of rebel captivity and subsequent family reunion? How do human beings cope and strategize in this kind of environment? What do people experience, and how do they articulate this when the basis of social belonging violently changes, when their sense of direction and their ability to exercise control have been violently challenged? One of my aims with this book was to try to understand how these experiences were communicated and rendered meaningful; thereby I am both a listener to stories and a storyteller.

Much as Ross found in her work on the South African Truth Commission, I too found that it is an act of intimacy to talk of pain. "Harm is not easily expressed and attempts to probe deeply may jeopardise strategies to cope, often tentative and fragile, that may already be in place" (Ross 2003, 3). Still, although some things were clearly not expressible, during my fieldwork many women did talk, a lot. They talked about the pain inflicted on them, their bodies and their social worlds, but this was not always an easy task, neither for them, nor for me. There was always a constant fear that in enticing my informants to speak, I too was doing violence to them, because "narratives can be coercive, doing violence to the memories they strive to tame or contain" (Linden 1993, 18).

There is a great difference between telling one's story in a circle of friends and family, within a particular storytelling tradition, and telling one's story in the formal venues provided in Sierra Leone by the demobilization programs, the Truth and Reconciliation Commission, and the Special Court, all of which operated within a very different storytelling tradition. In postwar rural Sierra Leone, for example, these nontraditional public spaces were often perceived as being culturally and socially inappropriate for women. While women did talk to me about their wartime experiences, this was almost always done in private conversations, and some of them made it clear that they did so against the expressed wishes of their families. After hours of talking in private spaces, and after promises of anonymity, only slowly did images of their experiences emerge. I got the feeling that to talk about what had been done to them was in the realm of what was possible to verbalize, but that to talk about the pain some of the women as fighters had inflicted on others was still taboo. Often they would speak in a general language of metaphors and avoid specificities. Some said that they knew how to fire guns, and others admitted to having fought, but most would say nothing. A few told of cutting hands, often in the plural, "we cut hands," and only in rare cases would some speak of having killed, but never in detail and most often framed in terms of their own survival.

In Sierra Leone at this time, stories about female fighters' extreme brutality had become widespread, although in all probability these were exaggerated, but this was something my informants could neither refute nor confirm. As I will show, in the context of postwar Sierra Leone, people had good reasons not to talk about being perpetrators. Considering the tricky and delicate character of the social and cultural circumstances my informants faced in postwar Sierra Leone, I wanted to examine how they remembered and talked about war and suffering. I focused on what their stories could tell about the society they lived in, and why, in certain social situations, it was dangerous to remember.

In most war narratives the experience of spending years, sometimes up to ten, with the rebels was often reduced to a few sentences with a clear narrative structure with a beginning, the abduction, and an end, the escape or release. There is often an emphasis on the initial events of attack and abduction, thereby reducing time "to a single event of horror" (Löfving 2002, 171). Even if women's generalized stories tell little about their actual experiences (apart from framing them), they are not necessarily symbolically "thin." The narratives often contain defining moments or critical events that altered the life course of the women, and these defining moments are something they have to deal with in rephrasing their relationships with not only their abductors but also the families and communities they had to leave and subsequently return to after war. One way to access information about these processes of change is to examine what Veena Das (1995) has labeled "critical events" Critical events are moments that have changed the way people conceive of things. In Sierra Leone, the war in itself can perhaps be viewed as such a critical event, and as such it is important to examine what, if any, changes the war has produced in the dominant gender discourse. But as I have argued, war is not only an event but a process, and to understand the complexity of social transformation, which is often a slow process, I argue that it is the essentially noncritical events, the mundane events of everyday life, that need to be researched. War changes everyday life, allegiances shift, roles and authority revert, and although the changes may not be permanent, they nevertheless affect postwar society. Daniel Hoffman and Stephen Lubkemann remind us that in focusing on small scenarios, we may also speak to larger patterns, and in studying specific moments we may be able to "reveal the unremarkably common patterns that operate at the general level" (2005, 317). The often very standardized narratives of abduction and abuse were framed by the events of everyday life. Not the ordinary every day, but the everyday of war and rebel life, such as finding food, looting, killing, disciplinary action, and quarrels with co-wives. I was interested in finding out how one adapted to that kind of life, and what that life was constituted of. I was also curious to see how the reversal of the order of things had in some ways become permanent for women who had lived with the rebels for so many years. These more standardized narratives can also give an indication of how the women conceptualized suffering and hint at the location and content of cultural taboos. My informants' narratives of war and postwar life were to a large extent shaped by their return to their societies from the bush. Some tried to adapt and kept quiet and assimilated, while others could not or would not, which in many cases led to a break with their families.

In material about people's experiences of war and the public telling of these, time and memory seem to be crucial. For instance, it is only now, some thirty years after the end of the U.S.–Vietnam war, that Vietnamese publicly narrate in personal detail the horrors of the war. The past decades of nationalistic celebrations of national heroes (and their mothers) are being exchanged for more personal stories.[13] And it took many decades before we heard the personal narratives of Holocaust survivors that today are so familiar (Handelman 2004; Linden 1993). Will we ever know the extent of human brutality and vulnerability in the Sierra Leonean war? For now, these experiences are still fresh in memory, often associated with shame, especially, I argue, for women. Their telling is made the more difficult by circumstances such as the postwar economy and cultural convention. Although women's war experiences are often not part of official local discourses, they might be present in other forms or contexts. This book aims to research those alternative spaces.

Working in a War-torn Society

In a war-torn country, it is evident that information is hard currency. During the war it was knowledge about events, people's whereabouts, attacks, atrocities, war stories, and the like that interested fellow Sierra Leoneans as well as members of the international humanitarian community. One can speak of new sources and new forms of knowledge tied to the economy and politics of war, of which the *language of rights* is an integral part. Important and powerful knowledge was knowledge that was of interest to those in power at the moment, politicians and commanders during the war, and in the case of postwar Sierra Leone, the donors and more immediately their field staff. Information's next-door neighbor, however, is rumor. As I explored stories of wartime experiences within a larger framework, it became apparent that they were infused with rumors, especially rumors about particularly gruesome atrocities. Rumors, locally referred to as *bush radio,* are an integral part of Sierra Leonean rural life. Also, most of my informants were illiterate, and even if they could read and write there were no newspapers, no television broadcasts, and the first local radio station in Koinadugu District, where I worked, opened four years after the war ended. The only reliable source, as many saw it, was the BBC on shortwave. The spread of information was gendered; it was still men who owned radios and promptly congregated in the shadow of a tree at 3:00 P.M. for the first edition of BBC *Focus on Africa.* People thus often have to rely on information provided by travelers, friends, neighbors, and strangers. Rumors abound and can be about witchcraft, the abduction of children by powerful politicians, or how many and who died in a traffic accident. In this environment, eyewitnesses are afforded an elevated status. Information is a weave of facts and rumors interlaced. I realized that what I sometimes took for a display of inappropriate curiosity was in fact a demonstration of people's anxieties about having lost someone they knew, but also of being in control in the very uncertain world of rumors. In my work I do not dismiss rumors or deem them false; they play an integral part in the life worlds and the cosmology of my informants. They may be of little value when quantitatively measuring the number of atrocities committed against civilians during the war, but they nevertheless reveal a lot about how people experience their place in the social world.

Sierra Leone, at the time of my fieldwork, was a war-torn country infused with humanitarian aid, something which undoubtedly affected the way in which potential beneficiaries of that aid presented themselves. Some of the girls and women I met with had been interviewed before by various UN agencies, by the National Commission for Disarmament, Demobilization, and Reintegration (NCDDR), by various NGOs recruiting beneficiaries for their programs, by journalists, and some by the TRC and the Special Court. The effect of these encounters on the way women narrated their war experiences should not be underestimated. I found that women with experience of NGOs or other professional bodies were less detailed and less personal in their narratives, followed a more structured and standardized storyline, especially when I was still unfamiliar to them. Over the course of my fieldwork, however, informants would alter or add previously unknown or even contradictory information, and their stories became both more individualized and independent of the grand narratives. But I have to conclude with Argenti-Pillen that the ways women "talk about violence can...no longer be studied in isolation from the ways they have learned to present themselves to humanitarian agencies" (2003, xii).

When I set about doing my field research I was adamant that I would speak to women who had been affected by the war, mainly those who had been abducted by rebels or other fighters. I consistently tried to avoid the grand narratives of government officials, traditional chiefs, or UN officials and NGOs. I was more interested in *how* violence and war, as well as life in a postwar society, was experienced and expressed by the women living in its midst, and how the war affected social relations, than in whether the government granted the rebels a political agenda, or the contents of the various peace accords. But anthropologists working in war-torn societies often do this in the midst of humanitarian agencies, and we are often forced to relate to the interpretations of these as well as to their impact on our subject matter. There is an interaction between NGOs and my informants, between what I know and produce and the knowledge produced by those very NGOs, and most importantly between myself and my informants.

Considering the circumstances described above, working with war-affected women and interviewing them was far from easy. Working in a postwar society, I frequently felt anxious about asking them to talk about what had happened to them or what they had done during the war. While a few women seemed to have no problems in narrating their stories, others did it with much anxiety. I have had to end many interviews or steer them away from sensitive topics. Many of the issues we touched on, such as rape, are still looked on as taboo in society, and this required a lot of sensitivity and discretion on my part. Like Linden when working on the stories of Holocaust survivors, I frequently questioned my own enterprise in terms of its effects on my informants. As Linden wrote, "Who am I to be recording accounts of the most unspeakable and unspoken atrocities of human history? Would I not bring more pain to the people I interviewed by asking them to dredge up their memories of concentration camp and hidings? Would they be racked by pain? Would they even be able to speak at all?" (Linden 1993, 61).

Conducting interviews with abducted women like Aminata entailed many challenges, such as overcoming distrust, unease, and suspicion. I nevertheless persisted in the sometimes intrusive task of collecting and analyzing these narratives. My encounters with Aminata were of the more difficult kind as she was so obviously depressed, whether because of her war or postwar experiences I did not know at first. Occasionally she agreed to talk to me in the presence of my assistant, Mary, provided I did not tape our interviews: "Do you want me to go to court!" she said accusingly when I asked if I could tape an interview.[14] Aminata was often quite sullen and short tempered, she disliked trivial questions, and I only once saw her smile. When walking in town I would sometimes see her at a distance, but she frequently avoided me in public, turning a corner or entering a house. To Mary she once said, "The white people always come and write our names in books and then leave and we never get anything to show for our cooperation!" Though Aminata's reluctance to talk to anyone about her experiences sparked my curiosity, I did not want to provoke her or bring back bad memories, so after some time I decided to leave her alone, but Mary continued to meet with her. Although Aminata once asked Mary, "What does your white woman want to do again with this when all has finished and is forgotten?" she still continued to visit Mary and often initiated conversations herself. She obviously wanted to talk, just not with me. She was aware that Mary related their discussions and showed her field notes to me. Since Aminata was quite outspoken and her story so well highlights many different aspects of how it was to be a young woman in war-torn Sierra Leone, despite her initial reluctance to talk to me personally, I decided to work with her story.

To work with the narratives of Aminata and women like her obviously has its limitations. As I have described above, because of their stigmatized position in postwar society, many were afraid of talking about their experiences, and this sometimes made interviews difficult to conduct. Methodologically, my work was difficult, for several reasons. I was initially interested in *everything* relating to my informants' lives: abduction, fighting, rape, abuse, healing, divination, marriage, initiation, income generation, migration, trading, division of labor, childbirth, to name the most salient—as many aspects as I could think of relating to women's life in war-torn Sierra Leone. However, as it was not only the issue of gender that was relevant to my study of how Sierra Leonean women had experienced war, but kinship and age as well, the individual sociocultural/economic position of my key informants begged to be examined at the level of the household and the family. The relevance of family for my informants cannot be emphasized enough; as anthropologist Linda Green (1999) wrote, marriage and kinship are one of those social spaces where structural and political violence are felt. Therefore inquiries had to be made concerning issues as diverse as birth order, the relation of relative age to authority, and inheritance and ownership rules, among many other things. The strength of this work lies in its focus on women: to their experiences of war and postwar society, how these experiences are articulated, how the women relate to and interact with people in their proximity, and how they in turn are interpreted by their surroundings.

When conducting fieldwork in 1998, 2001, and 2003–4 for a total of fifteen months, I worked mainly with a variety of war-affected young women. From initial work in a Sierra Leonean refugee camp in Guinea, to Freetown, I ended up doing the bulk of my research in the northern district of Koinadugu and settled in the district capital, Kabala (see maps 1 and 2). The town of Kabala lies at the intersection of three chiefdoms: Sengbe chiefdom, which has a Kuranko Paramount Chief, and Wara Wara Bafodia, and Wara Wara Yagala, chiefdoms that are ruled by Yalunka and Limba Paramount Chiefs respectively. There are also a great number of Fula cattle herders and traders in and around Kabala, but with increased migration, all ethnic groups in Sierra Leone are represented in the town proper. In Kabala I had the good fortune to meet Mary Kursarow Kowa, a Kuranko-speaking Sierra Leonean with good knowledge of both people and the area, and also blessed with great social skills. Mary came to be not only my research assistant and interpreter but also a good friend.

One of the reasons I chose to work in Koinadugu was the relative lack of NGOs operating there at the time. In a country otherwise dominated by the economy of humanitarian postwar projects, this was unusual. This was nothing that was celebrated by people in Koinadugu, however, who often displayed a very real sense of abjection and of being marginal to the work and world of the international community. They claimed to see little effect of rights conventions or poverty eradication schemes on the quality of their daily lives, and they welcomed any new agency coming to work in their community for the promises it held of a better life, but as much, I argue, for recognition, for someone to see that they are there and that they too have suffered.

It is difficult to position oneself in the field as an anthropologist in these circumstances. It took me a couple of months to convince my female ex-combatant informants that I was not working with an NGO, the TRC, or the Special Court, and I readily admit that much of my work would have been impossible to carry out had it not been for Mary.[15] Sometimes understanding is less a result of methodology than mastery of basic social skills, to paraphrase Jackson (1995, 21). I have interviewed more than one hundred women who were abducted during the war. Of these, I worked closely with ten. Among these there are some who stand out and whose names will recur often throughout this book. These are Aminata, whom we have met above, and also Mariatu, Musu, Kadi, Mateneh, and Finah.

The bulk of my material is in the form of field notes and interviews with these informants, some of whom I came to know quite well. Most informants, but not all, were Kuranko speakers, and those interviews were often carried out in that language and then translated into English by Mary. Still, a good number of my informants could speak Sierra Leone's lingua franca Krio, as did I. Mary was a teacher at a local school but had also before my fieldwork volunteered as a basic literacy teacher for women who had been abducted during the war. Therefore she already knew many women within my proposed target group. Also, Mary's personality inspired confidence, and I am quite certain that without her I would not have had the privilege of interviewing so many women about issues so sensitive. Nevertheless, I alone am responsible for all interpretations and conclusions based on this material.

The women we worked with differed in many respects. They were of various ages and belonged to different ethnic groups, although the key informants were all younger women and most were Kuranko speakers. They came from various social settings, and some were illiterate and others college graduates. What they all shared was the experience of being taken forcibly from their homes by "the rebels."[16] They also showed great diversity in how they talked about and dealt with their wartime experiences, which were also very varied. Some women had positions of authority while others were treated as slaves, as will be discussed in chapters 3 and 4. Their experiences of returning to their families and communities after the war also differed, as I will show in chapter 7. But for all this diversity, it is possible to discern some similarities and commonalities: most of them were sexually and physically abused, many were subjected to forced marriage, and some became fighters. My main female informants with whom I discussed war and postwar experiences begged me not to expose their identities. Many of them only confided to me in private and some against the expressed wishes of their families and kin. I have provided these informants with pseudonyms and have altered or deleted private and geographical information that might otherwise harm them.

Whether I like it or not, I was part of a horde of "strangers" in Sierra Leone comprising not only anthropologists (of which there were many), but also aid workers, UN staff, peacekeeping soldiers, missionaries, and many others. Anthropologists sometimes eagerly renounce any affiliation with those *Others* and frequently write in flattering terms of how our informants actually can make out a difference between *us* and the *others*. As we at least try to learn local languages, eat local food, and take local transport, some of us feel that we are closer to the people we want to study, just by sharing, or trying to share, parts of their life worlds. At the same time, many of us also feel terribly inadequate and often wish we really could do something tangible for people.

One concern has been how one writes about these issues without, as Daniel warns, engaging in a *pornography of violence*. Robin Schott, in a similar vein notes that "the witnessing and recording of these events raises a number of questions: How should these horrors be described? Is any description a form of complicity and voyeurism? Or is the greatest form of complicity silence? Are there some people who can speak 'truly' or 'authentically' about these events?" (Schott 1996, 23). Or as Daniel asked, how does one "give an account of these shocking events without giving in to a desire to shock?" (1996, 3–4). My desire has not been to shock, but the material may still be shocking. I have left some narratives unaltered, not because of any sense of daring, but because I felt I had to honor my informants, and of course, I also believe that although uncomfortable, they do shed light on important issues in women's experiences during the war in

Sierra Leone. By being honest about some of the violence my informants have experienced, I also wish to expose aspects of humanity some readers may have been blind to or unaware of. However, calm composure was not the driving force behind the writing of this book, rather the opposite. Although my informants shared their stories, their memories, and their desires with me, they could not share their lives.

Although the war is over, and most of my fieldwork was carried out in the postwar phase, in Kabala in 2003–4, I was reminded of it daily. As when I passed the amputee camp, housing those who had lost their limbs to blunt machetes. Or when a young boy in the neighborhood died after finding an undetonated hand grenade, thinking it was something he could play with. Or when a teenage girl walking home one evening passed a pile of burning debris, and suddenly she was hit by the shrapnel of a Rocket Propelled Grenade (RPG) left in the ground. Or whenever I was walking around town seeing the empty skeletons of burned-out houses still standing on almost every street in town. My informants all survived, but their stories tell of so many who did not. For them, life will go on, in all likelihood unperturbed by my addition to the ethnographic body of knowledge of war-torn Sierra Leone.

1

A Decade of War — Centuries of Uncertainty

Although the war started in 1991, for many of my informants the war did not really begin until November 1994, when the northern town of Kabala in Koinadugu District was attacked by the Revolutionary United Front (RUF).[1] The war was something that had been going on in the remote southeastern part of Sierra Leone and had something to do with diamonds, of which there were none in Koinadugu District. Few people seemed to know what the war was about and felt that they had nothing to do with it.[2] Was it a revolution against the corrupt state, or perhaps a conflict between disgruntled soldiers, a rural crisis due to unresolved tensions between elites and peasants, or maybe a war over natural resources? In fact, the reasons for this decade of war were many and stretch back in history.

Although this book does not attempt to explain the war in Sierra Leone, there is still a need to contextualize the conflict, which displaced more than half of the population, caused tens of thousands of deaths, resulted in many thousands of amputations and abductions, and gave a face to the phenomenon of the child soldier.

The war that Aminata returned from was part of the long and at times violent history of what we today know as Sierra Leone, which began with slavery in the sixteenth century and continued with the many small internal wars ravaging the country throughout the following centuries, to independence and the subsequent regime of the one-party state in the 1970s, up to this war. Since independence in 1961, Sierra Leone's political history has been marked by coups, two attempts (one successful) to make the country a one-party state, and severe economic mismanagement. Although the transition from colony to independent state was relatively peaceful, the first decade of independence saw much political strife.

Sierra Leone in recent history has been the recipient of much humanitarian aid and interest. In the late 1990s it was the location of the UN's largest-ever peacekeeping force, with some 17,800 peacekeeping soldiers at its peak. Operating in Sierra Leone outside the UN mandate were also British soldiers (see Williams 2001; Keen 2005).[3] At the height of the humanitarian intervention there were some 250 NGOs operating in the country, of which half were international. To really understand the country's relationships with these actors, in particular the British, I believe it is important to historically contextualize these events.

Sierra Leone is a small country, 73,326 square kilometers, and home to around 6 million people. The country is situated along the West African coast in a region also referred to as Upper Guinea, with the Republic of Guinea to the north, Liberia to the southeast, and the Atlantic Ocean to the south and west (see map 1). The climate is tropical, with hot, humid summers between May and November, and hot, dry winters between December and April. During the rainy season the coastal areas receive up to 495 centimeters of rain a year, making it one of the wettest places along the coast of western Africa. Except for the Freetown Peninsula, with its long sandy beaches, the coast is lined with a belt of mangrove swamps. The upland areas receive less rainfall and are characterized by wooded savannahs, plateaus, and a range of mountains in the east and northeast reaching a peak at Mount Bintumani of 1,948 meters.

There are seventeen ethnic groups in Sierra Leone that can be divided into categories based on language. First there is the Mande, which consists of the Mende, Vai, Kono, Loko, Kuranko, Susu, Yalunka, and Mandingo. Then there is the Mel group, which consists of the Temne, Bullom/Sherbro, Kissi, Gola, and Krim. The remaining ethnic groups do not form a consistent linguistic group. Among them are the Fula, who have a significant presence all over West Africa; they are also known as the Fulani, or in French speaking countries Peul or Pular. The Limba are not related linguistically to any of the other groups and believe that they are the original settlers of the country. Krio is the common name for all those descended from liberated slaves. Lastly, there are a few Kru, who hail from Liberia, where they are more numerous (see, e.g., Alie 1990, chap. 1). Ethnic groups in Sierra Leone do not form bounded cohesive groups, and migration and intermarriage are and have been a prevalent feature of the region. Most of my informants could speak at least two or three local languages as well as Sierra Leone's lingua franca, Krio, and those who were educated also spoke English.

Sierra Leone is one of the poorest countries in the world and has ranked lowest in the UNDP's Human Development Index for more than a decade.[4] Approximately 60 percent of the population is Muslim, 10 percent profess to what are called indigenous beliefs, and there is a growing number of Christians in the country, roughly 30 percent. Although a majority of the population consider themselves Muslim, there are great variances between Islamic practices here and in other West African countries, especially countries such as Senegal and Nigeria, which seem to have much stronger indigenous Muslim traditions. For example, intermarriage between religions is not uncommon, the most famous example being former president Tejan Kabbah, who is a Muslim and who had married a Catholic woman who kept her religious affiliation after marriage. Sierra Leone can be characterized as a society where religion is very important, although type of faith or denomination is not always important.

A Brief History of Sierra Leone

Centuries of tumultuous events preceded the political chaos that has marked the last decade and a half of violence in Sierra Leone. What emerges is a history marred on the one hand by exploitation of human and natural resources by colonial powers, and on the other by the misdirected good will of missionaries and, later, development aid, the IMF, and the World Bank. Although now famous for its diamonds and minerals, those kinds of resources were not what initially attracted European traders to Sierra

Leone from the fifteenth century onward. With one of the few natural harbors along the Upper Guinea Coast, the Freetown Peninsula was a perfect shipping center for the trade of slaves. Ironically, or perhaps because of it, the English abolitionist movement, chose this place for its project to settle liberated African slaves (see, e.g., Braidwood 1994; Kup 1972). Later, these liberated slaves came to be known collectively as Creoles and later as Krios.[5] It was hoped by the abolitionists that this settlement, the Province of Freedom, "would serve as a nucleus for the spread of Christianity and European civilisation in Africa" (Alie 1990, 51). The first group to settle in 1787 consisted of roughly four hundred people, mostly freed African men, women, and children, but the group also included white doctors, artisans, a chaplain, and about seventy white London prostitutes (Fyfe 1962, 17).[6] Land for the settlement on the Freetown Peninsula was "bought" for a pittance from the Temne chief Naimbana (Caulker 1981, 399). In 1808 the Freetown Peninsula was transformed into the first British Crown Colony in West Africa.[7]

However, the first Europeans to come to the region were the Portuguese in 1447, and it was also a Portuguese who gave the peninsula its name, Serra Lyoa, the lion mountain. Initially these traders were interested in the supply of fresh water and wood for ships on their way to India, but with the establishment of plantations in the Americas, slaves became the major trading commodity. During the next century the Portuguese trading monopoly was challenged by the British, the French, and the Dutch. Local rulers welcomed these foreign traders but limited the European trade to the coastal areas, and as a result became important middlemen between Europeans and traders from the interior (see e.g. Dorjahn and Fyfe 1962, on the relationship between traders and local rulers). In the late seventeenth century an Islamic jihad from the north dispersed many peoples over vast areas and signaled the advent of Islam in the country. According to recent historical sources, however, the expansion of Islam in Sierra Leone owed more to peaceful traders and missionaries in the eighteenth and nineteenth centuries than to the jihad (see e.g. Alie 1990; Ojukutu-Macauley 1997; D. E. Skinner 1976). By the late nineteenth century, a large part of the Sierra Leonean population had become Muslim. The first recorded Christian missionary to visit Sierra Leone arrived in 1605, but it was not until the early nineteenth century, when the Church Missionary Society sent its first missionaries, that the evangelization of Sierra Leone seriously began.

Despite the many missionaries, however, the great expansion of Christianity did not take place until the twentieth century.[8]

Trade has always been important to all the peoples in Sierra Leone, first in ivory, gold, and slaves with northern neighbors and, after the arrival of the Europeans, increasingly along the coast (Fanthorpe 1998, 15).[9] Initially, slaves sold to Europeans were a by-product of local warfare but due to an increase in European demand, in the seventeenth century, "the supply of slaves to Europeans became an end in itself" (Shaw 1997, 862), and in its turn gave rise to new wars and new patterns of migration. The introduction of European weapons also changed the manner of warfare (Siddle 1968, 50). The height of the Atlantic slave trade affecting what we now know as Sierra Leone was during a period from around 1680 to the early nineteenth century. Slave trade in the British Empire was abolished in 1807; however, the slave trade in the British West Indies was not abolished until 1834, and Holsoe among others have noted that for the Vai of southeastern Sierra Leone, just outside British jurisdiction, slave trade actually increased sharply after 1807 (Holsoe 1977, 294–95). From having been just one among many objects of trade, slaves now totally dominated even at the expense of agricultural production until it was terminated around 1850. The Atlantic slave trade was not only part of trade relations between peoples in the interior, middlemen along the coast, and Europeans, and was not only grounds for internecine warfare, but also came to fundamentally influence social and political structures among the peoples of Sierra Leone. These new structures altered relations between owners of the land and strangers, and clients and patrons; changed the institutions of marriage and domestic slavery; and created new patterns of migration and social mobility, the effects of which may still be seen today.[10]

After the abolition of the slave trade in the British Empire in 1807, the colonial administration in Freetown encouraged Africans in the hinterland to trade in new products targeting the European market, such as ivory, palm oil, kola nuts, and timber (Caulker 1981, 401). What the colonial administrators did not anticipate was the amount of labor demanded for the production of these, and instead of diminishing, the internal slave trade increased as chiefs and big men needed cheap labor. In a 1925 account, Migeod estimated that a third of the population, in what was then called the British Protectorate of Sierra Leone, were "slaves" (1925, 10). The domestic slave trade in the British Protectorate was not abolished until 1928

(Grace 1977, 415), when it was decreed that "any person born in the protectorate in or after that year was a free man" (Alie 1990, 151).

The Sierra Leonean hinterland, as opposed to the Crown Colony, did not come under British rule until 1896, and then only as a protectorate. This decision was taken in part as an action against the French, who had begun to claim large parts of land in the north, but also in response to the effects of the holy wars fought by the famous Samori Toure and his Muslim Sofas (Fyfe 1962, 448). The establishment of the protectorate was followed by a new type of local government, the British colonial system of indirect rule. The protectorate was divided into five districts, each under the administration of a British district commissioner. The districts, which cut across ethnic and linguistic barriers, were further divided into chiefdoms under the rule of paramount chiefs who were elected but could be deposed by the British governor. It has been argued that rather than promoting the interests of their subjects, these chiefs became servants of the colonial administration, for which they were given financial incentives (Alie 1990, 150).[11] The system of indirect rule enabled the British to concentrate on running the center, the colony, and letting the hinterland, the protectorate, sort itself out.[12] Also established during this time was a new system of courts separating the "natives," people from the protectorate, from the "nonnatives," who were people from the colony, mostly Krios.

As in most of Africa, women were politically and economically subordinate. In the colony of Sierra Leone in the late eighteenth and early nineteenth centuries, however, Krio women seemed to inhabit what was, for the region, a rather unique position (see, e.g., White 1987). Alie, for example, goes so far as to argue that the independence of Krio women "had no parallel either in European or African cultural life" (Alie 1990, 80). They were renowned traders and travelled all over the country, and in fact all over West Africa. They were often economically independent from their husbands, and some even owned so-called factories. But this was a small group of women, and their influence on rural "native" women in the protectorate was moderate. Women were legal minors and rarely held political positions, with the exception of the Mende, where women could become chiefs (see Day 1994; Hoffer 1972), and the Temne, where women could become subchiefs (Ojukutu-Macauley 1997, 92). There were also other positions some women could attain, such as "mamy queen." The responsibilities of a mamy queen were often to mediate between parties, settle disputes within households, between men and women, and also between women. The female leaders of the so-called secret societies could also be very influential in political life of their communities.

Unlike the population of the hinterland, the Krios were British subjects. During the nineteenth century they had a privileged position in society. Many were well educated and had jobs in the civil service, and others were successful traders. In the late nineteenth century, however, their influence diminished substantially as the colonial administration increasingly employed white civil servants (see, e.g., Spitzer 1968).[13] European and Asian (Lebanese and Indian) businessmen also came to occupy important positions in trade and effectively outmaneuvered the hitherto successful Krio and other African traders of the protectorate (A. Zack-Williams 1995, 39–44), something that was also to have serious effects on the independence of the female traders (Kaniki 1973, 98).

The period just after the First World War was characterized by a rise in the cost of living, mostly the result of poor harvests that led to a scarcity and increase in price of the country's main staple food, rice.[14] This eventually led to strikes and riots in the capital in 1919 (for more on this see Abdullah 1994). The riots of 1919 are also sometimes referred to as "the rice riots" or "the Syrian riots."[15] The world depression took a serious toll on the Sierra Leonean economy, which was particularly vulnerable as it had depended on only a few export items and as the prices of these fell dramatically (A. Zack-Williams 1995, 45). In the 1930s, the socioeconomic changes taking place in the country relating in particular to the expansion of mining, agricultural production, and trade, and facilitated by the construction of the railway and road networks, created both opportunities and problems. Although the postdepression years were promising in terms of the increase in mining and the fact that Freetown's harbor was now a key port for the British imperial fleet, large-scale migration from rural to urban areas meant that the labor force was larger than the number of job opportunities, and this created increased antagonisms (Spitzer and Denzer 1973, 566). As in much of Africa, political activism aimed at mobilizing urban labor, ameliorating working conditions, increasing the pay of Sierra Leonean workers and civil servants, and ending colonial rule, gained momentum during the 1930s and 1940s (see, e.g., Abdullah 1995). There was a lot of resentment in the country because the economic boom had not been translated into higher wages or increased employment opportunities (Spitzer and Denzer 1973, 569).

The schism between the Freetown educated elite, mostly Krios, and the peoples of the protectorate increased during the preindependence years. For example, the British had invested minimally in providing education in the protectorate.[16] At the dawn of independence, the Krios, who constituted 2 percent of the population, had a literacy rate of 80 percent, while the rest of the country had a literacy rate of 6 percent (Gberie 2005, 22). Because educational services during the colonial era were concentrated in the capital, and also grossly inadequate, colonialism "left behind a large illiteracy problem and an education system that was not suited to the needs of the people" (Alie 1990, 221). Further, as in most of Africa at this time, the educational facilities that did exist were heavily biased toward the education of boys. Nonetheless some improvements in the status of women occurred during the 1950s. In the protectorate, rights were given to women who paid tax and were literate or owned property, and also in the colony to "men and women over 21 years, who had resided in the colony for over six months, and who could meet some minimal financial requirements" (Alie 1990, 210).

From the 1930s, diamond mining, particularly in the southeast, had an important effect on the country. The earlier trend of trade monopoly among the trading houses continued, and now mining companies such as the Sierra Leone Selection Trust (SLST) received exclusive rights to mine certain areas. These companies initially also dissuaded locals from engaging in mining, and paramount chiefs were paid off at £30 to prohibit "strangers" from settling in the mining areas (A. Zack-Williams 1995, 52). Alfred Zack-Williams has argued that although a few individuals benefited greatly from diamond mining, for Sierra Leone in general mining generated underdevelopment and marginalization of the masses, and damaged the diamondiferous areas and agricultural production. These trends were "largely the result of the dominant position of SLST within the industry" (1995, 180). By the late colonial period, the economy of Sierra Leone had been transformed from one based on the export of agricultural products produced by farmers to an economy completely dependent on mining, and in 1940 minerals accounted for more than 73 percent of total domestic exports, the revenues of which went primarily to European shareholders (A. Zack-Williams 1995, 54–56). The diamond industry also increased the importance of the chiefs, as their consent was needed to prospect and mine the lands, and created large reserves of targeted laborers and so-called tributors (ibid., 54–55).[17]

In the period following the Second World War, British Sierra Leonean policy was geared toward a rapid transition to self-government. During this time, political representation from the protectorate increased, much to the dismay of the Krios and others, who complained that many of these rural representatives were illiterate (Kandeh 1992, 88). As a result, conflict increased between the educated Africans in Freetown and those from the protectorate. At this time, many people from the protectorate organized themselves into the Sierra Leone People's (SLPP), led by an English-trained medical doctor, Milton Margai, a Mende who was a conservative and also pro-British. Margai abstained from the anticolonial rhetoric common to his contemporaries in such countries Ghana and Guinea (Gberie 2005, 20). When the British handed over the country to its inhabitants they left a country fraught with problems, as there were huge gaps between the rich and the poor, and between urban and rural areas. The British focus on cash-crop production and mining had been at the expense of both industrialization and subsistence agriculture. On the other hand, these were also exciting times, and many believed that the new African political leaders would "provide a new moral leadership, a short-cut to political and economic development," and that these leaders had "the drive and charisma to move the post-colonial state from its period of suspended animation into the twentieth century" (Hayward 1984, 19).

As in most newly independent African former colonies, the high expectations and optimism that characterized Sierra Leone in the early 1960s came to naught. There were vast discrepancies between expectations and reality, and perhaps the issue was, as Hayward has noted, that the transition from colonial rule to independence "was seen primarily as a change of personnel, neither requiring nor warranting major changes," and where "the role of the state and the nature of political process were not at issue" (Hayward 1984, 22). Siaka Stevens, whose autocratic and patrimonial regime many believe sowed the seeds of the rebel war, took office in 1968 after much turbulence (see Alie 1990; Hayward 1984: 25). After having won the 1967 elections by only a small margin, and after having been sworn in, Stevens was deposed in a coup by the commander of the armed forces, Brigadier John David Lansana who then seized control of the government.[18] Only a few days later Lansana was overthrown by junior army officers giving the reign to Andrew Juxon-Smith, a senior military officer, who led a National Reformation Council (NRC) for one year before being himself overthrown by other junior officers in 1968 who then proceeded to hand over the office to Stevens.

Stevens's first years in power were characterized by violence and intimidation (see, e.g., Forna 2002), and the 1970s became a turbulent decade in the history of Sierra Leone. During this time, the country became a republic, there were new coup attempts, and independent and opposition newspapers were harassed and eventually forbidden. The 1973 elections were held during a state of emergency, and there were violent labor union and student demonstrations. In 1978 Sierra Leone became a one-party state and was to remain one throughout the rest of Siaka Stevens's reign. He stepped down from power in 1986 after almost two decades of corruption and mismanagement, handing over the largely bankrupt state to the successor of his choice, Joseph Momoh (Gberie 2005, 34–35; Kandeh 2002, 181).

The Revolutionary United Front

When the RUF emerged in the early 1990s, it presented its political agenda in its manifesto, *Footpaths to Democracy.*

> We can no longer leave the destiny of our country in the hands of a generation of crooked politicians and military adventurists.... It is our right and duty to change the present political system in the name of national salvation and liberation.... This task is the historical responsibility of every patriot.... We must be prepared to struggle until the decadent, backward and oppressive regime is thrown into the dustbin of history. We call for a national democratic revolution—involving the total mobilisation of all progressive forces. The secret behind the survival of the existing system is our lack of organisation. What we need then is organised challenge and resistance. The strategy and tactics of this resistance will be determined by the reaction of the enemy forces—force will be met with force, reasoning with reasoning and dialogue with dialogue.
>
> (Basic Document of RUF/SL)[19]

Although its ideology was outlined in this manifesto, the authenticity and purpose of its mission quite soon came to be disputed. This had to do with the atrocities committed by the rebels during the war but was also a result of the government's stubborn refusal to acknowledge that the rebels did in fact have a political agenda. This was even more so after 1996, when the elected government of Kabbah, the international humanitarian community, and many others claimed that the rebels had never had a political agenda, much less an ideology. Nevertheless, few dispute that if it is not an intellectual movement today, the origins of what came to be the RUF lie in what could be called a student movement or student culture (Abdullah 1998; Abdullah and Muana 1998; Gberie 2005; Richards 1995, 1996). In the 1960s and 1970s, the youth culture in Freetown changed with increased class consciousness and when the predominantly male, educated middle class began to socialize with what had previously been considered society's outcasts, in Krio often referred to as "rarray boys" and "savis men." Unemployed marginalized male youth followed the lead in the student-led protests at Freetown's Fourah Bay College in an effort to voice their dissatisfaction with the politics and corrupt practices of President Stevens. These events coincided with similar events around the world, and just like their contemporaries in Africa and elsewhere, young men in Freetown became politically active, and various revolutionary texts circulated widely. The students were engaged in Pan-Africanist movements and also organized anticapitalist and anticolonialist study groups, for example, the Green Book study group and the Juche Idea study group.[20] According to Paul Richards, Khadafy's Green Book populist argument of "participatory" politics was particularly appealing (Richards 1996, 55). One result of these social changes was that urban male youth culture became "an arena for a more broad-based political socialization" (Abdullah and Muana 1998, 173).

As Sierra Leone became a one-party state in 1978, the first protests against the government came, not surprisingly, from these students.[21] However, according to Bøås (1997), the students lacked focus and were not able to create links to wider segments of civil society, which is why they remained politically marginalized and failed to achieve any real political change at that time. Still, the students managed to expose "the weakness of the state, and the potential for small groups of dissidents to shake it to its foundations" (Gberie 2005, 44). Later, groups of students, political dissidents, and uneducated and unemployed youth, as far as I know only men, went to Libya for military as well as academic training. Among these were Foday Sankoh, a former corporal and army photographer, "whose sole claim to intellectual sophistication is a military signals course" (Richards 2002, 31). Sankoh later became the leader of the Revolutionary United Front.

Students and teachers were initially important figures in the movement but many of the early RUF leaders with intellectual ambitions were out-maneuvered and some were killed. In the early and mid-1990s, RUF still seemed to have intellectual pretensions insofar as they still educated their new recruits in the ideology of the movement (Abdullah and Muana 1998, 179).[22] In Freetown in 2001, I met Commander Cool, a twenty-seven-year-old ex-fighter with both the Sierra Leone Army (SLA) and the RUF.[23] He told me that while fighting as a soldier in the SLA he had been captured by the RUF, and that he together with all the other captured soldiers had been transported to the RUF base "for ideological education." Here, he said, they had to listen to Foday Sankoh's speeches about government corruption, poverty, and oppression. According to Cool, Foday Sankoh had been quite explicit in his speeches about how the country's resources had to be more evenly distributed, and how women were equal to men as fighters and revolutionaries.[24] However, as Gberie noted, Foday Sankoh was full of "rhetoric and rage," and "would never have threatened society...had it not been for the geopolitical adventurism of Libya's Colonel Gaddafi" (2005, 48).

The political climate had undoubtedly changed among student intellectuals by the late 1990s; a new generation of war-weary students had emerged who felt little solidarity with the older former students and their leftist revolutionary ideas. The students I met in 1998 had little faith in any aspirations to democracy that the rebels might have, and during this time an increasing number of male college and university students instead joined the ranks of the various Civil Defense Forces (CDF) to fight against the rebels. The CDF was allied to the government, and its overall commander was also the SLPP deputy defense minister at the time, Hinga Norman.[25] In 1998, almost everyone I talked to, whether they liked the current government or not, respected the outcome of what they thought had been free and fair elections in 1996 (Coulter 2001).[26]

The Youth "Problem" and the OAU Meeting

Though they may not be the only cause for the war, it is clear that frustrated and marginalized youth played a major part in the conflict. Why then were youth marginalized? Sierra Leone is described as an extremely hierarchical society ruled by male elders, and the war can be seen partly as an expression of discontent with this system (see, e.g., Abdullah 1998, 2004; Abdullah and Muana 1998; Archibald and Richards 2002; Richards 1996). But this alone cannot be the reason for the outbreak of violent conflict. To illustrate the generational divide, Archibald and Richards argued that as a consequence of the declining economy and post–Cold War aid budgets in the 1980s, chiefs lost many sources of income and, to procure funds, imposed arbitrary fines on young men to compensate for their losses, often in the form of "women damage" (Archibald and Richards 2002). It has also been said that in this gerontocratic and also predominantly polygynous society, young men have been especially vulnerable (see, e.g., Nyerges 1992, 869). Older men were often married to several younger women, and younger men were often too poor to marry, although this did not stop the latter from having girlfriends. The practice of accusing young men of "woman damage" in these circumstances seems to have played an important part in alienating young men from this system (Archibald and Richards 2002, 344). It can also be assumed that many young male diggers in the diamond area (where many fighters were recruited) were increasingly discontented with their position in this social system. They were often at the lowest rung of the diamond digging hierarchy and, unlike some chiefs who made fortunes, frequently received scant compensation (Zack-Williams 1995, 150, 189).

With economic recession, the conflicts between younger and older men were exacerbated. Indicative of this was perhaps the fact that the main victims of early rebel violence were seniors in the village hierarchy (see, e.g., Bøås 1997, 16; Jackson 2005). This age-biased violence has also been noted by David Keen (2000, 294), who writes that the "civil war has seen repeated attempts to humiliate traditional chiefs and local "big men" by teenage fighters lacking status or adequate employment within their own communities." One can surmise that many paramount chiefs and other senior servants in the administration of the country (police, army, schools, etc.) were all in one way or another in Stevens's, and later Momoh's, pocket (Kandeh 2002, 180–82). But the generational hierarchy that had until then been "normal" now became an affront and a deprivation to young men.

Education and the position of intellectuals have also been an issue of contest in Sierra Leone. As in most of Africa, education has historically been the prerogative of elites, who have in turn exploited it and thereby further increased rather than reduced educational and other inequalities (cf. Bledsoe 1992; Cruise O'Brien 1996, 65). In Sierra Leone, the educational situation had increasingly deteriorated since the 1980s, and to illustrate this, young students would often mention to me a public speech by President Momoh in which he is claimed to have said that "education is a privilege, not a right" (see also Kandeh 2002, 185). Geographer Barry Riddell, who has worked extensively on Sierra Leone, is quite explicit in his analysis of the war. He claims that "Sierra Leone's chaos and violence were a result of the policies, programmes, and plans of the post-colonial governments of the country, especially those of the All People's Congress (APC)" (Riddell 2005, 118; cf. Kandeh 2002). Many of my educated Sierra Leonean friends viewed the 1980 meeting of the Organization of African Unity (OAU) in Freetown as a turning point in history, or when things really went from bad to worse. One man explained that if I was really interested in the war I should start by looking at the events of and following the OAU meeting. There is of course no one factor that can explain the Sierra Leonean war, but the visibility of the OAU meeting and its bleak economic aftermath makes it a potent symbol of government corruption.

The OAU meeting was ostentatious. More than sixty luxury houses were built in Freetown for the African delegates, as well as conference centers and luxury hotels. The total cost was US$200 million, and money was taken from all other realms of society, including education, health, and the army, to finance it (Alie 1990, 272; Conteh-Morgan and Dixon-Fyle 1999, 113; Riddell 1985a, 537). The period following the meeting was a financial disaster, forcing the government to request financial assistance from the IMF. This was not the first time; the World Bank and the IMF had been an integral part of Sierra Leone's economy since the mid-1960s (for more see Conteh-Morgan and Dixon-Fyle 1999). One of the early strategies of Stevens's government to consolidate its power had been to create employment opportunities in the civil service and state corporations to "prevent the growth of a disenchanted and unemployed educated urban mass" (Riddell 1985b, 400–401). When the IMF called for austerity measures to be imposed on the national budget as a condition for credit, at least one-third of all civil servants were fired (for more see Conteh-Morgan and Dixon-Fyle 1999, chapter 5). This resulted in mass unemployment, in particular among educated youth, and also increased political opposition. But as opposition increased, so did the repressive measures from the government.

Consumer prices on imported items, including rice, skyrocketed, another result of the austerity measures, and public spending was cut to a minimum, affecting in particular schools, hospitals, roads, and communications. The conditions demanded by the IMF worked, according to Riddell, "at the expense of certain members of the population, those already disadvantaged, particularly the poor and unemployed" (Riddell 1985b, 396; see also T. Zack-Williams 2002, 3). But the government also feared the political implications of fully complying with the conditions set up by the IMF and so at times ignored them. This became clear in a statement in which Siaka Stevens likened the IMF austerity measures to "political suicide" (Conteh-Morgan and Dixon-Fyle 1999, 94). According to Riddell, the amounts of money spent by the Stevens government on the OAU meeting "exemplify how funds have been diverted from projects that could have benefited the nation as a whole to those that only serve the needs of specific segments of the political economy, especially the well-educated, urbanized elite, who were mainly government supporters" (1985b, 400). This continued under Momoh's reign. In 1987, despite some efforts by Momoh to improve the economy, IMF and the World Bank blocked further loans, causing inflation to rise to 170 percent and plummeting the national economy ever deeper, with prices increasing and salaries unpaid (see Conteh-Morgan and Dixon-Fyle 1999, 125–26).

The Sierra Leonean War

> In the beginning people said: the rebels are like the rain—when it comes
> it washes away all the debris.
>
> Interview with Sierra Leonean refugee in Guinea, March 1998

When Foday Sankoh and a force comprising roughly one hundred crossed the Liberian border into Sierra Leone on 23 March 1991, no one could have guessed the extent of the violence and brutality that would come to signify the decade-long war. The RUF had trained in Liberia under the courtesy of then rebel leader Charles Taylor and initially gained control only of the eastern and southeastern parts of the country. At this time, the RUF was considered by many in the capital to be a marginal phenomenon and did not pose a serious threat to the power of APC and President Momoh. This did not mean, however, that all was well in the Western Area. Although many Sierra Leoneans disliked the APC and were discontent with the political and economic situation in Sierra Leone, they did not rally to support the RUF. On the contrary, many considered the rebels "mercenary bands of ruffians who should be hunted down and exterminated as a threat to the very notion of society" (Gberie 2005, 72). When President Momoh was removed from power in April 1992, it was not by the RUF but in a military coup by the National Provisional Ruling Council (NPRC) under the leadership of the twenty-eight-year-old Captain Valentine Strasser. The coup was applauded by many Sierra Leoneans, who thought that now the rebel war would end. After all, RUF's aim had been to overthrow the APC, but the RUF continued fighting, undeterred. Although allegedly initially supported by the RUF, to enforce its own legitimacy among the Sierra Leone population, the NPRC hit hard against the RUF (Keen 2005, 94).[27] The rebels, now faced with major losses, changed their tactics and in an attempt to regain military strength withdrew to the bush, where they erected inaccessible camps for the purpose of training new recruits. In 1994, the RUF began what came to be known as Phase Two of their war against the state. This period was marked to a large degree by guerrilla warfare, and according to the TRC report it was during this period, 1993–97, that the RUF was responsible for more violations and abuses than either before or after (2004, 2(2) § 132). It was also during Phase Two that the northern district of Koinadugu, where I later came to work, was first seriously affected by the war. During this time that the government turned to private security companies, such as Executive Outcomes.[28] Executive Outcomes was a South African-based company, which in exchange for the provision of military training received large diamond concessions. During this period the war intensified and fighting came as close as forty kilometers from Freetown, reminding the population of the capital that the war involved all Sierra Leoneans and was not only, as had been assumed by many, a rural concern.

In Sierra Leone, as I have mentioned before, youth culture and massive unemployment, in combination with widespread political corruption, have often been seen as the main reasons for the eruption of the extremely violent conflict. Some deemed it rather "the coming of anarchy" (Kaplan 1994), while others pointed to economic aspects such as control of the country's diamond trade and political corruption (Kandeh 2002; Reno 2000; Reno and Bah 1997). There were also those who emphasized youth dissatisfaction

(Abdullah and Muana 1998; Bøås 1997; Richards 1996), or the urban-elite bias and the unrest of hundreds of thousands economically marginalized farmers (Peters 2006), in combination with the burden of debt servicing that was common to many Third World countries (Riddell 2005). Unlike so many other wars in Africa during the same time, ethnicity and religion were never major issues of contest in the Sierra Leonean conflict. Although early on, many international analysts pointed to local rather than international factors, emphasizing banditry and local corruption, later this turned out to be just another way of containing the conflict, ignoring international and regional interests in destabilizing the region. Today we know that external and international actors were involved from the earliest phase. Numerous foreign companies showed an interest in destabilizing or influencing the government in an attempt to make money, and influential diamond dealers from Europe and elsewhere have unquestionably fomented the conflict in search of cheap high-quality diamonds (Smillie, Gberie, and Hazleton 2000). The British and South African so-called security companies, in reality mercenaries for hire with dubious, but not completely covert, motives, also participated actively. Rumors that international gun, drug, and sex traders have been actors in the conflict in various ways were also widespread.

In January 1996, the NPRC wanted to postpone the elections planned for March of the same year, and then Strasser was brought down by his deputy and chief of armed forces, Captain Julius Maada Bio (see Keen 2005, 154–55). Bio's power did not last long, however, and public opinion was for elections. Especially women's groups, which had negotiated with both government and rebels, had worked hard to ensure the elections. In February and March 1996, parliamentary and presidential elections were held. In the second round of the presidential election a majority (almost 60 percent), voted for the Sierra Leone People's Party (SLPP) led by Alhaj Ahmed Tejan Kabbah, a former UN official, thus ending four years of army rule.[29]

Despite the elections, sporadic fighting of varied intensity continued unabated in the hinterland between progovernment forces and the RUF rebels. Peace remained elusive, as it was unclear if the rebels would really demobilize, and the new government became increasingly suspicious of the national army and sided instead with what came to be called the Civil Defense Forces (CDF), which consisted of groups of ethnically organized traditional hunters (see, e.g., Alie 2005; Ferme and Hoffman 2004; Hoffman 2004b). Then, in November 1996, a peace accord was signed in Abidjan, the capital of Côte d'Ivoire, officially ending the war yet again, but both RUF and CDF forces failed to observe a cease-fire agreement signed in March (Keen 2005, 196–97). This was not brought to international attention, as the CDFs were not a party to or subject to the demands of the Abidjan Peace Accord. The UN had played a key role in the Abidjan Peace Accord and the previous year had established a UN Special Envoy and a Joint International Observer Group. The Organization of African Unity (OAU), the Economic Community of West Africa (ECOWAS), and the British Commonwealth had also involved themselves in fact-finding missions and in negotiations. In fact, international support to promote democracy in Sierra Leone is perhaps unmatched in post–Cold War Africa (Conteh-Morgan and Dixon-Fyle 1999, 154; Ferme and Hoffman 2004, 73–74; Hoffman 2004a, 211–12).[30]

On a visit to Nigeria in February 1997, RUF leader Foday Sankoh was detained by the Nigerian authorities, charged with arms trafficking, and held under house arrest until late 1998. The capture of their leader did not deter the RUF fighters, and contrary to the hopes of the government, fighting did not stop but instead increased. In May 1997, events took an unexpected turn when a group of ex–Sierra Leone Army officers, calling themselves the Armed Forces Revolutionary Council (AFRC), headed by Major Johnny Paul Koroma, overthrew the fourteen-month-old government in a coup has been described as "the most bloody, destructive, and repugnant in the country's nation-building history" (Conteh-Morgan and Dixon-Fyle 1999, 136).[31] President Kabbah and most of his government nevertheless managed to flee to neighboring Guinea. In the meantime, AFRC invited its former adversaries, the RUF, to join the new regime. This period saw a great dispersion of people as refugees to the neighboring countries or as internally displaced people. The population of Freetown saw the period of AFRC/RUF rule as an occupation, and the capital came almost to a standstill as schools and banks closed and people refused to go to work; members of civil society also organized acts of civil disobedience (see, e.g., Mansaray 2000, 154).

Playing a very important part in the conflict at this time was the Economic Community of West African States Monitoring Group (ECOMOG), a West African peacekeeping force led by Nigeria (see Gberie 2003). Its mandate was to restore peace and to reinstate the Kabbah government with the use of force. On 12 February 1998, ECOMOG intervened in Freetown and managed to take control of the city, dispersing AFRC/RUF fighters mainly to the east of the country, where fighting continued. One month later, on March 10, the elected President, Ahmed Tejan Kabbah, returned from Guinea to claim his position of authority. My first visit to Sierra Leone coincided with this event. I traveled from the border town of Pamelap in Guinea with a bush taxi, stopping at thirteen ECOMOG checkpoints before reaching Freetown on 4 April 1998 (see Coulter 2001).

In Freetown in April 1998, the rebels were generally demonized and characterized as monsters. People said that they were not human. If the RUF had at one time had a political agenda, by 1998 they had lost a lot of credibility among the majority of the Sierra Leonean people. By all accounts, in March 1998, the rebels had lost the war. This naturally influenced my material at this time. Suddenly no one admitted to having been a rebel. All rebels were considered evil, and the violence they used was beyond the pale. The Sierra Leone Army, and even more so the ECOMOG soldiers, were heroes and the abuses they inflicted rarely debated. This closely reflected the official view of the government and the ECOMOG at that time, according to which the RUF combatants had no political agenda.[32] Today we have a more nuanced image and know that the RUF were not the only ones that committed atrocities and human rights violations (see, e.g., Keen 2005).

Despite hopes to the contrary, the war was not over. On 6 January 1999, Freetown was attacked by fighters from a new fighting force primarily made up by former army fighters, the West Side Boys, the AFRC, and also RUF, who took control of parts of Freetown, including State House (for details see Keen 2005, 222–23). During this attack mainly the eastern parts of the city were burnt and looted. Five thousand people were killed and approximately two thousand women and girls were raped. The fighters targeted police officers, army personnel, journalists, and many political activists. The fighters were eventually repelled by ECOMOG forces, who in their zeal to drive away "the rebels" were also accused of indiscriminate killing of civilians, rape, and widespread looting.

In July 1999, yet another peace accord was signed in Lomé, the capital of Togo. The Lomé accord was very much "an agreement between warring leaders, with a marked lack of participation from civil society or even

young combatants," (Keen 2005, 257) and as during the Abidjan negotiations, "women's organizations had been excluded from a place at the ne-
gotiating table—this despite their pivotal role in bringing peace and some
kind of democracy in 1996" (Keen 2005, 252). In October 1999, a UN Assistance Mission to Sierra Leone (UNAMSIL) deployed troops to Sierra
Leone to support the implementation of the peace accord and to assist in
the Demilitarization, Demobilization, and Reintegration (DDR) process.
Power sharing as the most constructive solution to the conflict was the basis
of this peace accord, and RUF leader Foday Sankoh was given the title
of vice president and made head of a new mineral resources commission
(Keen 2005, 251). The accord also granted a blanket amnesty to all RUF
fighters, and as a result became "a bitter pill to swallow for many Sierra
Leoneans" (Squire 2000, 63). Being war weary and seeing no other options,
many people had to accept the government's cooperation with the rebels.
Fighters from all factions, notably RUF, AFRC, The West Side Boys,
and the SLA repeatedly violated the agreement, most notably by holding
hostage hundreds of peacekeeping soldiers, and on 8 May 2000, members
of the RUF shot and killed around twenty people demonstrating outside
Sankoh's house in Freetown. This led to the subsequent arrest of Sankoh
and senior members of the RUF in Freetown (Keen 2005, 264). The signing of the peace agreements Abuja I on 10 November 2000, and Abuja II
on 2 May 2001 further strengthened the peace process. The war was officially declared over by President Kabbah on 18 January 2002. While awaiting trial at the Special Court after having been indicted for war crimes,
Sankoh died in a Freetown hospital on July 30, 2003.

Atrocities—Rumors and Realities

> The rebels entered Kabala in the afternoon. First I thought they had come
> to surrender because they had tied white pieces of cloth around their heads
> and they were so young. We stood on the side of the road and clapped and
> sang for them.
>
> Interview March 2004 with a young woman who was abducted
> by rebels during the 1998 "Five Day attack" in Kabala[33]

For many of the people in Koinadugu District whom I talked to, whose
houses had been burnt and properties looted or destroyed and whose children

had been abducted, the violence of the war was often interpreted as something coming from the outside, something extrinsic to their culture and social relations. "We are only farmers," some said. "We don't know anything." They portrayed a life in which they had felt little incentive, apart from trying to stay alive, to engage with either government forces or the rebels. I got the impression that many of the villagers I met felt marginal to the war between the rebels and the government. I was often told that the rebels sometimes punished villagers if they were suspected of being allies of ECOMOG or the SLA, and many were definitely punished by rebels for having voted for President Kabbah in the 1996 election. There were stories that have been recounted many times of rebels cutting off people's hands and saying, "Go and show this to Kabbah," or "This was the hand you voted with."

Any legitimate reasons the RUF had initially presented for starting the war were seldom if ever mentioned by my informants, and neither was the sad state of Sierra Leonean politics and economy prior to the war. Few people talked about the widespread corruption of the 1980s, the deteriorating standards of schools and hospitals, the irregular payment of civil servants; these issues were at that time dispatched to oblivion. After all, the rebels had lost the war and had thereby lost the prerogative to interpret or shape history. For the local population, to deconstruct the conceptual and experiential boundaries between victims and perpetrators was obviously not an issue; rebels were "wicked" and more so child and female combatants, as I will discuss further in chapters 3 and 4. Perhaps this was because the vast majority of the Sierra Leonean population did not take up arms and was not actively involved in armed activities. They were merely trying to survive, and the majority of the population felt that they had few interests vested in the war.

Like Aminata, thousands of girls and women were abducted during the war. No one knows exactly how many, and all numbers must be regarded as estimates. It is believed that there could have been from ten thousand to twenty thousand women in the RUF.[34] Not all abducted girls and women were fighters, however; many more were so-called bush wives through forced marriage, domestic workers, or slaves, and most were never counted or registered in any postwar program.

The Sierra Leonean war has often been described as one of the most brutal and vicious in the late twentieth century. For example, amputations,

rape, and random killings were common, and references to cannibalism
have also been commonplace in the reporting of the war in Sierra Leone.
Hinga Norman, deputy defense minister in the SLPP government and
leader of the Civil Defense Forces, was charged by the Special Court in
Sierra Leone for war crimes, including cannibalism, but died while in custody. Cannibalism as a mythical phenomenon has been present in Sierra
Leonean history since long before the war (see, e.g., Beattie 1978; Ferme
2001; Kalous 1974; MacCormack 1983; Shaw 2002). Many people I talked
to believed that anyone who has become a successful politician must have
sacrificed humans and consumed them, especially the bodies of young children. According to Mariane Ferme, the consumption of humans "reflects
an excessive greed for power, which inevitably results in trespassing the
boundaries of legitimacy" (2001, 183). Ideas about getting strength and
power from eating the human heart abound (cf. Shaw 1996, 2001, 2002;
and also Moran 2006 on heartmen in Liberia).

According to testimonies to the Special Court, cannibalism did occur
during the war, and although I do not refute this, I am skeptical about how
it has been used, in particular in Western media as a means of making the
conflict seem bizarre and exotic, thereby reinforcing Kaplan's anarchy and
barbarism thesis at the expense of a more complex analysis of the war. As
in the following statement by a former mercenary from Executive Outcomes who fought in Sierra Leone during the NPRC regime:

> If you capture the enemy, you want to interrogate them. For the Sierra
> Leone army, they wanted to eat the heart and or other vital organs of their
> enemies. We would have to fly out the prisoners we wanted to interrogate
> on the helicopters back to Freetown so they wouldn't be eaten. The MI-17
> would fly over and the Sierra Leone soldiers would look up and say, "There
> goes dinner." They would look upset. In certain parts of Sierra Leone can-
> nibalism is rife.[35]

Nevertheless, for many of my female informants who had been abducted by the rebels, the issue of cannibalism held other concerns. One
example of the many rumors that flourished about cannibalism was that
many said they had often been afraid of eating the food served when they
were with the rebels. One of my informants to whom we will return later,
Mariatu, said that while she was with the rebels she only ate rice, because

at the sight of any meat she would think it was from humans. She said that sometimes when they were served meat she had not seen any animal from which it could come, so therefore she assumed it was human flesh, and this was repeated in many interviews. Still, it has to be emphasized that no one I interviewed had actually witnessed the preparation of human flesh for consumption, and in a later conversation, Mariatu said that her group "did not eat people." One of my youngest informants, Kadi, who was only nine when she was abducted, said that her mother believed she had eaten human flesh in the bush, and had insisted on offering sacrifices for forgiveness when her daughter returned home after the war "to let God forgive me."

One of the most widespread stories of rebel atrocities is about the evisceration of fetuses from pregnant women. The most common version is about two male rebels and a pregnant woman. The two rebels start to argue over the sex of the baby, one saying it is a boy and the other a girl. To find out, they have to cut open the stomach of the woman and pull out the fetus. This is a story that has been repeated many times in official NGO documents and reports (see, e.g., Human Rights Watch 1998, 2003; and the report by the TRC 2004). In a confidential TRC interview with a girl who had been very young when abducted, the following incident was narrated:

> I came across a pregnant woman who strayed into our camp. I threatened to stab her with my knife. The others came around and were curious to know the sex of the baby she was carrying. I said male and others said female. The boys opened her up in front of me and brought out a boy. I jumped with joy that I had won.

> (TRC 2004, 3a: § 51)

Almost all Sierra Leoneans I have met can recount this story, although with variations. It was often told as an example of extreme rebel brutality. In the film *Woman See Lot of Things* by documentary filmmaker Meira Asher (2006), about the lives of three female fighters in Sierra Leone, a young girl reenacts exactly how she disemboweled women on direct orders.[36] This act of disemboweling women constitutes one of the Sierra Leone Truth and Reconciliation Commission's official findings, and they write that according to human rights law, the practice of disemboweling pregnant women

with the intention of removing the fetus constitutes "enforced steriliza-
tion" (TRC 2004, 2: note 41). However, although the TRC recorded only a
few incidents of "disembowelment," they suspect that "the figure is not indicative of the actual number of women who suffered the violation" (TRC
2004, 3b: § 264). The final TRC report emphasized that victims and witnesses may have suppressed memories of such events; the TRC felt that
this could explain why more people did not testify about it. I find it curious that these memories in particular should be suppressed when other
equally horrific memories have been narrated quite openly and in frank
detail. Whereas many people could tell of firsthand experience of, or being
eyewitnesses to, the cutting off of hands, not one of my informants had actually witnessed rebels debating the sex of an unborn child before eviscer-
ating the mother. Other, equally horrifying stories about extreme violence
on women's genitals, for instance, were not as widespread, but many people admit to having witnessed it.

The RUF did commit a lot of atrocities, and this made it difficult for
many people to understand or have sympathy for its cause. In general it
seemed very difficult for people to understand how child and female combatants could be so "evil." Stories of "long sleeve," "short sleeve," where
the rebels cut off arms above the elbow or at the wrist, or the cutting off of
noses, ears, and lips were prevalent. This is where we detect perhaps one
of the major incongruities of how this war has been described and interpreted by Western media and policymakers. On the one hand we have the
children, considered by most Westerners as innocent victims, and on the
other we have the "evil" rebels whose brutality has been condemned by all.
The discrepancy lies in the fact that the wicked rebels consisted mostly of
these innocent victims. This argument can also be related to the presence
of female fighters among the rebel forces. If women are always victims,
how is the violence of female fighters explained? There is no doubt that
the rebels committed brutal atrocities, but the rebels also consisted mostly
of girls, boys, young women, and men.

Although the rebels would be blamed for all kinds of atrocities, only
a handful of people I talked to said that they actually believed that RUF
child soldiers were personally guilty of the crimes they had committed.
Most pointed to drugs as the main reason explaining the absurd level of
violence; "that is how they are brave to do all these things, without the
drugs they cannot do it. Because I cannot stand and see my mother and kill

her! But because of the drugs you can't recognize who is standing in front of you," said Musu, one of my informants. Others blamed the "wicked" rebel leaders but more rarely the corrupt political system.

Concluding Remarks

Working as an anthropologist in a war-torn society usually means that the area will be covered not only by many journalists and UN and NGO staff but also by many academic researchers. The majority of academic studies on the war in Sierra Leone have focused on political corruption, anarchy, neopatrimonial rule, the weak state, and warlords. Others have focused on the rebel movement, child soldiers and young fighters, refugees, the rural crisis, or the problem of humanitarian intervention and security issues, and some have examined the role of diamonds and other resources in the war. More recently some have also focused on the role of the Truth and Reconciliation Committee and the Special Court. As this summary shows, it is not my intention to *explain* the violence of the Sierra Leonean war; I leave that to others. I merely want to point to some of the complexities surrounding both the actual violence and the myths surrounding it.

As this summary of Sierra Leonean history also reveals, not much is written about women's contributions and position in the country in general or in the context of war. This is not unique to Sierra Leone, to Africa, or to the rest of the world. At best, what we get is a fleeting glimpse of women in history. When they do appear, it is often as wives, migrants, slaves, or mothers, and more rarely in connection with issues of politics, nationalism, and resistance (cf. Geiger 1999, 26). When women emerge as influential and successful members of society, these are often the exceptions rather than the rule, as when women diverge from traditional African gender roles: the successful female traders, the Mende female chiefs, and the powerful women leaders of the "secret societies," for example (see MacCormack 1974; Ottenberg 1994; White 1981).

Despite the lack of "women" in the writings on Sierra Leonean history, I have still found it important to give an account of longer processes of Sierra Leonean history. This is because I wanted to show some of the complexity of Sierra Leonean politics leading up to and following independence. "Anthropologists who study civil war without mentioning its translocal context and its distant protagonists," wrote Argenti-Pillen, "are in danger of participating in a spurious indigenization of violence" (2003, 202). The Sierra Leonean war was neither a war only over diamonds or other resources, nor only of disgruntled youth, although both these factors have played important parts in the rhetoric of and reasons for the war; but they alone cannot account for it. An historic background of this sort can help contextualize the conflict and make it seem less exotic and strange. However, it lacks the potential to explain the current social relations of the country's population—between men and women, parents and children, and families and their kin. In the next chapter I will deal more explicitly with the social structure of Sierra Leone, with a preference for the area where I have worked longest, the northern district of Koinadugu.

2

Gendered Lives in Rural Sierra Leone

An Ethnographic Background

Most of my informants were very young when they were abducted; only a few had married and had children. When they returned home after the war they were mature women, and many had also become mothers but had never been married. As I will discuss later, the ambiguous position of these young women—they were neither girls nor fully women according to cultural convention—created many problems for them, their families, and communities, as has been indicated already in the introduction with the case of Aminata. Many of these problems revolved around issues of morality and sexuality but also spoke to issues of social organization and social reciprocity. In this chapter I will discuss some important aspects of local social organization focusing on gender, age, and kinship. My emphasis will be on social relations among Kuranko speakers in Koinadugu District, but I will touch on issues common to many peoples in Sierra Leone.

It is difficult to present a unified and generalized system of gender for Sierra Leone, or even for the people living in Koinadugu District, as there seem to be as many exceptions as there are assumptions about proper roles for men and women. Nevertheless, in Sierra Leone, as elsewhere, it is important to make a distinction between women's and men's lived experience and lived expectations of gender norms (cf. Dolan 2002). The normative model, or set of ideas, defining what constitutes men and women is a model to which men and women aspire and against which they measure themselves, and against which they are also measured by their society. In rural Sierra Leone this is a model based on the polarization of men and women with regard to what their positions and roles in society should be, what women and men should do, and how they should relate to each other, as illustrated by marriage, the sexual division of labor, and status under the law. This is also a relational model in which men and women occupy multiple subject positions, and one that offers different masculinities and femininities. Both men and women are "embedded in nexuses of specific opportunities and obligations associated with kinship, friendship and patron-client relations," and both men's and women's "experiences depend on their ability to manage and draw on these effectively" (Leach 1994, 206).

The roles women and men occupy in this system of gender division are mostly complementary and interdependent. The idea of complementary gender roles is not restricted to the division of labor but permeates many other spheres of life and cosmology among most groups in Sierra Leone, and is a recurring feature of gender in much of West Africa (cf. Oppong 1983). Men and women are assigned separate but complementary roles and duties, but men are superior to women, particularly in the legal and political domains. Women rarely own or control land, and property inheritance is often reckoned through the male line (Tejan-Cole 1998; Thomas, Harding, and Kabbah 1998). Women in northern Sierra Leone are thus considered to be subordinate to men, first to their fathers and later to their husbands. Male stereotypes about women during my fieldwork were that they were always gossiping, they were lazy, they were also dangerous and needed to be controlled (which is why they are circumcised, according to both men and women), and they "belonged to the house." It was understood that a woman cannot *be* for herself; she is always *of* or *for* someone else (see, e.g., Ferme 2001). In reality, in northern Sierra Leone, women are not lazy at all but extremely hardworking; they perform the most tedious tasks on farms, and produce, process, and cook almost all food. In the little time they have when not farming, they are involved in petty trade, cleaning the house, and bringing up children. Most wives and mothers were not alone in the household with these responsibilities. Due to the practice of polygyny they were often one of a number of wives, who may or may not cooperate in the household. For example, depending on socioeconomic status, some wives took turns cooking, while others cooked separately and lived in separate households.

This set of gendered ideas is also reflected in Sierra Leone law, where formal and customary laws coexist.[1] Whereas in the 1991 Constitution women and men are equal, in customary law women are often treated as legal minors. Also, the constitution has until recently not covered adoption, marriage, divorce, burial, devolution of property on death, or other interests of personal law, which have been subject to common law. This has in effect been discriminating in many areas of concern to women, such as education, inheritance, property, and divorce laws (Amnesty International 2006; Tejan-Cole 1998; Thomas, Harding, and Kabbah 1998). Three years after my fieldwork, however, on 14 June 2007, after years of lobbying by women's groups, the Sierra Leone Parliament passed three "Gender Bills" into law. The new acts are the Domestic Violence Act, the Registration of Customary Marriage and Divorce Act, and the Devolution of Estates Act. The last one, the Devolution of Estates Act, governs intestate succession, that is, inheritance between spouses. Previously this varied under the three sets of laws.[2]

In Sierra Leone, as in most of West Africa, just as society is organized along male-female distinctions, age is also a relevant factor of differentiation (see, e.g., Leach 1994, 58). Therefore, a senior wife will have authority over junior wives, an older sister over younger brothers, and all adults over all children. It is often said that women have a "duty to serve" their husbands and juniors their elders. This focus on the differentiation of gender, age, and status has meant that the region has been characterized by the simultaneous "tension between the production of gender boundaries and processes [age and status] that undermined them" (Ferme 2001, 63). There are also considerable differences between rural and urban women, between the educated female elites and the illiterate female farmers. Among educated urban women there has been a long struggle for political recognition and participation. There are a number of strong women political and community leaders and also many outspoken women's grassroots organizations, mainly based in the capital. These women are well versed in the language of rights and are often supported by NGOs, and they work hard to include women in decision-making processes on national as well as international levels. In the rural north, most women were not engaged in political activism, and there were few women's organizations. Many women led very "traditional" lives; most were farmers or petty traders, they married, had children, and had little overt interest in politics. Many older rural women said that politics was no place for women, and they also felt that women should be subordinate to their fathers and husbands, "because that is how we met it," as they would often say.

Women are nevertheless not subordinate to men in all aspects of society. In the village of Kamadugu Sokorala, for example, the women cherished their initiation society. In fact, any infringement on their activities by men for any reason, Islamic or otherwise, was seen with distrust and skepticism. For example, Muslim leaders have of late displayed a dislike for some practices of these "secret societies" of both men, the Kome and Gbangbe, and women, the Segere, which has resulted in a substantial decrease in male traditional rituals and ceremonies. But the women's society, Segere, is still very active.[3] The women's society gave them access to public space in ways not possible for individual women. The society could, for example, unite against abusive husbands. I will provide one example where women as a group showed that they had the means to effectively correct male behavior. Once in the village I was sitting outside on a mat taking notes when suddenly someone screamed what I first thought was "snake, snake!" Everyone took to their feet and ran off as fast as they could. I did too. Only moments later did I realize that in fact they had shouted "Segere, Segere!" When they enter public space, all men, children, and uncircumcised women have to flee indoors, for to be caught by the Segere can entail various sorts of gruesome punishments. The men, boys, uncircumcised girls, and I, hid in the houses while the women's society paraded through town. There had been no previous warning that they would come. It was not a time for initiation or other ceremonies. Eventually I found out that one of the women's husbands had beaten her, and the Segere marched through town, stopping outside his door. I did not hear it, but from what I was told afterward, the *society devil* had threatened the husband, and it was understood that the husband would get a huge hernia on his scrotum if he continued. Segere is no laughing matter. People take them seriously, and I did not hear of the man's beating his wife again. I think few would argue on the relative subordinate position of women in Sierra Leonean society, and from this perspective then, the Segere, its activities, and the sanctioned appropriation of public space become all the more fascinating, and the women's reluctance to give it up because of Islamic (or Christian) constraints on so-called pagan activities, more understandable (cf. Ferme 2001, 64).

The Village and the Town

Like many rural villages lying along the rebels' paths, the small village of Kamadugu Sokorala in Koinadugu District was hit hard during the war (map 2).[4] The villagers lived for months at a time in the bush while rebels occupied their village, later leaving it burnt and looted. Despite the upheaval of war and displacement, some routines persisted; villagers discussed and debated prospective engagements, youths flirted, children were born, some married, and others divorced. The war obviously brought changes to the village, but other changes had already started to take place well before the war, and also since anthropologist Michael Jackson did fieldwork in Kamadugu Sokorala in the late 1960s and 1970s (see Jackson 1977).[5] Winding paths are no longer the means of navigating from house to house; instead, most houses today stand side by side facing three rather straight but dusty intersecting roads, and houses are no longer round but rectangular or square. Despite a high level of out-migration, especially among young men, the population has increased in the past thirty years. The village of Kamadugu Sokorala is home to little over six hundred people. They are all, with very few exceptions, Kuranko speakers. The village is situated about twelve miles southwest of Kabala, the district capital of Koinadugu District (map 2), along a very poor road, almost impassable by vehicles during the rainy season. After the war, through donor-funded rehabilitation schemes, a clinic and a new school were built in the village. The village is dominated by Muslims, but there are also four Christians: the schoolteacher and his wife, and two converts. People basically live on farming and remittances, although there are also two male petty traders. During the war the village was attacked and occupied by the RUF twice; the second time, the rebels left with all they could carry and burned down all but five houses. At the time of my fieldwork there were sixty-five houses, most built anew with mud bricks, thatched roofs, but a few had salvaged bits and pieces of the old and rusty corrugated iron sheets for roofing from the debris. Most people lost everything they owned during the war. Although many people at the time of my fieldwork had houses and were farming, they were poor. Perhaps this is not a perfect indicator of level of poverty, but most women I met owned only one pair of slippers, one T-shirt, and at most two *lappa*.[6]

Even though the Kuranko as a people were one of the first in Sierra Leone to become Muslim, in small villages like Kamadugu Sokorala, many people have not strictly followed the tenets of Islam and instead privilege what they term "Kuranko customs." The fact that Islam spread so quickly was also because it was indulgent of traditional religious practices and beliefs, as I have described in the previous chapter. So far, religion has not yet become politicized to the extent that is the case in many other West African countries, and Islam in its present stricter form came quite late to Kamadugu Sokorala, from the 1960s onward.[7] This has changed somewhat during the last three decades, especially with the spread of Wahabiyya Islam from Saudi Arabia. Wahabiyya enforces more rigorously the doctrines of Islam. For instance, only ten years ago the Muslim leaders in Kamadugu Sokorala had the children destroy all effigies of the hunting societies, and as I mentioned above, some Muslim leaders today are not in favor of the traditional male and female societies. However, in both Kamadugu Sokorala and Kabala, imams were important and respected community leaders with influence on both religion and local politics, and they were also generally consulted on issues of domestic problems. Many of my informants in the urban areas had converted from Islam to Christianity, or the other way around, and some Muslims went to church and some Christians to the mosque. Religious tolerance and diversity characterize the region but are perhaps more pronounced in urban areas, where families will sometimes consist of both Christians and Muslims.

Only twelve miles away, the situation in the district town of Kabala, where I lived with my family, was more diverse. Some of these differences had to do with education and financial possibilities that did not exist in the village: for example, a higher degree of in-migration, pluralism in regard to ethnicity, educational facilities, and more job opportunities. While almost all people in Kamadugu Sokorala were Kuranko, Kabala was very heterogeneous when it came to its population. Almost all ethnic groups were represented here, although the Limba, Kuranko, and Yalunka, the three groups that are the traditional custodians of the land, constituted the majority, and there were also substantial numbers of Fula cattle herders and traders. In Kabala there were several generations of town dwellers, recent arrivals from the surrounding villages, and also a number of civil servants temporarily stationed in town. Although Koinadugu District is predominantly Muslim, there were a number of Christian congregations and denominations in Kabala, and Pentecostalism in particular is increasing rapidly.

Migration

> Nowadays young men, looking beyond the village, face confusion—a nation in name only, summarily carved out of the continent by colonial powers, a place whose centre had never held and whose infrastructure is as fragmented as it is surreal—a modern highway that runs eighty miles through the middle of nowhere, a fleet of unused ambulances rusting away in a city yard, a school without teachers, a clinic without pharmaceuticals, a petrol station with no petrol. Young men drift into opportunism and fantasy as orphans sometimes do, hoping for some fantastic change of fortune, of a second chance in another country, or a powerful benefactor or political leader who will guide them out of the wilderness.
>
> MICHAEL JACKSON, *Existential Anthropology: Events, Exigencies, and Effects*

One of the more striking phenomena in the village was the absence of young men, but while some had been absent for more than a decade, they nevertheless still *belonged to* the village. Wherever they resided in the country, they would claim the village as their home and were also regarded by others as natives of that place. Out-migration has a long history in the region, and although fewer and fewer return to the village, social and symbolical relations with one's origin remain. I did not meet anyone in Kamadugu Sokorala who did not have relatives in the diamond districts (cf. Jackson 1977, 6). Thirty-odd years ago, young Kuranko men went to dig diamonds for a few years, amassed some money, and then returned to their village, settling down, building a house, and marrying (cf. Nyerges 1992, 864).[8] Most of the men I interviewed today, however, had stayed in the diamond areas much longer.[9] Many had married there, and their children were born and raised in the diamond area and belonged to a second generation of migrants in the diamond areas. The war has in many obvious ways affected residence patterns in the country. Some people born in the village had lived in the diamond-rich eastern district of Kono for decades, but when the war came they decided to relocate to their own or their father's native village. Today, some of these resettlers are still in the village, as they lost everything in Kono due to the war and could not return because of poverty. In contrast, a majority of my informants in Kabala had just recently moved there after the war, mostly because of the difficulties of surviving on farming in rural areas. There are extremely few livelihood opportunities in rural areas apart from the hard life of farming.

Even before the war, Kabala, like most district capitals, was the center of secondary education and commerce in the district, attracting a substantial number of migrants. Still, Koinadugu District as a whole has had one of the highest male out-migration rates in the country.[10] Migration is also part of girls' and women's life trajectories, although on a lesser scale than for boys and men. Some girls from Kamadugu Sokorala were sent to relatives in Freetown or to the diamond areas, where it was hoped they would be able to attend school, but unfortunately most ended up doing domestic chores or in other ways working for their relatives. Today, it is more common for men who move to urban areas to bring their village wives, and not, as before, leave wives and children in the village and return occasionally. Female mobility has also historically been regulated and legislated in ways different from men's. Anthropologist Kenneth Little wrote more than half a century ago that "a significant evidence of female mobility in this respect is the fact that a number of native administrations have enacted a fairly wide range of bylaws to restrict the movement of women about the country. Women are to be kept under 'proper control,' and the onus of reporting and returning a runaway wife is placed on husband, parents-in-law, and other persons normally in charge of the female sex" (Little 1948, 14). Today no such laws or any legal restrictions on women's movement exist, but there are still cultural conventions among some groups, and some families may not look kindly on young women travelling alone. Still, notions of proper control of women remain. I, however, often met young women travelling alone or in company to resettle, marry, work, trade, or just to visit friends and family. To migrate—for work, marriage, or education, or for other reasons—can be a result of conscious strategies to enhance one's quality of life, but, I argue, migration also belongs to the realm of fantasy and opportunism. For many young people I met, both men and women, dreams of the village were no longer their dreams. Many young men still dreamt of wealth through diamonds, but the young women I met mostly dreamt of education or of becoming successful businesswomen.[11]

In Kabala there was more variety in the configuration of households than in Kamadugu Sokorala. This is due partly to the war, as the population increased dramatically when displaced people from the rural areas took refuge in town, and also after the war, when every day new people came in from the countryside in search of job opportunities, NGO aid, education, and with hopes of a better life. They came because they could not produce more rice than they needed for consumption, sometimes not even enough for that, thereby generating no surplus to pay for clothes, school fees, or other material goods. They came also because in the rural areas there were few educational or medical facilities. Kabala could not really accommodate the needs of all settlers, as there were not that many job opportunities, and land for housing was becoming scarce. Most new arrivals would rent a room in town at a monthly cost of between Le 5,000 (US$2) and Le 10,000(US$4). Still, because of the increase in population, Kabala was expanding and many houses were being constructed, which meant that those new to town could always make a couple of thousand leones every day by carrying stones or other construction materials.

Gendered Livelihood Strategies

Like the majority of the Sierra Leone population, my informants came from rural farming backgrounds, although few young people were interested in pursuing the hard life of farming and had other dreams. Still, farming is the main economic activity with 70 percent of the population of Sierra Leone living in rural areas.[12] In 1999, despite the war, agriculture made up as much as 50 percent of the GDP.[13] The country's main agricultural products include rice, coffee, cocoa, palm kernels, palm oil, and groundnuts. In Koinadugu most people are primarily subsistence agriculturalists, except for the Fula, who are cattle herders and traders. Paramount chiefs are the custodians of the land and get a share of all crops and meat. Traditionally, in the district as a whole, there has been low population density, and farmland has been easily available. Land itself is not inherited, but the rights to use it are, often through the male line. The ruling and senior lineages generally have farm land closer to the village, while newcomers and strangers sometimes have to walk some distance to reach their farms. Rice is the staple food, but sesame, millet, maize, peppers, and cotton are intercropped with upland rice. Although rice farms will lie fallow for five to six years, they are reused for groundnuts, millet, and cassava during the second season. Farmers usually start their upland farming at the end of December to early March and harvest between October and January. The rainy season, June to October, before harvest, is called the hungry season (for more on farming activities in the region see, e.g., Leach 1994).

Most aspects of rural life are organized around sexual difference, and there is little overlap in female and male activities. People often said that men slash, burn, and clear farms, while women are responsible for planting, harvesting, and processing food. It has been considered quite inappropriate for a woman to clear any kind of bush for the production of rice, and such women might even be labeled "men-like women" (Leach 1994, 77). This has changed somewhat due to the war when labor became scarce, and where women were obliged to assist in activities formerly regarded as male. However, the war alone cannot account for changes in the organization of rice production and "therefore in exactly what farming roles 'say' about social relations" (Leach 1994, 79), and some of these changes have been noticeable during the past thirty years. When brushing and clearing the farm is completed, it is time to plant the seeds, and in postwar society this too has become problematic, since the quality of seed rice has declined in the past decade, according to informants.[14] After the war it has also been difficult to procure seed rice; there was a shortage and it was expensive.[15] The villagers had received some seed relief after the war from various NGOs, but because of an almost constant food shortage, many farmers had to sell this seed rice or have even had to consume it.

Despite all these postwar changes in the production and economy of farming, being a farmer is still important to the notion of adult male identity. A "man" is someone who can support his dependants, and according to Leach, a man who does not have his own farm is often referred to as "only a small boy" (1994, 85). Traditionally, men's failure to clear the bush for farming could well constitute grounds for divorce. Sierra Leone also follows the common pattern in Africa and even other parts of the world, where the production of food has been the responsibility of women, and where men have instead been more involved in the production of cash crops.[16] One could say that although women provide the majority of labor for food production, processing, and distribution, men have greater access to "ownership" of land and to the control of cash crop production. As I will show in chapter 3, women's substantial input in productive labor would come to play a significant part in the rebels' use of abducted women. When commercial cash crops were introduced in the colonial period, this was followed by a considerable shift in gender roles, where women's opportunities were restricted by regulations relating to marriage and ownership of property (see Leach 1994, 36), the effects of which are still to some extent in force today. During the past thirty years or so, the production process seems to have gone from a cycle of mutually dependent male and female tasks to "a process initiated by men and carried through by women" (Leach 1994, 93).

People make a distinction between farming and gardening. The latter is performed mostly by women, who grow cassava, groundnuts, sweet potatoes, onions, tomatoes, pumpkin, cowpeas, okra, and peppers; men may also have gardens but with a focus on cash crops. My host in Kamadugu Sokorala, Pa Morowa, had a garden in which he grew pineapples, bananas, cassava, and palm-oil trees. Fishing with nets is women's work, and in some areas fish is the chief source of protein. Traditionally, men have been associated with the farming of upland rice and women with swamp rice. Swamp rice has long been considered inferior, in taste, in cultivating, and in maturing, and Jackson gave its association with women as a reason for the unwillingness of Kuranko male farmers to turn more attention to its cultivation (Jackson 1977, 7; see also A. Zack-Williams 1995, 67). In postwar Koinadugu, however, swamp rice was a lucrative business for both men and women. While many upland rice harvests failed after the war, swamp rice was considered a safe bet, although it was more labor intensive.[17]

People, even in rural areas, have become increasingly dependent on cash, perhaps more so in postwar society with the rehabilitation of houses and property. Cash is also needed to pay taxes and school fees, and to buy medicines, blankets, clothing, lamps, zinc sheets, cement, and other items. Yet, to quote Leach, "Just as the importance of money has grown, so its value seems to have diminished" (1994, 185). For many farmers the only way to make money was to sell their rice and other agricultural products

on the markets. Because of a constant cash shortage, but also due to inflation and the rise of the U.S. dollar against the leone, prices increased all
the time and farmers were often in a position where they were not able to
keep as much rice as they needed for household consumption. Therefore
they increasingly encountered rice shortages when they most needed food,
in the hungry season. Worrying about the constant lack of rice, my friend
Pa Morowa once said, "This year hunger is not hunger, but death." To get
rice, often bought on credit, to feed their families during the hungry season, women sometimes had to walk for days carrying heavy loads of rice
on their heads.

Another commodity with economic value, which is also seasonally varied, is palm oil. Women process palm oil, but the kernels have to be picked
from the tall palm trees by young men. Women with teenage sons would
ask them, while others had to pay young men in cash for help. The price of
palm oil is seasonally varied, so some people tried to buy palm oil when it
was cheap and then sell when the prices had increased, but due to the fragile postwar economy this has become increasingly difficult. Now, when the
shortage of products such as palm oil and rice is not limited to the months
of the rainy season, it is difficult for many farmers to save money or make
a profit by storing or hoarding farm products for later sale. Pressures from
family, kin, and neighbors to share or sell also increased these difficulties. Those who are able to sell palm oil, rice, and other products on credit
used this as a form of saving money, on other people's deeds. Leach writes
that "people with money 'invest' in other people by giving or lending it
to them or contributing to social occasions" (1994, 184). This is a way of
both enhancing one's status and saving money that is common in the area.
Pa Morowa, who had been a relatively wealthy trader before the war, by
Koinadugu standards, told me that people all over Sengbe chiefdom and
as far as neighboring Barawa chiefdom owed him money from as far back
as the early 1990s. But during the postwar period, it was almost impossible
for him to procure this money, as many people had lost everything in the
war, and he feared being disliked if he sued them in court. Traditionally,
someone who could not repay their debts would be brought before the
local court and be fined, but now this seemed mostly to apply to debts incurred after the war, with the exception of outstanding bridewealth.

Thirty years ago, Jackson noted that transport was seen as the major
problem for people in the village. The Kamadugu Sokorala villagers, he

wrote, "want to be able to market their rice, to have a road link with Kabala, to encourage trading and marketing in their own locality" (1977, 19–20). Although our fieldworks were separated by thirty years and a war, transport was still perceived as a major problem. The road was still there, yet the vehicles passing were as a scarce as before, and most people could not afford to use them anyway.[18] Instead, people walked to the market in Kabala, carrying their goods on their heads and backs, a walk that could take between six and thirteen hours depending on load and agility.[19]

As seen above, livelihoods and personal economies are gendered. There is a notable difference, for example, in the strategies women and men use to obtain money. For instance, the proceeds from the sale of groundnuts are women's property, and women can also make money on other goods that they farm, such as palm-nut oil and groundnut oil. Petty trading in nonagricultural products was not very common among women in Kamadugu Sokorala as compared to Kabala, where a majority of petty traders were women. Women and men also have different and separate economic responsibilities, and there is no shared conjugal budget (cf. Bledsoe 1990; David 1997; White 1987, 19). This is not a recent phenomenon, for as Leach writes, "Husbands and wives have always maintained separate income streams and expenditures, whether in cash or kind" (1994, 189).

> Husbands and wives do not know the full extent of each other's resources and expenditures. It is accepted that men and women keep their financial affairs private. While this can lead to ambiguity and suspicion, too much openness is also thought to invite problems. Wives often suspect husbands to be withholding resources, spending them on co-wives, or depleting them unwisely such as on "unnecessary" litigation or social investments. Keeping cash stores and flows private is considered to maintain marital harmony partly because such flows remain hidden, rather than being brought into the open where they might invite palaver.
>
> (Leach 1994, 195)

I often got the impression from my married female informants that they suspected their husband of favoring one wife and her children over the others, and this often resulted in arguments between the wives. In view of this, men preferred their wives not to know the full extent of how they spent their money. But with the destruction of personal property and resources during the war, certain changes have occurred. Take Morowa, for example. Before the war he had built one house each for his wives, but now they all lived in the same house and took turns cooking for the whole household, whereas previously they only had to cook for people in their own house. After the war, everyone in Kamadugu Sokorala was poor.

Not only do men and women make money from gender-specific activities, but men make money intermittently—Leach (1994, 190), uses the word "lumpy" to describe men's incomes—while the incomes of women, though they make less money, are more regular and come from many different sources. Women and men also have different purchasing responsibilities. Men usually purchase in bulk and cater to long-term needs, such as rice by the bag and oil by the drum. Women, on the other hand, are concerned with the day-to-day needs and smaller purchases. As a direct result of the war, however, in both the village of Kamadugu Sokorala and the town of Kabala, hardly anyone could afford to buy in bulk, and the war affected men's purchasing ability a great deal. This resulted in an ever-increasing burden on women's spending. Since women have customarily been obliged to provide smaller items, day-to-day necessities, and as men could no longer afford to buy in bulk, practically every purchase now became the responsibility of women, much to their detriment and annoyance. Whereas before, men had always provided the staple food of the household, rice, now women had to buy rice by the cup and cooking oil by the pint every day on top of what they needed to buy to cook the daily sauce.[20]

Also, it was still mostly women who paid school fees and bought school materials and uniforms for their children. Pa Morowa's junior wife, Adama explained, "We used the groundnut money for our affairs. As the children are in school, whenever they [the teachers] ask for anything from the parents, there we take the money. For the children's book fees, so we also buy clothes, shoes out of this. Farm rice we use as food. The groundnuts help us for our children's affairs." Men's prior responsibility to provide food and clothing for their dependants has been considerably more difficult to realize since the war, but even more than a decade ago, Leach (1994, 191) noted that wives were taking over previously defined male responsibilities, such as buying clothes. Men's decreased willingness or capability to assume responsibility has also had consequences for marital relations and notions of masculinity.

Because women in West Africa have historically been involved in trade, and due to the fact that they have had some control of their own income and expenditure, they have sometimes been described as "independent" (Hart 1985; House-Midamba and Ekechi 1995; Little 1975; White 1987). Already in the late 1940s anthropologist Kenneth Little noted that "another sign of the times is the increased ability of women to obtain money for themselves, if necessary, outside the patriarchal system of the family. This is the product in recent years of improved communications by rail and lorry between and from the tribal areas, which have provided women with greater opportunities for petty trading" (Little 1948, 13). And thirty years after that, Jackson argued that the "economic independence of women and their ability to determine how they will use their production from gardening is certainly not customary, but is increasing in importance as Kuranko villagers get access to roads and markets and as trading shops are established in the villages" (1977, 11). But what does the word *independent* signify in this context? And what do women choose to do with that independence? It is a mistake to strictly equate West African women's independence with being in control of one's life, or having, as many dictionaries phrase it, "freedom from control or influence of another or others," as few people in this region are independent in this Western sense. How is this independence to be analyzed in a country like Sierra Leone, which has the highest infant and maternal mortality rates in the world, extremely low literacy rates for girls and women, and one of the world's lowest life expectancy rates? Just because women have some amount of economic independence, or separate incomes from their husbands, does not automatically mean that they vote, have a right to choose how many children they want, or are represented in local politics. To refer back to the case of Aminata in the introduction, if she had been independent, she could easily have left her family and married her bush husband despite their refusal, yet she could not. In this region, people are tied to kinship relations in a way that may seem foreign to Westerners. But this is a mutual dependence and includes restrictions and obligations as well as favors and assistance, depending on position in an age and gender hierarchy.

Having said this, although women in Sierra Leone in general are less educated, make less money, and are legally and politically subordinate to men, and despite the fact that Sierra Leone is still a largely patriarchal society, many Sierra Leonean women are nevertheless both resourceful and ingenious. Some are extremely successful businesswomen with both power and prestige, and just as there are "big men" in Sierra Leone, so are there "big women" (see, e.g., Ferme 2001, 159). Many of my informants dreamt of becoming just like these "big women." Sierra Leoneans accept that women, just like men, can become wealthy patrons; still, as Leach reminds us, "Men's and women's relative opportunities are uneven, because of their respective positions in the social relations," and that "while women do become 'big women', they do so with more difficulty—and in different ways—than men become 'big men'" (1994, 60). Although there are female chiefs in the Mende area and many "big women" throughout Sierra Leone, the majority of Sierra Leonean women have no such opportunities for power and prestige. For example, most of my informants were positioned on the lowest rung in this hierarchical and patriarchal society. In this context, gender alone is not a sufficient tool of analysis, and one needs to look at other aspects of social stratification as well. Just as women cannot act independently of their social relations, neither can men. Although male heads of households face increasing difficulties in providing for their dependants, they are still under social pressure to do so, and failure to do so frequently resulted in divorce.

Education

I described above how many young women admired successful businesswomen, and it is not difficult to understand why: they are generally better off; they invest their money in houses, their children's education, and nice clothes; they have authority; and they are respected members of the community. It is less obvious, perhaps, why young women would find education an attractive alternative. Teachers and other educated people have paltry salaries, if at all, and have few chances of being promoted and even fewer of furthering their education. Material wealth was not one of the reasons teachers were admired; this had to do with other, less tangible aspects. In Sierra Leone one often encounters what Jackson (2005, 67) referred to as "the mystique of literacy." Education has been highly valued in Sierra Leone since the time of colonization, when educated people were few and most were employed in the civil service, while illiterates were relegated to menial jobs (cf. Alie 1990, 70–71). Still today, as Susan Shepler

noted, the "educational system in West Africa has always seemed myste-
rious and unequal to rural Sierra Leoneans, but a path to a hugely desirable future" (2005, 173; see also Peters and Richards 1998a, 1998b). Shepler
explains the reasons for this are that people overvalorize education and
that many also assume that an educated person will not have to work. Literacy has on occasion conjured up fantasies of a better life in which one
would not have to engage in hard physical labor, but there are also, I believe, other factors contributing to the desire for education: namely control and authority. Being literate includes being in the flow of information,
and being able to read and write means that one does not have to rely
on others for writing or reading letters. Educated people in rural Sierra
Leone command respect. Education was obviously something important
to young women in Sierra Leone, but sadly, the reality is that very few girls
attend school.[21]

Northern Sierra Leone has been discriminated against regarding educational opportunities, as I showed in the previous chapter, with most
schools being in the south and in the capital. Further, most people in the
north are Muslim, and according to Ojukutu-Macauley, as "Islam defined
women by their roles as wives and mothers, post elementary education for
girls was viewed as a waste since, according to this definition, they would
eventually be limited to the domestic arena" (1997, 93). Nonetheless, in
her survey on women and education in the north, she found that more
than half of the women believed that "education—formal or vocational—
would increase their earning capacity either by qualifying them for an office job or enhancing the skills necessary for operating highly profitable
businesses" (Ojukutu-Macauley 1997, 99–100), and she interprets this as a
"realization by these women that education is the key to their 'liberation'."
In my survey in Koinadugu I found that among girls and women younger
than thirty, one-third had between four and five years of primary schooling. Of women in Kabala older than thirty, only 13 percent had received
any education at all. Still, this is an indication that things are improving. In
Kamadugu Sokorala, none of the women older than thirty had ever been to
school. I remember talking to women in Kamadugu Sokorala about girls
and education, and one of Pa Morowa's wives, who was around thirty-five
years old, told me that her mother would not let her go to school when
she was young, fearing that she would become a prostitute (cf. Ojukutu-
Macauley 1997, 102–11).

Although many older girls and young women told me that they dreamed of education, just because girls now can go to school does not mean that everyone wants to. This was more noticeable in the village than in the town. For example, a few of Pa Morowa's teenage daughters told me that they preferred marriage to education. This I attribute partly to the lack of role models to emulate, but it is also because it is difficult for many girls to see any immediate benefits of education. In the rural villages there are only primary schools, if any, and the school year also interferes with their parents' farming activities, for which they seasonally require the assistance of their children. Like most girls and young teenagers, my young female rural informants wanted to grow up and become women. In this region, to become a real woman required marriage and children. Girls' education has nevertheless been high on the Sierra Leone government's postwar agenda, financially supported by the UN and donor governments.[22] Primary school is now free for everyone, and girls are exempt from school fees for the first year of secondary school. Just after the war, certain measures were also introduced to cater to those children who had missed out on school completely due to the war: Complementary Rapid Education for Primary Schools (CREPS) programs, Nonformal Primary Education (NFPE) projects, and Community Education Investment Programs (CEIP).[23] Even so, as I will discuss in a later chapter, for abducted women to return to school was not easy.

Myths of Marriage

The hegemonic model of femininity in the region was one of being a wife and a mother. During my fieldwork, old people often told me that "there is no such thing as an unmarried woman." I was intrigued by this statement, which was repeated many times. In northern Sierra Leone, when a girl is born into a family she is by social convention destined to leave when she becomes "mature." Converging in the life worlds of rural women are the ideals of patriliny, clan-exogamy, viri-locality, and bridewealth. In a patrilineal society people reckon descent through the father. Since they are clan-exogamous they marry outside their own descent group, and since they practice viri-locality a woman will go and reside with her husband after marriage, or more often in his family compound. Bridewealth is generally explained as an exchange for a woman's reproductive and productive labor. These transfers are also ideally seen as definitive and irreversible, or as Jackson (1977, 97) put it, "The transfer of rights in genetricem and in uxorem is considered to be absolute and in perpetuity." A girl's life trajectory according to Kuranko ideals is quite clear: she is born, engaged to a man of her parents' choosing, she is initiated, circumcised, married, and becomes a mother. Yet, as I will describe below, this ideal was not always realized.

The main reason people gave for the supposition that all women have to be married relates to the belief that a woman cannot be buried by her own kin, only by her husband's. This has to do with the transfer of rights between the families and is also related to the concept of *being for* or *being of* someone as mentioned above. Under customary law, as I have noted earlier, women have until recently in many ways been considered legal minors, and as such could not be expected *to be for* themselves. Still, patrilineal reckoning, viri-patri location, and also the levirate are models that quite often do not conform to practice, but they do exist in the cultural imaginary. They are the models against which individual lives are measured. They are also often invoked when someone feels wronged or wants to state an example. As I will show, some women felt shackled by the restraints these models of social organization imposed on them, while others were quite upset when they could not count on the kind of support such a system of social organization was believed to offer. With the outbreak of war and the social disruptions that it entailed, diversions from this ideal model, or norm, have perhaps become more pronounced, although, I argue, they surfaced already long ago.

It is assumed with regard to society and culture in precolonial or pre-Islamic Sierra Leone that most groups, in conventional anthropological terms, were patrilineal; that descent and inheritance was reckoned through the patriline, except for the Sherbro where the kinship system was matrilineal (Alie 1990, 20); and that households consisted of a man, his wives, children, and other close kin, as well as other dependants and slaves. Households were considered the basic social unit, although one needs to bear in mind that the household itself was extremely fluid. Polygyny was widespread and, according to Joe Alie (1990, 20–21), an economic necessity due to the nature of farming and the sexual division of labor and the many wars and slave raids. It is apparent that the Atlantic and also the regional slave trade to a large extent altered local social relations, and Ferme has thus argued that marriage must be understood in the context of slavery (cf. Ferme 2001, 18). Rosalind Shaw (2002, 32) also makes a note of this; most slaves destined for the Atlantic trade were men, and those destined for the internal African market were women (who were also largely used as agricultural laborers). This produced a gender ratio that facilitated polygyny, and Shaw also links this with the emergence of wealthy merchants who particularly benefited from this system and were able to marry large numbers of wives (ibid.; see also A. Zack-Williams 1995).

As in many accounts of the past, I found that today, in the village, preferred marriage is clan-exogamous and also frequently village endogamous with matrilateral cross-cousins (see, e.g., Jackson 1974, 1977). Marriage is usually negotiated between families and bridewealth exchanged. Postmarital residence is generally viri-patri local, and children belong to the father's lineage. Widow inheritance was practiced, meaning that at the death of a husband, the wives were often "inherited" by one of his kinsmen. But marriage and settlement patterns in the village of Kamadugu Sokorala have changed somewhat in the last thirty years, and customs in Kamadugu Sokorala also differ from the situation in the town of Kabala only twelve miles away.

Kabala, as I have described above, was more diverse in terms of language, religion, and ethnicity, to name a few aspects, but also regarding marriage practices. Marriage and parenthood is still, especially for rural women, one of the most important trajectories of life. Of course, "marriage" cannot convey the lived realities of my informants, as these are also tied to aspects of gender relations, the sexual division of labor, religion, education, history, and politics. To marry is not really a single event among peoples in northern Sierra Leone, but rather a process that traditionally could even begin with the engagement of an unborn girl (cf. Gage and Bledsoe 1994, 151). The engagement process leading up to marriage and ultimately parenthood is also intimately connected to wider social networks of reciprocity and exchange of labor.

Initiations and Engagements

In the village of Kamadugu Sokorala, all girls go through the initiation ceremony (*dimusu biriye*), and after initiation they are prepared for marriage.[24] In some cases the future husband has paid for all costs relating to the initiation, and this constitutes part of the bridewealth (*yilboi*). In the town of Kabala on the other hand, although a majority of girls go through initiation, there is a significant difference in that in town the initiation event is not as focused on the actual ceremonies, the songs and the dances, but more on the circumcision, or "the operation" as they called it, whereas in the village ceremonies are both elaborate and costly.[25] Another shift, which became apparent to me during the initiation season of 2004, was that in town the initiation of very young girls, sometimes as young as three, was becoming increasingly common.[26] Elderly women in Kabala told me that they had been much older when they were initiated; they had been "mature," they said. I recall sitting with one old woman talking about marriage, when she laughed at the young initiates and said that she had not been initiated until her "breasts were hanging." Something the two locales shared, however, was that whereas previously girls would "go to the married house" quite soon after recovering from initiation, girls today may take many years between initiation and marriage.

Informants told me that traditionally the fathers of the bride and groom planned the marriage, often while the girl was still an infant (see also Jackson 1977, 96). Today such alliances are few, and this was explained by both men and women as a result of girls, when they became "mature," rejecting the men they had been engaged to. Girls more often wanted to choose for themselves and have increasingly been given the opportunity to voice their wishes and concerns. Because of this, informants explained, men often did not want to enter lengthy and costly courting when they knew that there was an ever-growing risk that infant fiancées would end up rejecting them when they got older. These rejections caused problems for the girls' families, who had to repay everything spent on the girl, an amount which is often carefully and meticulously recorded. If the girl had another potential husband in mind, this man would most likely reimburse the bridewealth of the first man. Pa Morowa's wife Adama explained that young men were afraid to commit to paying for initiation and bridewealth when a girl was still too young to marry, because "in doing so [paying for initiation] you will suffer for her, and when it is time to be married, another man will just come and take her." Instead, parents often found that they had to pay all expenses covering the initiation, but unlike a rejected potential future husband, they would not be reimbursed for the actual costs by the man who ultimately marries her, bridewealth notwithstanding.

While "in the olden days," as my informants used to say, a potential marriage could be planned well before a girl child was born, today it was more common that men would court a "mature" or newly initiated girl by giving her or her family kola nut (*wureh*). The parents of the girl would then discuss the matter with her, and they would together reach a decision. Parents still have a pretty good idea about who they think would be the best candidate, and often try and convince their daughter. Still, if she refuses they see little point in forcing her, realizing that it would never be a happy or stable marriage. But they might also be afraid of the social and financial ramifications of a failed marriage agreement or divorce, and many therefore quite carefully consulted their daughters before making any final or official announcements of marriage. In order not to offend the suitor and not to cause bad feelings between the two families, Pa Morowa explained to me, a girl's parents would tell the parents of the rejected man that they had tried to "talk for" the man, but that the daughter would not budge on her decision, thereby at least exonerating themselves of responsibility and any suspicions of ill feeling towards potential in-laws. If a girl accepts the suitor, this type of marriage would be considered an "engagement marriage" (*mabira yaneh*) and is validated by bridewealth and the offering of four kola nuts (*wureh nani*).[27] For the girls who were initiated during my fieldwork, prospective husbands, by way of their families, also presented kola nuts to the girls' families, often in connection with the actual initiation ceremony. In many cases the prospective husbands themselves were not even present; most were in Kono digging for diamonds and were not very involved in the marriages their parents performed on their behalf. One may suspect that many of these marriages were arranged by parents not only to create alliances but also to safeguard the return of their sons. However, I recall one girl who had been engaged to one of these absentee men and had waited for him to come back for three years; she had not "gone to the married house." Her parents had grown very disconcerted with the whole process and had decided, much to the chagrin of the husband's family, to break the marriage and repay the bridewealth in order for their daughter to marry another man, "for her not to be sitting down."

Some young men I talked to said that they had not married yet, but that their parents had arranged an engagement for them, and as soon as they got some money they would marry. A few young men, if they returned from labor migration, brought wives they had married on their own while away, wives who often belonged to other ethnic groups; they had married "strangers." This is not something new. The parental generation also consists of men who spent many years away from the village during their youth, and some of them also brought wives from other places on their return to the village. However, people still say that they prefer it if their sons "marry their neighbors," as has been the custom in this area. By arranging marriages of their absent sons to girls from the village, parents of young men also wanted to show their good will toward the families they were marrying into, and from whom in many cases they have "received" wives in former unions. In so doing, they also retained a degree of control, which was important, as it was not only a wife that entered their compound, but a whole complex of social relations with in-laws. As Stone put it, "Perhaps the only generalization one can make about marriage is that everywhere it entails intimate, if not emotionally charged, relationships between spouses, and everywhere it creates in-laws" (Stone 2006: 191), or in Jackson's words, "marriage makes people kinsmen" (1977, 106).

After marriage, a wife is entitled to food, clothing, and shelter, which the husband is obliged to provide (cf. Bledsoe 1980, 50). In return, ideally a wife must be totally obedient or else risk being returned to her family. In bearing the responsibility of providing for wives and children, men not only fulfilled their obligations, they also became "men." The incentive for a man to assume this responsibility is that it "reinforces his image as a patron and provider, of 'holder' of dependents, and strategic planner" (Leach 1994, 190). The image of provider had been intimately associated with adult masculinity, and Leach even goes as far as arguing that "failing in these duties to wives and dependents implies failing as a man" (1994, 190). The ideal masculinity in this area was one in which men strove to become "big men," to have many dependants, which is also referred to as "wealth-in-people" (see, e.g., Bledsoe 1980; Ferme 2001; Nyerges 1992). I remember talking to a group of young women who were laughing heartily and making a parody of a "traditional" Kuranko big man, dressed in fine garb, walking along the road followed by an entourage of wives and children dressed in tatters. "Those traditional men," they said, "he will have so many wives and children that he cannot even feed or cloth them, but he will be proud when everyone looks at him." The area in question fall under that which Igor Kopytoff (1987) termed "the African frontier," where the social organization is described as patriarchal and gerontocratic, and where older men try to control the labor and loyalty of women and junior men (Nyerges 1992, 862), and according to Frances White, having dependants became increasingly important during the nineteenth century. White quotes a European who at that time noted that "slaves and wives make a man great in this country" (1987, 28).

Although, officially, a married woman *belongs to* the husband and his kin, even after marriage most women maintain close contact with their natal families, even if they have "married out" (cf. Leach 1994, 187). In my research location, marriage did not entail a severing of ties to women's natal families, and it was actually quite common for a woman to return to her family on the gestation and birth of her first child, sometimes for months or even years. Melissa Leach writes that "a woman usually sustains strong links with her natal family, both as a source of personal support in the short term, to ensure support if her marriage founders, and to assure her rights to land and residence if she later returns to live there, perhaps on widowhood" (1994, 187). As we shall see in the following chapters, this was also an important aspect of abducted women's return home after the war. In some cases husbands no longer wanted their abducted wives, in other cases it was difficult for abducted women to get married, and in those cases where the women's own families rejected them they faced many difficulties in postwar society.

The Diversity of Marriage

Thirty-five years ago, the villagers of Kamadugu Sokorala distinguished between three types of marriage: engagement, "God-gift marriages," and bride-service marriages (Jackson 1977, 95).[28] Most of my informants explained that this belonged "to the olden days," but have things changed that much? They still classify the most common form of marriage as an "engagement marriage" (*mabira yaneh*), and bride service still occurred as described above, although no one spoke of it as a particular form of marriage. Today, I found the most common types of marriages to be (1) *mabira yaneh,* or engagement, which can also but does not have to be a family marriage (*kebilε fureh*), where a woman ideally will marry her father's real or classificatory sister's son (matrilateral cross-cousin marriage from the perspective of a male ego);[29] (2) *sumburi,* which literally is translated as wife stealing; (3) love marriage (*dienye fureh*), in which a man and an unmarried woman choose each other because they like each other for whatever reason; and lastly (4) *keyaneh,* in which a widow marries another man after the death and mourning of her husband, ideally the husband's brother (widow inheritance). There has been a decrease in the number of engagement and inheritance marriages in Kamadugu Sokorala in the past three decades. Simultaneously, there has been an increase in so-called love marriages and wife stealing, among younger men in particular.[30] The number of inheritance marriages will probably increase, as well as the number of wives to a man, as younger men grow older and continue to marry. There seemed to be a consensus that family marriages (*kebilɛ furehnu* pl.) are still preferred, ideally between classificatory if not real cross-cousins. Older men and women often said that the best marriages were those between the children of a mother and father who were half-siblings of the same father (*Fa keli*).[31] *Sumburi,* which means both elopement and divorce, but also "wife stealing," is also still common in Kamadugu Sokorala. A woman who is already married leaves her husband for another man, and this man has to pay "damages" to the estranged husband, in reality reimburse him for the cost of bridewealth (cf. Jackson 1977, 98). Added to the bridewealth may also be costs that have been incurred after the marriage; some men will note every cent spent on the wife, such as clothing, cooking utensils, and medical costs. These damages symbolize the transfer of rights from one man to another over the wife and any new children born in the relationship. However, an often quoted reason for *sumburi* is the inability to conceive children.

Love marriage (*dienye fureh*) is a type of marriage that needs some explanation. *Dienye* is a term denoting friendship among same-sex relatives as well as between women and men (see Jackson 1977, 120). However, I have found no references to this term being used in relation to marriage in the literature of the Kuranko-speaking area. Nevertheless, friendship marriages, or what my informants all refer to as "love marriages," are becoming increasingly common. A man and a woman like each other, make frequent visits, go to see a video show, stroll around, sometimes even hand in hand—a type of public courting that was unheard of for the older generations—and eventually marry. Some of the older men in the village said that some of their wives they had married for love, but this had at the time been considered *sumburi,* probably because almost all girls at that time had already been engaged. Although I would argue that there are differences between *sumburi* and love marriages, they do share one feature: they are not arranged.

What can we infer from the increase of a type of marital alliance such as love marriage? Has there been a shift in relations between men and women, or perhaps between generations? Three decades ago Jackson wrote,

> In Kuranko society marriage is assimilated into the world of rights and du-
> ties, the inescapable rules and constraints which characterise kinship. *Love
> and friendship are not emphasised in Kuranko ideology;* in fact they are often
> regarded as symbolically inimical to marriage. *Personal preferences or ran-
> dom choices often conflict with social imperatives.* Thus should a woman take
> a lover she is in fact confusing marriage with friendship.
>
> (Jackson 1977, 121, my emphasis)

Today, the use of the term *love marriage* as a label for interpersonal relation-ships between men and women is widespread, although still much more common in a town like Kabala than in rural areas.[32] Although love mar-riages are becoming more common, most first marriages are still arranged (*mabira yaneh*). In fact, of 151 marriages in Kamadugu Sokorala only 7 per-cent were love marriages while 70 percent were engagement marriages.[33]

Generally, parents seemed to assert less authority over their children's choice of spouses than before, which can be one of many expressions for this change. It was often said that it was above all fathers who gained from being in control of such issues in terms of alliances, bridewealth, and bride service, and although I was told that it is still primarily fathers who arrange marriages, I found much pointing to the fact that mothers are very much involved in their children's conjugal liaisons. As the mother of the husband is an influential person in the new wife's life, and the future relationship between wife and mother-in-law would to a degree dictate everyday life, I found that many mothers of sons thought that this was such an important liaison that they could go quite far in arranging their sons' marriages.

As I mentioned above, polygyny is quite common in this area and is still the ideal for men in rural Sierra Leone. In Kamadugu Sokorala I found that almost 50 percent of the married men only had one wife, which is almost the same rate of monogyny that Jackson found in the early 1970s (Jackson 1977, 140), but there were changes in relation to the number of wives of polygynous men. For example, I found that not one man had four or more wives, while thirty years ago this had been the case for quite a few adult married men. Younger men in general said that they did not intend to marry more than one or two women, as they did not think they would be able to support a large family. Masculinity and fatherhood are still synonymous in the ideology, however, and young men seemed to be torn between the desire for prestige and the reality of their position as providers in a fragile economy, perhaps even more so after the war. Men in their thirties complained about the burden of providing for the wives they already had and the cost of sending their children to school. Young educated men in cities were even less likely to marry many wives, and among these there was often also an ideal of monogamy, irrespective of whether they were Muslim or Christian. Some men who had been brought up in town had married women they had met there, women who were also educated and had initially assumed that their husbands would stay monogamous. Some men explained, however, that it was still seen as prestigious as a man grew older to have more than one wife, and many would also succumb to family pressure and marry a second or third wife. These later wives were frequently from rural areas, and some would live with their children in the husband's village, often taking care of his mother if she was a widow and also tending farms and gardens, while the husband would live in town and only visit occasionally. It is not uncommon, therefore, that the children of a "town wife" and a "village wife" will grow up under very different circumstances despite having the same father.

Men are generally younger today when they first marry.[34] To some extent, the decrease in age at first marriage across the younger male generation probably has to do with the decrease in infant betrothal, making the number of marriageable women higher for all men, young and old. For the older generation it had been different, as Goody noted for another West African setting: "Men of marriageable age have to get betrothed to infant girls; all other girls are already engaged. Since they have to wait some fifteen years before they can get married, the age of marriage for men is late" (Goody 1973, 184–85). This may also be why there has been an increase in love marriages, as well as a decrease in the amount of bridewealth, both of which may make it easier for younger men to marry. Younger men today simply do not have to amass the same amount of money or goods to marry as the older generation did. Older men report having paid cows, goats, sheep, forty bags of rice, and a lot of money in bridewealth. This is completely unheard of today, where young men struggle to rebuild houses burnt by rebels and to procure even a fraction of the amount of rice they used to harvest. When one of Pa Morowa's teenage daughters was formally engaged to a man from a neighboring village, his wives complained bitterly that the money they received in bridewealth, Le 50,000, would not even cover the expense of giving their "strangers," their guests, food. The first marriages for all women I interviewed in Kamadugu Sokorala had been engagement marriages, and frequently also "family marriages" (*kebile furehnu* pl.) to sons of their fathers' often classificatory sisters. Women in Kamadugu Sokorala have generally married when they were somewhere between fourteen and eighteen years of age. Younger women in the village were slightly older than the older female cohort when they first married, and one would assume that this has to do with education, yet the fact is that while none of the married female informants older than thirty have had any education at all, only one of those between fifteen and thirty had gone to school, and then only for one year.

Religious affiliation also seemed to affect marriage practices, and one difference between Kamadugu Sokorala and Kabala was that in the latter there was a large minority of Christians. Some of these still classified their marriages as traditional engagement marriages, or *sumburi,* while others just stated that theirs had been a Christian marriage. Those who identified as Christians were generally older at the age of first marriage.[35] Christian women were also more likely to be the only wife of their husband, although polygyny among Christians did occasionally occur. Judging by my survey, there seemed to be little intermarriage between Christians and Muslims in Kabala, but when discussing the matter, most people said they did not object to intermarriage and quite often gave the example of the marriage of former president Kabba mentioned earlier. Although most of my informants were Muslim, when asked, none of the informants in Kamadugu Sokorala categorized their marriage as being specifically Muslim, but rather a Kuranko marriage. In town, on the other hand, it was much more common for people to state that theirs was a Muslim marriage.[36]

The Dissolution of Marriage

Despite the emphasis on village endogamy as a means of safeguarding marriage unions from being dissolved, divorce was quite frequent in the village.[37] More than one in three marriages in Kamadugu Sokorala have ended in divorce. In the 1970s, many more of Jackson's male informants' marriages ended in death (Jackson 1977, 99). According to some older women I spoke to, divorce was extremely rare when they were young. One woman said that her parents would have killed her if she had left her husband, although she was probably speaking figuratively. On the other hand, we have to remember that although these women were the same age as Pa Morowa or slightly older (he was around sixty-five), they had entered marriage when they were much younger, marrying men who in some cases were as old as Pa Morowa's own father. Therefore, although born of the same generation, their marriage experiences might well belong to different generational traditions.

Although divorce is more common today, it was still quite rare for a divorced woman to live on her own; rather, she will divorce one man in order to marry another (cf. Jackson 1977, 102). This has to do in part with bridewealth. A new husband will compensate the former for costs incurred during and in association with the previous marriage arrangement, whereas a woman would have difficulty amassing this money on her own, and most parents could not afford to reimburse an estranged husband. A commonly cited reason for divorce was that a husband had failed to provide for his wife (cf. Leach 1994, 190). Today, men seem to have difficulties in meeting these obligations, difficulties that are further emphasized by the fragile postwar economy, as has been described above. In a conversation with one of my main informants, Finah, a young woman who had been abducted during the war and since returned to her home area, where she married the man who had engaged her when she was young, she explained that many women were not satisfied with their marriages because of this.

By right the man should take care of the wife, the woman should be under the man, but provided that the man is doing everything for her. But if you have to feed yourself, you have to buy your clothes, you have to buy shoes, chain [jewelry], dress your hair, you have to care for the children, your family, your mother, your father, [now] the man doesn't care. So how can you be obedient, submissive to the man? If a man says "Don't go there," if he is doing everything for you, or gives you a big market, and says "Sit down here, do trading for you to get something to feed," you will sit down. But if not! Then how? And you don't have anything at home, unless you have to go and find trading, to go to your parents, or to friends, or to where you can get work.

However, things are not the same in the village and in the town, and the differences in divorce ratios in Kamadugu Sokorala and Kabala were significant. The divorce rate among men in Kamadugu Sokorala was considerably higher, for example, than among men in Kabala.[38] It would seem that men in town marry fewer wives and stay married to them longer. The higher divorce rate in Kamadugu Sokorala was somewhat surprising, as there was a heavy emphasis on village endogamy and family marriage as a means of sustaining marital unions, while such practices are less emphasized in Kabala. However, among female informants the situation was the reverse, where the divorce rate among women in Kabala is almost twice as high as in the village.[39] Some relate the increased fragility of marriage relations to economic factors (Ferme 2001, 18), but it may also be due to a general increase in urban migration and the level of education, especially in urban areas. Perhaps women's changing position in society may also have been a contributing factor.

The dissolution of marriage through death is still quite common and is in some ways viewed as a divorce as well as grounds for a new marriage. As the Kuranko practice widow inheritance (*keyaneh*), widows may marry a real, classificatory, or a compound (*kebilɛ*) brother of the deceased husband. After a period of mourning, the deceased husband's property and wives are distributed among the husband's male kin, often referred to as "brothers."[40] A real brother seemed to be preferred from the perspective of the widow and her children, as he would probably feel closer to and take better care of his brother's children. The children of the deceased would legally belong to the new husband but would trace their lineage through their genitor. Any children conceived in the new relationship would belong to the new husband and not the dead brother, and thus would not constitute what in anthropology has been called a "true levirate" (cf. Abrahams 1973, 165). Some women were content with this arrangement, but there were also cases where young widows with children had been shunned or where the new husband did not fulfill his responsibilities. However, according to many of my informants, many had been maltreated as children by their own mother when she entered a new marriage, claiming she had only cared about her new children.[41] An inherited wife would also frequently enter the new household as the second, third, or fourth wife, meaning that she and her children would not only have to get along with the husband, but also his other wives.[42] If the widow is young she is expected to enter a new marital union with a new husband. If older and past childbearing age, she would be expected to marry officially but would not need to consummate the marriage and frequently does not need to live with her new husband but can live with her own grown children. Nonetheless, she *belongs to* her new husband, and he or his kin are responsible for burying her at the time of her death.

Widows in Kabala town were more likely to be abandoned by their late husbands' families and forced to fend for themselves, especially if the husband's family lived far away, as was often the case with increased urban migration. On numerous occasions, I met young widows who after the husband's death had been completely abandoned by the husband's kin, women who had wanted the support of their husband's kin but who did not receive it. These women wanted the security of the old "traditional" system and saw few possibilities of making it on their own, and they would often seek council with the elders and even go to local court to sue their late husband's kin for breaking with tradition. One of my female informants said that on the one hand she thought that widow inheritance was good, because someone would provide for the widow. On the other hand, she said, although a widow could refuse to live with the "brother," she may in reality have little choice because he might have taken control of the assets of the deceased.[43] Of course, there were some young widows who simply did not want to remarry at all, but tried to make a living in town by trading and farming, often staying with their own kin or friends. Lately, people seem to be more tolerant of divorced women and widows remarrying outside their husband's *kebile,* and sometimes the husband's kin would even welcome being released from the burden. One of my informants, Neneh, an elderly widowed woman, the mother of four daughters who had all been abducted during the war, told me that the institution of *keyaneh* was becoming difficult.

In this of our environment, Kabala, when your husband dies, for another person to take you it is very, very difficult. Unless you the wife will have to get him up your trousers and be firm and fine and hard working to find money, you will see the husband's brother coming for you but he won't take care of you, or the children. If you go to his house you will see him giving money to his own children and leave your own. Most women are now rejecting to marry keyaneh, even if she is young—some, not all. Some men will think of what their brother has been doing and take care of his children but for some, they won't take care, they will say yes, she is my wife, but when they have something they will give it to their own children. They will give food to their own children, to their own wives, but for the keyaneh they leave. Most women are rejecting it now.

Women are still not very likely to divorce on their own, and an informal separation is sometimes more beneficial than an actual divorce, as bride-wealth does not have to be repaid. A separated wife can take lovers and does not have to share the proceeds from her work, farming, or trade with her official husband. Just as there are different types of marriages, entailing different rights and obligations, divorces can be very different depending on postmarital residence, educational level, income, kinship alliances, and so forth. Although women do initiate divorce, the process is different than for men (cf. Ojukutu-Macauley 1997, 95). Divorce cases were settled in the local courts, which are governed by older men, preferably from the ruling lineages (cf. Leach 1994, 196). With the passing of the Registration of Customary Marriage and Divorce Act in 2007, these practices will probably change. In a village like Kamadugu Sokorala where village-endogamous marriages are more common, a woman is more likely to have the support of her family; still, women who have divorced a man from the same village will frequently leave and "marry out" in any subsequent marital union. To stay with one's natal kin for an extended period may also be an act of protest against wrongs committed by the husband. In such cases a wife would force the husband to approach her family, or more likely a third party, usually the same one who had negotiated the marriage, to settle the matter. This mobility meant that women could raise questions of marital disharmony to a public or semipublic level in their own, rather than the husband's, village.

Reasons for divorce also differ somewhat between men and women. Women gave as reasons that they had not become pregnant and had therefore left for another man, or that they had left their husband because he did not provide for them. Reasons stated for divorce among men were often a wife's refractory behavior: she did not obey, did not accept his control, or abused in-laws. Some also mention that the wife did not get pregnant, or more commonly that "God put something between us." And one man said that he divorced his wives because they refused to farm. This is

interesting, especially when comparing material historically and regionally. Melissa Leach wrote that for women, "the phrase 'he does not make
farms for me' encapsulates the deterioration of marital relations" (Leach
1994, 87), and as has been mentioned above, it is a husband's responsibility
to provide for his dependants. Still, as has been shown above, since women
contribute a substantial amount, if not the majority, of farm work, a woman's refusal to farm is problematic for the husband, as he depends on her
productive labor.

Husbands and Wives, Brothers and Sisters

As I described in the introduction, Aminata said that her brother was the
only one who cared for her, and that had it not been for her brother, her
family would have rejected her. Although in northern Sierra Leone a husband is an important male person in a woman's life, he is neither the only
one nor always the most important. There is often an even stronger emotional tie between a woman and her brother(s), particularly uterine brothers (*Na keli*). Considering that divorces are so common, it is thus reasonable
to assume that the relationship between a sister and her brother is more enduring than that of a wife and her husband. Relations between affines are
often fraught with tensions and conflict, and wives more than husbands
experience this, as women in a sense belong to both their own and their
husband's families, and have to negotiate between the two. Ferme, who
worked among the Mende, noted that the "connotation of stability implied
by the terminology of marriage (*hei,* which also means 'sitting') is decep-
tive" (2001, 18). This is partly because of the tensions between the demands
by a woman's kin on the one hand, and her obligations toward her husband and in-laws on the other, which are frequently conflicting. As explained above, the prevalence of matrilateral cross-cousin marriage in this
region has often been explained as a way of maintaining marital alliances
between men. Although writing about the Tamils of South India, Margaret Trawick (1990) proposes another very compelling interpretation of
cross-cousin marriages. Trawick suggests that for cross-cousin marriages
there are other reasons than alliances between men, which have more to
do with the emotional dynamic between, in particular, brothers and sisters
in Tamil culture. Trawick's proposition is convincing also for the Kuranko

exactly because of the close relationships between brothers and sisters that can be found here too, and which have been extensively covered by Jackson (1977, chap. 7).

Few would argue against the fact that in Sierra Leone, women as wives, or women as daughters, have relatively little authority in relation to their husbands or fathers. However, a life-cycle perspective is important, as "woman" is not a fixed category, and there are many generational and relational differences regarding rights and privileges. "A range of identities describe women's familial relationships: daughter, sister, wife, co-wife, mother, grandmother, aunt, cousin, and niece. In different cultural situations, and throughout the life cycle, several of these identities become more or less salient for specific women" (Sered 1994, 71). Further, the social organization of sexual difference is more complex than merely male/female. There is no one definition of "woman" but many, which vary according to age and economic status; moreover, and perhaps more important, any definition of "woman" is also relational. Wives have different opportunities and means of power and influence depending on position and status in the household. Among the Kuranko-speaking peoples in northern Sierra Leone, women as sisters have been a completely different matter. Women as sisters, both traditionally and to some extent today, have had much higher status than women as wives. There are also other relational positions that have granted women in this society more authority. For example, women as mothers have exerted indisputable authority over their children, and a first or senior wife will have more authority than subsequent wives.

Although Sierra Leone is frequently characterized as a hierarchical, patrilineal, and patriarchal society, there are still strong elements of matrifocality. In matrifocal societies, the mother is the focus of the household, and women are identified primarily as mothers rather than wives. In such societies, there is generally an absence of adult males in the household, control of many key economic resources is maternal, and decision-making authority (in the household) is vested primarily in the hands of mothers (Sered 1994, 47). In northern Sierra Leone, a woman's control and authority were less often exerted over her husband than over other relations such as children, siblings, co-wives, affines, and other dependants. Likewise, a woman's most important relationships in life are with those in her natal family and with her children, not necessarily with the husband. Women frequently said that they did not really trust their husbands the way they trusted their brothers. To focus on the more enduring relations of sibling-ship rather than the apparently more tenuous marriage alliances is to aim the analytical focus on relations among the living, not on abstract prin-ciples, and also on relationships among individuals of the same relative generation—on key social relations.

From a relational perspective one can see that during the past century there has been a gradual transference of rights and authority to women as wives. Today women have more say in the choice of when, with whom, and how to enter marriage, and they can also increasingly decide when to end marriage. Girls are encouraged to go to school; postwar legislation has increased women's rights in terms of rape, domestic abuse, divorce, and inheritance; and there are now social welfare services and Family Support Units within the Police trained to protect and implement women's rights in marriage. Simultaneously, there has been a reverse development in the status traditionally accorded sisters. Men today do not need to symbolically share the first harvest with their sisters to ensure prosperity, and they are less and less often in need of their sister's blessings and less and less afraid of the previously so dreaded sister's curse (cf. Jackson 1977). What we are facing is thus a situation in which women as wives are gaining influence while women as sisters are losing status and recognition. At the same time, and this may appear contradictory, women as wives can no longer depend on their husbands to provide for them; women as wives can no longer trust in the system that granted them not only the chance of marriage, but the right to be married.

Concluding Remarks

The proverb "There is no such thing as an unmarried woman" may be-come an obsolete relic of the past. Many women, of course, welcome this development, as it signals a rise in women's opportunities and possibilities to make it on their own. Yet, being a change in progress, as we speak, it is also one that causes a lot of distress and creates ambiguity. Susan Sered speaks of gender disjunction, or gender dissonance, as occurring in situ-ations "in which culturally accepted notions of gender are either highly contradictory and/or rapidly changing" (1994, 43) and states that these are "manifested either as rapidly changing gender relationships or as important discrepancies between gender ideology and practice" (1994, 65–66). Although one could argue that West Africa in general has long been characterized as a region in which the ideology has been highly patriarchal and the reality fairly egalitarian, thereby producing ambivalence and ambiguity (cf. Sered 1994, 46), this ambiguity, at least in northern Sierra Leone, has been maintained within a system of sexual division based in part on complementarity. Today, however, this system is changing swiftly and can no longer be sustained by traditional moral values. Women and men today do not know what to expect from one another, neither as wives and husbands, nor as sisters and brothers. Women's rights are still not realized, nor can they rely on the security provided by convention. Still, as in the case of Aminata, her family was dependent on her brother's income and therefore had to accept her, since that was his will, and one can assume that the close relationship between uterine siblings, and the importance of sisters in this region, played some part in Aminata's brother's reasons for taking her in.

In this chapter I have emphasized the relational aspects of identity, whether it be gender or age. Although basically a hierarchical society, where women in general are subordinate to men, the hierarchical nature applies to all social relations—some women over other women, first born over last born, first wife over junior wife, and elder over youth. Moreover, a power structure based on different gender identities and one on seniority are not mutually exclusive but coexist, making up the lived realities for my all informants in northern Sierra Leone. However, considering that marriage still is one of the most important trajectories of women's life, I believe that the changes we have seen in marital relations reveal something about societal change at large, between men and women and between generations. Older men and women, as everywhere, grumbled of course about the youth of today, how girls were initiated before they were mature, how men married before they had sense, and they also complained about the number of divorces and the sexual practices of the young. Life has changed significantly since these old men and women were young; although most of them were born when rural Sierra Leone was a British protectorate and later a colony, few older women had travelled far enough to see the effects of modernity on the urban landscape during the second half of the twentieth century, while men in their generation had worked in the diamond areas or served in the Sierra Leone Army. Today both men and women are more mobile in terms of short- and long-term migration to urban or industrial areas, the major towns have cell phone coverage, and some have internet access as well, and as a consequence the pace of change is perhaps swifter than before. These long-term processes are probably more significant for changes in marriage practices than the war was. I have not focused on the marriage practices of abducted girls and women after the war in this chapter but will discuss these further in chapters 6 and 7. But without this background, I argue, it becomes very difficult to understand both the phenomenon of bush marriage as well as marriage strategies in postwar society.

What has been communicated throughout this chapter is that in Sierra Leone, diversity is at the core of social relations. Within one family there are illiterates and college graduates; rural peasants and cosmopolitans of the Western hemisphere; adherents of Islam, diviners, and Pentecostals; cell phones and infant betrothal; "traditional" marriages and "modern" love affairs. I have tried to give an account both of the official transcript of kinship ideology and of the heterogeneous society of Sierra Leone today. It has been my attempt to provide a sketch of how social actors organize themselves within the web of kinship and affinal relations, and of how people acquire and use resources to maintain those relations. My aim here has been to provide a background for the following chapters, which will deal with far more unpleasant topics. This background, I believe, will provide an increased awareness and contextualize the conditions and the experiences of war-affected women, in war and postwar society. As I mentioned above, I was often told that "there is no such thing as an unmarried woman." However, this ideal was often contradicted, leading me to believe that this had more to do with convention than reality. I was both right and wrong. There were many cases where I had assumed that the women were unmarried, divorced, or widowed, but as it turned out, this was not the case. Many were in fact, at least officially, married. Some of them had been abandoned by their husbands, had themselves left, or had been given to a "brother" of a dead husband but had never consummated the marriage and were not cohabiting. I was also right: there were many unmarried women in Koinadugu. Just recall what happened to Aminata when she returned home after the war. No one wanted to marry her, and the only man she wanted to marry, her father rejected. Although many women divorced and remarried, it is still implicit that the first marriage should be an "engagement marriage," and that girls should be virgins when entering their first marriage. Perhaps this was the problem with Aminata? She had left unmarried and returned as "damaged goods." In this context, however, it was very difficult to understand why Aminata's father refused to let her marry a man who had even offered bridewealth and the traditional kola nut. To explain some of the factors behind this, we need to understand what happened to Aminata, and others like her, during the war. To this I will turn next.

3

ABDUCTION AND EVERYDAY REBEL LIFE

> Survival in the camps was fundamentally a social process. I wanted
> to understand what circumstances enabled survival: its vicissitudes,
> precariousness, and uncertainties; the interplay of luck, determination, and
> careful calculation; the interdependence of human beings upon one another
> for life itself.
>
> RUTH LINDEN, *Making Stories, Making Selves*

In the introduction I argued that when fieldwork is done on war experiences after a war has ended, narratives take place in the register of
memory (see Shepler 2002, 2) that are filtered through a variety of postwar experiences: for example, humanitarian discourse, responses from society, family situation, health, and poverty. In this chapter I will give an
account of my informants' narratives of abduction, bush marriage, and
everyday life in the rebel movement. Many of these narratives of past experience were told in a sometimes hostile postwar environment. All of
my key informants had been abducted, most had been raped and taken
as bush wives. Some stayed with the rebels for a few weeks or months
before escaping, while others stayed for up to ten years. Everyday rebel
life, despite the violence and abuse, still had many similarities with "traditional" prewar life. The organization of rebel camps, the social structure
of rebel communities, hierarchies, and the division of labor, all had precedents in "normal" village life. The differences were substantial, however;
people were killed, age hierarchies were reversed, traditional relations of

reciprocity severed, kinship and language ties obliterated, and consciousness altered through the massive use of drugs.

The Abduction

Aminata, whom we have already met in the introduction, was around fourteen years old when she was abducted, and she was with the rebels for almost three years. I estimated her age to be around nineteen when I first met her in 2003. Through her story I slowly began to understand both her own and many other women's reluctance to speak about their experiences of war. Many found themselves back in a society that, if not openly, at least covertly ostracized them, or even actively discouraged them from speaking about the war, about what had happened to them, or what they had done. Aminata told me about her abduction on our first encounter, and it is very similar to many of the other first statements recorded and to abduction stories published elsewhere (see, e.g., Save the Children 2005; UNICEF 2005). These narratives usually start with the initial attack and abduction, rape, and departure from their homes carrying loads of looted goods for the rebels. In this type of narrative it is quite common for the narrator to begin by locating herself in time and space (cf. Ross 2003, 46–47).

> I was captured here by the rebels during the Five-Days attack....So when they entered everyone ran. I also ran but from here to...the swamp....There I met some [rebels] who arrested us. We were five in number at that time when they arrested us. There is a house here where they put all the captured people until their mission was accomplished. So we were put in that house. Men in some rooms, women in some rooms. So all of us that were captured in this area were kept in that house. When they went to central Kabala to fight, they left some rebels in charge of us. These will use us as they want. They will each choose one or two girls they will have sex with while the others fight. So after three days, on the fourth day we were sent ahead of them with the loads they have taken from the shops and people up to [the rebel base camp]. As we were going so they were firing [shooting] those that will say they are tired, and also arrested others in villages or roads. Those people took loads also.

Another of my informants tells a similar story. "When I was captured we were put in one room. As we were in that room any man, whether small or big, comes to have sex with me, you can't deny him. If you do, you will be killed. So they were sexing us as they feel. We were seven in that room. We were not allowed to go out. You can't go out unless someone guards you. They were giving us food only once per day." Different from most abduction stories was that of Mateneh. She had spent four years with the rebels. She volunteered to tell her story only if we promised not to tape it; she said, "Don't record me, but I will tell you and you will write it." Mateneh's story is more detailed, and she paused frequently while telling it.

> I was born in 1976. I was arrested in the year 1998 in the Alikalia area. I went with my sister to go in search of things to sell. At that time we were expecting them [the rebels] to be in the Kayima and the Yiffin area. Those people are very fast in walking. We were rushing to come when we heard about them in Nieni chiefdom. As such, we decided to pass through the bush paths from Kondembaya to the Kamadugu Sokorala road. But actually, these people were many. So we took the Kurekunema road to Sokorala. When we reached at Kurekunema, there we met a huge number of them. We were not expecting them there at that time. We reached there around 4 o'clock. When we were going on the road, six of us, four women and two men [she pauses for a while]....I was just twenty years. I was just married [pause]....When we went closer to the town, we didn't know that they were the people [the rebels]. This was because as we were nearing the village we met a man and a woman a half mile from the town, but they didn't have guns. We asked about the road, and they told us that the road was safe. When we went further we met three men. Among these were two Mende and one Kuranko. When we greeted them the Kuranko man answered us politely. Then we again asked about the road and the town. He gave us the confidence to go to the town, more especially when he told us that "Listen, you hear people pounding [rice] in the village." Also, he told us that they had just left the town to go to the river and bathe. But as soon as we passed them to enter the town, my body was weakened, not only I, but all of us. As soon as we entered the village we saw uniformed men with red cloth tied around their heads. We saw some civilians, men and women, pounding rice, and it was that pounding that gave us the hope that there were villagers in the village [she pauses again]....It is only now that it is good to talk about this [pause]....As soon as we entered we were arrested.

After they had been "arrested," Mateneh was separated from the others and raped, but I will return to Mateneh's story of rape in more detail in the following chapter. As I mentioned above, Mateneh's story was much more detailed. She accounts for where she was going, how they had heard rumors about where the rebels were, and how they tried to choose alternative routes to avoid them. In most other narratives, my informants were abducted when the rebels attacked their villages or towns, but the way she describes the approach to the town where she was taken, and the meeting with the people on the road, one gets the impression that she was lured into the lion's den.

Kadi, one of my youngest key informants, was only nine years old when she was abducted in Kabala in early 1994. She had gone with some of her friends to the community center to watch a commemoration ceremony celebrating the local CDF (*Tamaboroh*) leader, Dembaso Samura, who had been killed by the rebels a while before, when suddenly the town was attacked and she and her friends were abducted. The rebels had initially wanted to kill her, she said, but she had started to cry and one of the rebels said, "If you don't want me to kill you, let's go to the bush." Kadi told him that she did not want to go with them, she wanted to go to her mother. Then they said they would kill her, leaving her little choice. Kadi did not see her mother again for more than eight years. She was brought to the rebel camp in Koinadugu village, and from there she went with the rebels all over the country. "Where I went?" she said, "Many places! It's just to America that I didn't go."

In contrast, most of the narratives that I consulted from the local Kuranko NGO Christian Extension Services (CES) are even more condensed. CES started their work in Kabala as early as 2001 with local staff, when no other organizations were working in the area. Following is one such abduction narrative, with a twenty-one-year-old woman from Kabala. The only additional information provided about the woman, apart from her name, which I have omitted, is that she was twenty-one years old and was at the time unmarried, had two children, and had never been to school.

It was 1998 when they attacked and I was captured by Major Alusine—RUF....I was pregnant when I escaped from him and came to my sister to take care of me. I spent two years with him. I was with him as his wife doing cooking for him. But because of too much punishment in two months pregnancy I tried to escape.

Many narratives are completely devoid of emotion; they lack subjective references to pain, humility, suffering, anger, or even hatred. The stark contrast between the graphic details provided and the detached, almost clinical way they are told simultaneously emphasize the violence and keep the feelings of those violent acts at arm's length (cf. Kelsall 2005, on how witnesses at the TRC narrated their memories of war). In a sense, this is consistent with what I came to learn about feminine ideals, where women rarely speak of violence inflicted on them and the pain they felt. In the socialization of young women they are taught to endure pain, keep it hidden inside, and not to reveal any emotions, as is obvious, for example, in female initiation ceremonies and in childbirth (cf. Coulter 2005).[1]

Although an overwhelming majority were abducted, some girls and women did in fact voluntarily join the rebels or other fighting forces (cf. Brett and Specht 2004, 85; Mazurana and Carlson 2004, 13–14). In the postwar context, as I have mentioned, this was an extremely precarious topic. In Mazurana and Carlson's study, nearly all stated either that they had been captured or forcefully recruited (2004, 12). I met no one in Kabala who had voluntarily joined. Most, if not all, girls and women had been taken away by the rebels in one of the many attacks on Kabala (during the war the town was attacked thirteen times by rebel forces). The situation in Kabala differed somewhat from that in the southern and eastern parts of the country, because in Kabala so many girls had been abducted in groups, girls who knew each other from before. Also, as I was working in Koinadugu, I interviewed women who had been abducted from there and had since returned. Many people in the community, family and neighbors, knew exactly who had been taken and when.

Voluntary recruitment seemed also not to have been that common in the north. However, it has to be noted, as Brett and Specht write, that girls "may consider it to be in their own interest (retrospectively) to let it be assumed that they, like the majority, were abducted" (2004, 85). Although the situation might have been somewhat different for my informants in Kabala, I agree with Brett and Specht that in Sierra Leone in general there were women who in postwar society saw it as in their best interest to say they had been captured and unwilling participants in the rebel war. Binta Mansaray argues that initially, some women may have joined the rebels in a bid for gender equality: "Being marginalized by both customary practices and the APC regime, women's involvement in armed conflict can also be seen as a revolt" (Mansaray 2000, 144). While this was certainly possible, it nevertheless did not apply to any of my informants.

Those of my informants who did not manage to escape at once often stayed with the rebels, some for many, many years. This prompted my interest in finding out how rebel life was lived. A number of questions emerged. How was rebel life in war different from ordinary life in peace? How did they live; how did they sleep; and what, how, and with whom did they eat? Did they have friends? Did they take drugs, were they afraid, and who were they afraid of? What did they do if they got sick or gave birth? How many were in a group, how did the rebels control all those abducted, and did they have some form of "rebel justice"?

Everyday Life in "The Bush"

Most Sierra Leoneans spoke about the rebels as being "in the bush," and many abducted women I talked to also referred to their wartime experiences as when they were "in the bush." The terms *bush wives* and *bush husbands* were also frequently used by all informants. It is well known that the rebels' knowledge of the bush gave them strategic superiority during the war (see, e.g., Gberie 2005; Richards 1996). While the army with its battalions and big trucks could move freely only on roads and in towns, the rebels traversed the whole country on foot, effectively out of reach. "The bush" was the dominant rebel metaphor, and it was along bush paths the rebels mostly moved. The RUF rebels' first political manifesto was not surprisingly named *Footpaths to Democracy,* and Ibrahim Abdullah's 1998 article on the origin and character of the RUF rebel movement was aptly named, *Bush Path to Destruction.* It was through this idiom that most would cast their experiences of war. However, the rebels were not always in the bush; as one girl exclaimed, "We were not in the bush! The villagers lived in the bush, we lived in their houses!" This was indeed often the case in Koinadugu District, where during an attack the villagers would run away to live in the actual bush, while the rebels occupied their villages.[2]

"The bush" has important connotations in the region both historically and today, something that has been extensively studied among the Kuranko by Michael Jackson, who noted that "the wild is the direct opposite of village life, and their distinction between bush or wild (*fera*) and village or domestic space (*sue*) expresses this principle of opposition in many ways" (1977, 34). According to Jackson, a common way among the Kuranko to imply that someone was antisocial was to use the term *bush person* (*fera morgo*). Whereas in peacetime the antisocial elements of the bush could be staved off, during the war "bush people" were enemies against which "traditional" protective fetishes and medicines did not work. The bush was often conceived of as the village's opposite—the bush was wild whereas the village was domesticated. "The contrast between bush and town," writes Jackson, "signifies the extremes between exuberant disorder and social order, or between uncontrolled power and restraint" (2004a, 156). During my fieldwork, people also often used animal metaphors when speaking about the rebels; the rebels were not only from "the bush," they resembled animals, demons, and beasts—they were not human (cf. Hoffman 2003). This wartime dehumanization of the enemy is nothing unique to the war in Sierra Leone but is common to many wars (see, e.g., McC. Lewin 1993). This naming also worked both ways. Whereas the rebels were seen as dangerous and ambiguous creatures from the bush, according to some of my informants rebel commanders often referred to the civilians they killed as fowl (*sisi*). "The commandos killed a lot of civilians. They said [to the villagers], 'You don't know anything, we are killing you like fowl.'" Fowl, of course, are one of the more domesticated animals, not known for their aptitude or cunning.

Research has shown that in most wars, male enemies are often feminized; they are not like "our" soldiers—heroes and patriots—but are often pejoratively labeled cowards, wimps, women, girls, homosexuals, or something equally "unmanly" (see, e.g., Cohn 1993; Ruddick 1993). In Sierra Leone I heard many people talk about the enemy rebels in unflattering terms, but never as effeminate. They were frequently demonized, but the differences between rebels and others were phrased not so much in gendered terms as in the opposition of human/nonhuman. Rebels, male and female, were portrayed as nonhuman, but they were not a feminized or weak enemy. This becomes particularly interesting as male rebels in both Liberia and Sierra Leone, as I mentioned in the introduction, creatively challenged notions of a Western militarized masculinity when, during a period at the advent of war, they dressed up in women's underwear and wigs, engaging in what has been called ritual transvestism (Moran 1995). "The rebels, drawn from the rural population and staging their attacks from the forest, turned to an older and more potent, although less clearly Western, masculine ideal, that of the indigenous warrior," wrote Mary Moran on Liberia (1995, 79; see also Ellis 1999). As I have discussed in the introduction, this mix of feminine and masculine attributes did not weaken the rebels' sense of power; on the contrary, it enhanced it. It was the very act of transcending gender identities that infused them with power (Moran 1995, 80). This latter aspect nevertheless eluded many international observers, who dismissed them as bizarre drug-crazed tribal desperados.

When Aminata was taken from her home she was brought to a small rural village occupied by the rebels, which served as a base camp. They were in the group of one of the more famous rebel commanders, Superman.[3] The group consisted of around two hundred people divided into smaller groups comprising several household units. These household units can best be described as pseudofamily based, in which every commander would be the head of his compound with several "wives," many children, his junior officers, bodyguards, and sometimes even old people. These rebel villages thus in many ways corresponded to the structure and social composition of villages before the war. I asked my informants how the leaders were able to keep such large groups of people under control, with so many abductees and child soldiers, most of whom were under the influence of drugs. Aisha, who was in the same group as Aminata, said that every compound was headed by a commander who in turn had to report to his seniors, and ultimately to the rebel leader in the group, Superman: "If Superman says 'This is my law,' all the commanders have to obey." Aminata also explained that the entire rebel group only came together in the mornings for a parade, when they would pray for victory over their enemies (both Muslim and Christian prayers were performed every morning) and during looting expeditions and attacks, but most of the time they spent in their own smaller groups.

Many of the women who had been captured said that even if they had been with the rebels for many years, they had had little contact with the highest leaders and had little actual knowledge of their plans and strategies. Another of my key informants, who had also been abducted, thirty-year-old Mariatu, said that the leaders "don't even sit and discuss with us, unless when they were ready to go out and destroy, then you heard of them going to attack a place. You will never know their minds, you will only know it from their wives. Even then, it was very difficult to speak to them, they don't trust people." In the mornings after the parade, the commander would delegate tasks to everyone. Girls would often be sent to fetch water, firewood, or do the laundry, guarded at all times by younger boys, "smaller boys who don't have plan [sense or purpose] and can kill easily," as Aminata put it. In the rebel camp every household unit was more or less self-reliant in terms of food and other necessities. Although most women said that the commanders were always in contact with central RUF command, there was no central distribution of either food or weapons. When they ran out of food, each group would organize looting (*yaya*) expeditions. Aminata explained how this worked in her group:

> When the food was almost finished the commander will tell everyone to go. So when we enter any place those people will run and leave everything. Then, when we go, we will take as much as we need and go to another place. If we catch any woman or man, we will ask that person to take the load and to pound [the rice] for us. When we go, we will all give it to the CO [the commanding officer] and all the other leaders. But before we reach him we will hide some and then we cook it for [our] group. At times, after cooking they will only give you the remains if you are not with a good wife, but as for me, we were eating.

Clearly, a survival strategy for abducted women was to hide some of the food and perhaps other looted goods from their superiors. Aminata's narrative also shows how important the commander's wife could be in the distribution of food to the rest of the household, not unlike a senior wife in a polygynous household before the war. However, despite their power and influence, even commander's wives were not allowed complete freedom of movement, and commanders often left a group of bodyguards to protect them and prevent them from escaping while the commanders were away on mission. Kadi, who, as I have described earlier, was only nine when she was abducted, described her everyday life with the rebels in ways similar to both Aminata's and Mariatu's.

> KADI: The work the children usually do was to fetch water.... The women, they don't allow, only the girls go and fetch water, because they will feel that [the women] will run away. When we come with the water, the

children cook for them. When we cook we eat the rice. After that we play tape, music, and we dance. After that, in the night everyone will go to bed and sleep. Those that are on guard duty will sleep outside.

CHRIS: So even small children were guards?

KADI: Even they were guarding, even if it is a dog that is passing by you will say "Who is that?" Whatever thing passes by you will say "Who is that?" And you won't sleep.

CHRIS: How did you get food?

KADI: Yaya [looting]. It was not difficult because where we live, we were in the bush, but we were living very nicely. We were getting everything in abundance.

CHRIS: What kind of things?

KADI: We were getting food, we were playing music, we had many gallons of kerosene, we were lighting lamps, anywhere we go we will dig water wells, we have big pots to cook. We have everything.

CHRIS: So was your life better than now?

KADI: I was getting everything yes, but here is better than there, because there they were killing people a lot. That was a time of killing. They were just killing people. But here now, we live peacefully.

As Kadi describes, when a rebel group was in need of food they would attack villages and farms, but for other essentials such as kerosene, petrol, batteries, and medicines they would plan an attack on Kabala or other towns in the area. Spies would be sent out in advance on reconnaissance missions. Aminata said that the "most beautiful girls and brave boys will go to that town and make friends. The girls in fact will love the soldiers or other people in the town. Then after one week, or two weeks, they will come [back] and inform us about the set-up of the town" (cf. Mansaray 2000, 148–49). This is not something unique to Sierra Leone. In many conflict zones, armed insurgencies have used women as spies because soldiers often do not see women as potential enemies, and women can therefore manipulate soldiers' notions of women as innocent civilians (cf. Aretxaga 1997, 66). Mariatu explained that many of the girls in her group did not even want the war to end, because "they have been used to stealing or taking people's properties. Because when they say 'Let's go and yaya,' they will rush. They were always happy to get free things, won't they be happy? As for me, I was praying for the war to come to an end." However, Mariatu also explained that there really was no other way to get food at this time. "You are not trading, you didn't make farms, and you are not doing anything, so you are just sitting like DC [the District Commissioner]. So if you get anything it's just stealing." When I asked Mariatu about the lifestyles of some of the female ex-combatants in postwar society, she replied somewhat enigmatically, "*Monkey won't leave his black hand*—those that have been used to stealing won't leave it."

Although the rebels had to attack and loot villages to get basic supplies, not all villages were burnt or looted. Because of the lack of any centralized distribution of resources, the rebels needed villagers to cooperate and supply food and other necessities (see also Shepler 2005, 63–64). The village and its inhabitants would be spared as long as they cooperated with the rebels, but this cooperation was always coerced and the villagers had little room for negotiation. While working in one such village in Bombali District in 2004, Rosalind Shaw was given letters that had been sent to the village headman during the war, in which the rebels expected large quantities of clean rice, alcohol, kerosene, and many gallons of palm oil in only a matter of days.[4] Aminata also told of how Superman had instructed his group not to kill or loot in certain areas, and how instead they had made villagers provide food and other necessities in exchange for their lives. Different villages would bring a certain amount of rice and other necessities on alternating days. In some cases, the demands by the rebels were impossible to meet. Aminata mentioned one incident when a village had not delivered.

> Some people [villagers] took three days without coming to the [camp]. He [Superman] sent some boys to the farmhouses since we knew all their farms. So one day, many elders, young boys, girls, and some old women [from the village] came to the town. They were more than one hundred, if I didn't lie. When they came they were all put in one house.... Superman and two or three leaders entered while those appointed to put fire were around the building ready to obey their command. After five minutes we were up near the cotton tree, ready to go when we saw the smoke. None of them escaped. All of them died. When the fire caught, all [of us] left to go to Makeni. That was one of the worst incidents that happened in my presence.[5]

The rebel leaders punished not only recalcitrant villagers but also dissenters within their own ranks. During the morning parade, camp justice was meted out, and anyone who had killed without the expressed permission of the leader was in turn killed or severely beaten, and anyone who had violated the laws of the camp would be also be beaten. Aminata said,

> If you fight, quarrel, or beat a child, the commander will command one other person in front of all, during parade to flog [beat] you also. You will lie down and they will give you forty-eight lashes. The least they beat someone is twenty-eight [lashes]. If someone wrongs you, [you] instead tell the mamy queen and she will ask you to explain, and try to settle the dispute between you. So some they will tell the leaders, like lieutenant, sergeant, or commander. When these people are tired then you go to Superman, and for the women, we will tell the elderly women, or even [if] she is a small girl but married to any of the top-ranking people. We usually take our cases to them to settle....In fact, disputes are not many because there is not too much time. You won't be allowed to go out to friends in fact. And there, friendship is not too much.

Aminata and many others mentioned the presence in the rebel camps of mamy queens, whose responsibility it was to take care of young girls until they were old enough to become wives. As I described in chapter 1, a mamy queen is a "traditional" institution, and the fact that the rebels utilized this testifies to the continuity between the organization of ordinary and wartime life. I met one such mamy queen who had lived for three years with the group of another infamous rebel, Commander Savage. Her job was to take care of the girls, and she said that when a man found a girl he liked she would "do the marriage." In the rebel camp the mamy queen was held in high esteem, had more authority than most women, and would generally also be treated better by rebel commanders. Considering the similarities in the organization of the rebel groups with the social structure of the village, with its pseudokinship-based family units, the institution of mamy queen was an effective way to regulate and control behavior, enforcing sanctions if necessary but also encouraging and caring for children and young women. Being "traditional," the mamy queen's role and responsibilities were also well known to people from before the war. However, despite her authority, there was little a mamy queen could do to protect women from their own bush husbands; this too was no different from life in peacetime. Musu, another of my key informants, who was the bush wife of a senior commander, and who during her time with the rebels had become a renowned fighter, explained that despite the presence of a well-known broker such as a mamy queen, disputes were not, to her mind, settled in any customary way. She described instead a ruthless atmosphere: "To settle disputes is not there—you do me, I do you. There was no one to report to if your husband abused you.... There my husband was a big man, where will I report him? Nowhere! When he do me—I only hold God and sit."

Despite the presence of familiar "traditional" institutions, life with the rebels was described by most informants as one of hardship, in a society of strict rules and regulations, where seniority in the rebel hierarchy had little to do with chronological age or ruling lineages but rather a violent meritocracy. In a reversal of conventional authority, young boys and women could be commanders over older boys and men. One informant explained that a commander could be anyone. "It can even be a very small boy. They choose the commander according to his wickedness. You that are wicked will be the commander." Although Musu said that there were rebel rules and regulations, her story is one of uncertainty and arbitrariness, about unpredictable commanders and massive drug use. Musu was one of six bush wives to a commander. She became pregnant but miscarried, and thinks this was because she was so frequently beaten by her bush husband. The reason for the beatings, she believed, was that her bush husband usually took drugs, which made him "wicked." She said, "Whether you do them wrong or not, as long as the wickedness arose in them, even if you look at them they will beat you." Mariatu also told of drugs, "It's only the *jamba* [marijuana] and cocaine that made them to be bad. It was not everybody, some take it, but if they take that one, they will become wicked. Even your mother you will kill, you won't know or feel it until it [the drug] left you." In many narratives, drugs are often used as the main explanation for how children and women could become such tenacious fighters.

Informants also often talked of drugs being the reason bush husbands wanted to have sex so often. "Most men use their wives several times for a day, especially when they take cocaine. Cocaine makes them to like to sex women frequently, and also to kill. The woman won't say 'I am too tired to sex.' If you refuse, you will be killed. Some women don't do any work but to be sexing." Once I was sitting in the house of one of my informants together with some of her friends, who had all been abducted. We had talked about how their experiences of returning home after the war were very different, and had gone on to talk about sex and marriage. When I asked them if women enjoyed sex, they all started to laugh. I asked because it was not altogether clear to me that they would, seeing that they were circumcised and that most of them had been raped during the war and also had been married to men not of their choosing. One of the girls, Finah, laughed at my naiveté and said:

FINAH: We are all equal! Everyone enjoys sex!

[meanwhile, her friend Isatah is laughing her head off]

CHRIS: But you didn't enjoy it in the bush?

FINAH: Eh, in the bush you hate it.

CHRIS: Does it depend on the man?

FINAH: With the one that married you, you will enjoy.

CHRIS: Do men enjoy?

FINAH: Yes, the men enjoy, because they are the first people that will ask!

[everyone laughs]

CHRIS: Do men enjoy more than women?

FINAH: Yes, they enjoy, but some women also enjoy. But those men in the bush they love it more than all!

CHRIS: Why?

FINAH: Because of the drugs!

Aminata said that they were "injected with substances to make us strong and brave." They were given marijuana, cocaine, and something she calls *kubeyara*.

That leaf [*kubeyara*], they say it is to prevent snake. If they boil that, you take, you will go to fight with no fear and you will even kill your brother without knowing. In fact, when they capture people and they want to kill, they will ask you to fire at them.

Mariatu also tells of the frequent use of cocaine among fighters, and also of something she calls *pera-peran:* "They put it at the top of the match box and just passed in front of their nose. That one was more than cocaine. Well, they who smell that will be in trouble. They will kill, beat, ... take nails and remove eyes or cut hands and tell you to go to Tejan Kabba [the former President] to cure you." Drugs were used on a daily basis and included heroin (which is generally referred to as *brown-brown*), cocaine, crack, and marijuana (which is referred to as *jamba*). Apparently, jamba was the drug most commonly used, but also alcohol such as wine, beer and the local palm wine (*puyo*).[6] Many of these young children, girls and boys, belonged to the Small Boys Unit and Small Girls Unit, which were often sent out on dangerous missions and are known to have performed some of the most violent killings and mutilations (Mazurana and Carlson 2004, 14). The Small Boys Unit also worked as bodyguards to the wives of commanders. Musu said that she thought that the small boys were far more dangerous than any female fighter, because they were often very young when captured, and many had seen their families killed in front of them at the time of their abduction.

> It was the way they were trained up. Because they were giving them some drugs that were not good, cocaine, brown-brown, so they were giving them [this]. As such they had minds too much. When they killed human beings they put the blood in cups and give to the smaller boys to drink. So they were drinking that blood and they were not afraid of nothing. Even their mothers, if they meet them on the way they will [kill] her. They said the reason why they are not afraid, [like] one small boy, thirteen years of age, they cut his hand, they killed his mother and father. So because they did that, he said he won't spare no one again because they have killed his family in his presence. Father, mother, sisters, brothers. So he won't spare no one [when he himself became a rebel]. Anyone he hold he won't leave...anyone he met, even if you talk from January to December, he will kill you.

Mariatu also told me that she was more afraid of the small boys than the commanders. "In fact," she said, "they were more wicked. If they say 'We will kill you,' they will do it! They were not afraid of anything, because cocaine was working in the system. Those children knew how to shoot with gun. They slaughtered people like chicken, and also they will say, 'My father is dead and my mother is dead.' The drug also was in their bodies, so [they had] no sympathy for people."

Although the abduction was often a shocking event, for those girls and women who stayed with the rebels for many years, war was not only turmoil; there was also an everyday life "in the bush." Although one can point to many instances where rebel life was a radically transformed organization of social relationships, a violent exaggeration of regular life, there were also continuities, as indicated, for example, by the presence of mamy queens. To most girls and women, life in "the bush" was a far cry from life at home, but gradually some of the women became socialized into this existence, leaving both their language and their sense of belonging to their natal homes, and most of my informants became so-called bush wives.

Bush Marriage

Aminata was first taken as a bush wife by a very young man with low rank. She said that those who got bush husbands were lucky, "Because if you get a husband, during attacks you won't go, for you not to die." Together they lived in the household of one of the commanders and worked for him. Most informants said that life was easier as a bush wife than if they had been unattached. They did not have to go with the rebels on attacks but could stay in the *Joe bush* or *Jungle bush,* as they called it, although always with bodyguards to make sure that they did not escape. Favored wives of senior commanders could also have a lot of authority in rebel social life. Many had several people, young and old, both men and women, working for them, preparing food, laundering, and taking care of children. Often, senior wives were in charge of the distribution of arms and ammunition before an attack. Mazurana and Carlson noted the relative authority of RUF commanders' wives, writing that when commanders were away, wives "kept in communication with the commander and would select and send troops, spies, and support when needed. These girls and young women decided on a daily basis who in the compound would fight" (Mazurana and Carlson 2004, 14). In this sense these women had commanding responsibilities, although they were not referred to as commanders.

Commanders' wives had the power to punish or reward and were often in a position to get everything they asked for: clothes, shoes, jewelry, music, and videos, either by looting it themselves or having it done for them. They were therefore the object of much admiration and envy among girls in the lower rebel social hierarchy but were also feared and respected. Many girls and women told of frequent struggles between a commander's co-wives, some of which ended in death. Kadi said that her captor had always treated her nicely and had protected her from other men; it was the wives she was afraid of. A senior wife would have many privileges and would not take kindly to competition. When Kadi became older, her captor showed an interest in her and wanted her to become his wife. His first wife had then been killed because she had been caught having sex with another man, a punishment not executed by the husband but by his commander, Savage. Kadi explained that men would often fight each other over women. "When we were in the bush it was very easy for them [the men] to shoot each other for a woman. If you see someone loving to a woman that someone has intended to marry, she's your girlfriend, you will kill the other person."

Another of my informants, Mariatu, said that frequently, when a "companion [co-wife] do any wrong [to her co-wife] she will report to her husband and the husband will ask her what to do, and she will request to kill her companion." Theresa, a local social worker in Kabala who has worked with hundreds of captured girls, explained that those who were not wives would in essence be slaves: "They will be the slave for their [the commander's] wives [and] she has to work for the wives. So you'll be slave for that woman. So if you refuse that woman's order you will be killed. Anything that woman tells you to do you have to do it." In the case of Liberia, Mats Utas also mentions that in a rebel group the social dynamics between a commander's wives was often very hostile (2003, 180), which is not very different from the situation in ordinary families, where quarrels with co-wives are very common, the difference here being that the outcome of such quarrels could be death.

Fear was a constant factor in Aminata's life with the rebels. She said that she was most afraid of the leader of their group, Superman, and after him his commanders and her husband. Everyone feared Superman and the high-ranking commanders, also her bush husband, "because to kill you will be easy for them," she said. A senior commander was also free to take any junior man's wife, and once Aminata's low-ranking husband got into an argument with one of the commanders who had wanted to take Aminata for himself. When her bush husband did not return from the next attack, she was quite sure he had been killed by the commander. While one of the rules of the camp was that you were not allowed to kill at will, only by orders, Aminata said, "since they know that if you kill in [the camp] without command [order], you will also die, so some will wait until they go out [on attack]." After the death of her young husband she found herself without protection, and she was afraid of the commander, whom she now suspected of killing her bush husband. There was another young woman in the camp, Aisha, who had also been abducted from Kabala during the five-day attack and who had known Aminata, her former neighbor, since childhood. Aisha had been taken as a wife by one of the leaders, who she said had treated her well, and her relationship with him meant that she had some authority in the group. Seeing her friend in distress, she intervened and took Aminata into her own household to work for her as a cook, thereby probably saving her life. However, after some time in Aisha's household, Aminata was chosen by one of the other senior leaders, High Man, to become his wife, and Aisha told me that this time there was little she could have done to prevent it.

The period in between "husbands," or when a husband/protector was away on a mission, seems to have been a precarious one, as noted by both Utas (2003, 176) and McKay and Mazurana (2004). Utas writes of this period as "turbulent," and that the "struggles of daily life in the war zone were an immense pressure for most young women. The years of conflict were a constant battle for protection under the wings of the right commando. Young women in the war zone had no choice but to cling to a fighter with enough power to protect them" (Utas 2003, 176).[7] But whereas Utas emphasized women's agency in this context and described their strategizing to attach themselves to powerful commanders, my material shows the extremely haphazard ways in which some women were chosen by senior commanders while others became slaves. I will develop this discussion of women's agency further in the next chapter. Those girls and women who did not become wives were forced to labor, which could mean domestic work, cooking, cleaning, and taking care of small children, but it could also be farmwork or looting expeditions. According to most people I talked to, girls or women who had no "husbands" suffered physical hardship, lack of food, and frequent rapes. A "wife," on the other hand, would be protected from sexual abuse by other men and would also often have girls working for her, making her own situation less straining. Many informants said that women who were not taken as wives would be continually abused sexually by any number of men. According to one, new girls not yet chosen as wives would be offered to any man that wanted her, "so those [men] that would like, will take her for that day or days—so women were not enjoying." McKay and Mazurana (2004, 93) also make note of the fact that children not attached to a "family" had to live like scavengers, searching for scraps of food to survive. However, another of my key informants, Musu, said that whether formally or not, only very few women did not have husbands. "Let me say we all had husbands. This is because whether you agree or not you will have a man by force."

As I have shown, a bush wife who *belonged to* a high-ranking man was to some extent protected from other men's physical and/or sexual abuse. However, should a woman fall in love with another man, she could be killed. Mariatu said that the men were very jealous and that the punishment of death came easily during the war. "They are jealous more when they tell you that they love you, and [if] you answered another man's love, they will kill you." Although men quite frequently fought each other for women, they also protected their "wives" against other men. This sense of protection by the bush husband perhaps explains the sense of loyalty some women felt towards their "husbands," a loyalty which, to the families of abducted women, and to me as well, was sometimes quite difficult to understand given the level of abuse they suffered. Kadi said that "to live in the bush, I also supported the men because it was good for you, the one person that has captured you protected your life, it is good to be with him only." According to her, only foolish women would openly cheat their husbands. "If you see another one, like the head [the commander], and say 'I am going to leave this one,' if they kill you, you've found it for yourself."

In Aminata's household there were fifteen people. Her new bush husband was the head, and he had two wives and the others worked for them. As his favorite wife, Aminata did not have to do any domestic work and was actually prevented from this by her bush husband. She was not allowed to go and fetch water, to do the laundry, to cook, to go out, or even to go and take a bath on her own. Her only "duty" was to have sex with her husband whenever he wanted. He also gave her jamba to make her "brave." Although she did not have to do hard labor, and she said that they "were getting everything" in terms of material goods, she was not happy. "Because as they are killing others you will always be thinking that you will be killed."

This was also reiterated by another young woman, Mateneh, who said, "Well, they will say, even if you wear so many dresses, your heart is not at rest. Because the dress you are wearing is for nothing, you wear your dress and they kill." Many of my younger female informants emphasized that they had nice clothes during the time with the rebels. In this respect they seem no different from other teenage girls; coming from poverty, they sometimes reveled in being able to dress up and look nice. But even this illusion of splendor faded in the face of violence: "The dress you are wearing is for nothing," as Mateneh said. Nevertheless, many girls and women did say that life in "the bush" was not so bad. Because of the massive looting, they often had food, medicines, generators, kerosene, batteries, and many other things, making the alternative, to return home to poverty, not as attractive. In the situation they found themselves in, this kind of "militarized" life was sometimes seen as their best option (cf. Save the Children 2005). Although women under the protection of high-ranking commanders were protected from sexual abuse by other men, they were frequently sexually abused by their own bush husbands. One of the young women I met, Amie, twenty-one years old, had been a bush wife during the war. She described her life with her rebel bush husband like this:

> I was not working. I had people to work for me, only to sex, and at the time of attack I usually take his armor boxes for boys to fill it.... But for the sexing, I should always be ready for him. The day you will deny for him, for the rest of the day you will be pumping. That has really affected me. If I didn't accept for him to sex, I will be stripped naked and he beat and pumped me. I had all children working for me.

This girl, who was nineteen when interviewed and only twelve at the time she was abducted, starts her very short narrative by positioning herself in the camp hierarchy: "I was not working. I had people to work for me." It is not until she talks about having always to be ready to have sex with her bush husband and how she could not refuse or would risk being severely punished as well as sexually and physically abused, that the vulnerability of her situation really comes to the fore in the narrative. She interlaces the experience of being freed from manual labor and having people under her control on the one hand, with being constantly at risk of being raped and sexually abused by her captor on the other. When she says that the abuse "has really affected me," she may also be referring to the vaginal problems she tells of later in the interview; she is still suffering from venereal diseases as a consequence of the constant sexual abuse. The most dramatic shift, however, is that after graphically relating the abuse she had suffered, she reinstates herself as someone who had been afforded an elevated status: "I had all children working for me." By repositioning her status she was also escaping or playing down her vulnerability.

Like numerous captured young women, Aminata became pregnant. Children born of rebel fathers are frequently referred to as *rebel pikindem* (rebel children). These children are often thought to have "bad blood" and are often in a very vulnerable position in postwar society, as I will discuss in a later chapter, but suffice it to say that many mothers of these children would not unreservedly divulge information about their situation.[8] Only three months after the birth of her first child, Aminata's bush husband demanded to have sex with her. In Sierra Leone, especially in rural areas, there is a belief that if a pregnant or breastfeeding woman has intercourse it can endanger the child, who will get sick or die (cf. Bledsoe 1987; Jackson 1977, 83). To have sex with a breastfeeding woman thus violates a cultural taboo, and the potency of this transgression is one of the reasons men should not have intercourse with their wives from the time they become pregnant until they have stopped breastfeeding, up to two or three years in all. Fearing that her child would die, Aminata therefore stopped breastfeeding her child. Musu was convinced that the baby she was suckling at the time of her abduction in 1995, died because of the sexual abuse she was subjected to. The Kuranko word Musu used to describe the sexual abuse was *balfa*. She explained, "So they kill my son, *balfa,* which means they sexed me until he died."

In many rebel groups there were traditional midwives, sometimes nurses and even doctors. When Aminata gave birth she was attended by a nurse who helped her deliver and also gave her pain killers. Interestingly, I found that young women from rural areas, especially those who were illiterate and even those who were initiated, were quite ignorant of childbirth. I first thought this had to do with the fact that most had been abducted at a very young age and had no such previous experience. Mariatu said that when she was about to give birth she very reluctantly went to one of the older women (in Kuranko *musekòtεnu*), who eventually helped her and explained what it was that she was going through. I was often told that the actual birth was something they had been unprepared for and did not understand. It was not only Mariatu, but many other girls and women as well, who said that they felt ashamed because they thought that the pressure exerted by the baby on the pelvic area meant that they needed to defecate, and others told of feeling extremely ashamed of having to expose their genitals and "reveal" themselves to others. From a very young age, Sierra Leonean girls are taught to carefully cover their bodies from the waist to the knees, and never to expose their genitalia. I had assumed, before my fieldwork, that childbirth was one of the things young women were taught in the female societies they were initiated into. During my time in Koinadugu I started to understand that this may not have been the case, and after returning home and reading Bledsoe, among others, I found my suspicions confirmed. In her work, Bledsoe found that "contrary to previous belief, Sande [female society] leaders hide more than they teach about reproduction, and midwives try to keep the knowledge of child bearing secret. Many girls, I am convinced, do not find out how babies are born until the very moment their own children emerge from the womb" (Bledsoe 1980, 73). Therefore it seems to have been a strategy of older influential women to withhold information and thereby augment their own status. So, despite the inversion of hierarchies and the social upheaval of war, certain aspects of social structure were no different during war than in peace.

Sexual violence and exploitation have been the focus of most attention concerning women in the Sierra Leonean war, and rightfully so, but was this the principal reason for their abduction? I believe one important aspect has received too little attention in most writings about abducted women in the Sierra Leonean war: women's productive labor. As I have previously described, pregnancy, childbirth, and breastfeeding were all part of women's everyday wartime experiences, just like cooking, cleaning, doing laundry, and farming. Even during the war, the chores of everyday life had to be performed. According to Mazurana and Carlson, the rebels needed women and children to maintain their "war system" and kidnapped them for that reason (2004, 12–14).[9] Long before the war, women in Sierra Leone contributed substantially to the country's agricultural labor force.[10] Agricultural production in Sierra Leone is highly gendered, as has been described in chapter 2. During the war, rebel groups could not rely solely on looting and the cooperation of villagers. When the inhabitants of a village or farm escaped during an attack, this meant that the hard work of harvesting and preparing the rice left by the fleeing villagers had to be done by the rebels themselves. The processing of rice from harvesting to cooking is a long and complex process, and is also explicitly women's work. It involves harvesting, transporting, steaming, drying, pounding, separating husks from seeds, cleaning, and finally cooking. It is evident that without the logistics of centralized food distribution, the rebels would never have survived had it not been for the forced productive labor of women. This seems to be the case in many African insurgencies where armed forces live off the land and where women's agricultural labor is much in demand, as noted by Meredeth Turshen. She writes that control of "women's productive labour is one of the gains from rape and abduction in civil conflicts" (2001, 61). The lengths to which rebel commanders went in controlling women to prevent them from escaping, and as I will show below, from communicating with each other in their own language, demonstrates the value of women's productive labor. Thus my findings support the supposition that the roles women performed in rebel groups "went far beyond being simple 'sex slaves' or 'camp followers' [but] were essential to the functioning of the war systems" (Thompson 2006, 349). In fact, this has historical precedents, and although women's productive labor has been neglected in most studies of contemporary armed conflicts, it is a known fact in the literature on the internal slave trade in West Africa, especially in the nineteenth century where women were abducted in raids and wars (Shaw 2002, 32).

The Eradication of Language and Belonging

The language mostly used by the rebels was Sierra Leone's lingua franca, Krio. To speak any other language could invoke death. I have mentioned in chapter 1 that the war was not fought along lines of ethnicity or ethnic belonging. The prohibition of local languages in a multilingual country had more to do with control. Rebel groups consisted of people from many different ethnic backgrounds, and of people who did not always know the language of the area they operated in. Therefore Krio was given preeminence, as almost everyone knew it. Most informants also explained how their abductors suspected them of making plans to escape or plotting against them if they were speaking their native tongue. Aminata told me that they were not encouraged to make friends, and that she had had no friends apart from the girl who saved her; still, even they would not talk to each other in their own language in the presence of others because of the risk of punishment.

That the rebels had been especially afraid that the women were planning to escape or plotting to kill them if they were talking in their own language or showing bonds of friendship was confirmed by countless informants. Mariatu said that "we were not allowed to speak to our people, and we also pretended not to know that area for them not to kill us.... we will only talk to each other in their absence, but if they come from their patrol, we won't speak to each other because they only say we are making plot or plans to kill them or run away." Another expression of this culture of anonymity was the use of noms de guerre, war names, which was widespread among the rebels during the war in Sierra Leone. I was told that all rebel leaders took war names to protect themselves from future revenge and retribution, and also to boost their confidence and reputation. Some rebels chose names that emphasized their bravery, and others names that reflected their personality, while some were given names by their comrades. They were names like Cut Hand, High Firing, Hold Mi Cap (according to informants he always said, "Hold me cap, I'm ready to kill"), Blood (person measuring blood to drink), Necka (a man who frequently raped or had sex with any woman, young or old), Nylon (a person who drops melted plastic in people's eyes), and Mami Curse (someone who insults mothers). The more famous leaders operating in Koinadugu District and who are often mentioned in narratives were Savage, Bottlecap, and Superman. There were also famous RUF and AFRC commanders with creative names such as Rambo, Base Marine, Colonel Tiger, Cobra, Sawimbi, Mosquito, Five-Five, Bomblast, Mon Amie, Machiavelli, and Leather Boot.

This culture of anonymity is interesting in that it seems to be a renunciation of the "ordinary" order of things. In Sierra Leone even third-generation urban settlers will refer to their "village" when asked where they are from. Family, relatives, and origin constitute to a large extent the fabric of social life and are often the basis of networks of patronage and other social relationships. A person by the surname of Marah will become a family member when meeting a stranger by that name anywhere in the country. I have been present on innumerable occasions when strangers discuss at length until they find their common denominator, often a geographical area or an ancestor. This reversal of the order of things among the rebels during the war was a master theme with many auxiliary themes. There was the reversal of hierarchies of age (see, e.g., Richards 2005a; Shepler 2005, 116), the use of war names, but also the play with gender roles in the element of masquerade present in the beginning of the war in Sierra Leone, which, as I have described, was also an important element in the war in neighboring

Liberia (see, e.g., Ellis 1999; Moran 1995). On the other hand, this culture of anonymity also plays into the act of hiding and concealing true identities in order to evoke power as described by Ferme (2001).

Many were the accounts as well of pretending to not know one's own family members or pretending not to recognize certain villages or houses. If a friend or family member had been acknowledged, they all would have been killed. I was told it was better to feign ignorance. Musu explained this situation of social reversal. "I didn't have a friend, there was jungle. There, there was no friendship. Even your mother when you see her you won't even make people to know that she is your mother. Even your father that born you, you won't make as if he is your daddy." While she was with the rebels, young Kadi had returned to her hometown of Kabala during several attacks. I was curious to know whether she had gone back to her house or if she had tried to contact her family while there.

> CHRIS: Did you ever go to look at your house?
>
> KADI: At that time this place was all under our own [rebel] care, you in the bush, even if you were born here you won't say this is my house. If you say this is my house they will kill you, [they will] say you are a native born of Kabala so that you want to escape, that you want to prosecute us.
>
> CHRIS: Did you try to look without telling anyone?
>
> KADI: Whenever I was passing I will just glance at it.

Mariatu also told me that once when her group was approaching the village of her father's family, she just acted as if she had never been there before. "Even if you have relatives there you won't say it—eh, death has called you!" She explained that men and boys who were forced to rape their daughters and sisters would pretend that they were strangers to each other for fear of being killed.

> Even if they catch your mother, and yourself, you won't say it out. When they caught some men they will say, "Sex with your mother," you see! And you have to do it. Even your sister they will tell you to sex with her. You will even do it and pretend as if you don't know each other. And she is your mother or your sister! If you show it out, they will kill both of you. They will also give you knife to kill your mother. Would you say no? You won't, because you also want your life to be spared.

However, arriving at her father's village during the attack, Mariatu found one of the rebels trying to cut off the leg of her younger half-sister. She pretended she did not know the girl and instead feigned sympathy for a stranger and said she wanted the girl for herself. Mariatu's bush husband was a high-ranking commander, which made it easier for her to act on her own initiative, albeit shrouded in secrecy so that her motives would not to be questioned by the other fighters. However, every act and spoken word was measured in a dangerous balance between life and death. Both the case of Mariatu trying to save her sister and Aminata's old neighbor trying to save her, indicate that wives of senior commanders not only inspired fear in other women but would also sometimes use their position and influence to try to save and protect children, relatives, and fellow female abductees (cf. Mazurana and Carlson 2004, 14).

The Escape

A very important part of women's wartime experiences with the rebels in the bush was leaving it. Most of the shorter, less personal war narratives almost always end with the escape, or less frequently with release by the rebels. It was as if the stories of war could not come to completion without this last reaffirmation of their return to "humanity," for in a society where the rebels were "animals" and their domain "the bush," the escape carried important moral connotations. Most of my initial interviews actually ended with the act of escaping. Many said they managed to escape during an attack, when sent to launder by a river, or when fetching wood or water. Only a few said that they had been released, mostly toward the end of the war. One girl said that "I did not escape, but when we were in Makeni Colonel Issa told us civilians captured [that] if we want to go home he'll let us go. We were free to go."[11] In fact, as I came to know later, there were quite a few women who had not escaped at all, but had left the rebels after the cease-fire, or even later. In postwar Sierra Leone, the act of escaping was seen as a moral issue, signifying that abducted women had not been in collusion with the rebels. As will be apparent in the following chapters, returning home after abduction was not always easy.

The narratives of escape were delivered in a postwar society where the creation of a public metanarrative of "The War" had already begun, a narrative in which abducted girls had few available trajectories to follow. This is again one example of the intertwining of the past with the present in terms of narrating war experiences and their place in an explicitly moral order. During my time in Kabala, for instance, it became evident that those who had managed to escape after only a short time with the rebels, days or perhaps a few weeks, were seen as more "innocent" than those who had spent several years with the rebels, who had through their long exposure to rebel life become rebels themselves. One can say that through their long exposure to the rebels they had been contaminated. In our very first interview, Aminata had said that after her bush husband was killed, the suffering of rebel life became unbearable and she had escaped one day when sent to launder. Much later she admitted that "I was not released, neither did I escape. I was with them until after disarmament. And even after that, I was with the man for one year in Makeni." For family members and relatives, it sometimes seemed inconceivable that abducted girls and women who had stayed with the rebels for a long period of time could not have found an opportunity to escape earlier, and this was to have consequences for their return to their families after the war. Their having stayed with the rebels voluntarily meant that these women were complicit in the horrors of rebel activity. There were of course many reasons that some did not escape sooner. Some could not, as they were often supervised by bodyguards, but many were also afraid because there were many deterrents. Many told of witnessing many girls being killed when they were caught escaping. Some were also afraid to escape because of what they thought would await them when they returned home. These girls and women therefore faced a double threat; they were blamed by the rebels if they tried to leave and by their communities if they returned home. They were "caught in a cycle of recrimination: too scared to stay and too scared to leave" (Save the Children 2005, 12).

It has been said that for girls, "participation in the conflict tends to exacerbate this problem, because their participation is usually countercultural and is often associated, rightly or wrongly, with perceptions of them being sexually active" (Brett and Specht 2004, 101), and this would be related to the problem of return, as I will discuss in chapter 7. I believe this is an important insight to bear in mind when analyzing narratives by women like Aminata. For example, it has been suggested that the tight security measures and the wrecking of the social world were aspects of RUF's master plan for creating a "bizarre new reality" (Richards 2005a, 135), and many stories reveal that some girls and women slowly became socialized into this new, "bizarre" way of life. Yet, as I have described, some informants admitted that life with the rebels was not all that bad, and there were also those who were afraid to return to their homes with rebel babies, for good reason, as Aminata's case reveals. Quite a few women also told me that they had actually come to love the bush husband. I will return to this in the following chapters. Just as Aminata had begun our very first interview with the event of the actual abduction during the Five Day attack on Kabala, she ended our last interview with the same event.

> Well, the thing that I will never forget was the day I was captured during that five-day attack. We were many and kept in one house not to escape. We were *virginated,* not one person virginated me, although one person started, but there were four of them and that continued up to two months.[12] They got so many things here [in Kabala] and we were asked to take them to their base, running, fearing the soldiers are after us.... Also the day I was captured I was laid down so they could write on my skin, RUF. That was a big day for me. I nearly wanted to die. They had sharp instruments with which they wrote. To be sincere, my eyes were closed with cloth and after that they untied my eyes. And in fact, it took three months for the wound to be healed in the bush. I finally got well by the MSF [Médecins Sans Frontièrs had performed corrective surgery on her after the war]. They [the rebels] really treated us badly. Now I don't have money but I feel good and happy because I am free to move, talk, and do things. But in the bush, no freedom, no peace, only feeling or thinking of death.

Concluding Remarks

Some women made it through the war as fighters, but as I have shown, most female combatants in Sierra Leone were not exclusively fighters but served also in other roles during the war. This made their experiences complex and ambiguous, as I will discuss further in the next chapter. Almost all had initially been abducted, especially where the rebels are concerned, and most abductees had initially been given as bush wives to male fighters of various ranks—the higher his rank, the better their fate. A "wife" of a commander would have some amnesty from abuse by other men as long as she was under his protection. If they were not chosen as a bush wife, girls and women often became carriers or domestic slaves, in which case they were often raped and abused. Of those girls and women who had positions of authority, the majority were bush wives of high-ranking men. These women had more power and leverage and were generally more trusted and considered loyal. Most important, in this chapter I have shown how important abducted women's productive work was in maintaining and upholding the "war system" of the rebels.

The women I worked with often described a social landscape of war and rebel life that was completely devoid of any mechanisms of containment. Violence could flare up at any time, directed at anyone, even among the commanders. But they also describe an everyday life characterized by strategies of survival amidst the daily activities of preparing food, doing laundry, and taking care of children. To speak up against an injustice, to look someone in the eyes (defiantly or not), to say the wrong thing, or to be in the wrong place at the wrong time, could all mean death. This culture of fear was not, I believe, cultivated by the rebels as a conscious method of control but stemmed rather from their own fears of uncertainty and loss of control. Fear was definitely a motivator of violence, especially violence perpetrated by those rebels who themselves had been abducted by violent means. Many abducted men and women had witnessed the brutal assassination of their own families, and some had been forced to participate in them. Life with the rebels after such events consisted of few, but nonetheless complex, options: adapt, die, or try to escape.

On the one hand, I have followed the straight trajectories of many war narratives—from abduction to escape—in this chapter. On the other, it has been my endeavor to muddle the neat road of narratives into the fractured, ambiguous, and spidery paths I believe these women's rebel experiences were. I have described how the experience of abduction constituted a break with "normal" life, how ties of reciprocity were severed and hierarchies inverted, but I have also shown how everyday rebel life demonstrated continuities with "traditional" social organization as well. The continuities between prewar and wartime life should perhaps not be overly emphasized, though; in this chapter I have also given accounts of some of my informants' experiences of an everyday life in the rebel movement that consisted of forced marriage, continual sexual abuse, and consumption of drugs. But important aspects were also domestic chores and managing the tenuous relations between their bush husbands, their co-wives, and their commanders.

The closing note, however, has to be that many of my informants were caught in a cycle of recrimination: many were afraid to stay, but too scared to leave. In writing about the composition of rebel groups—about role reversal or the reversal of generational authority, or about how abductees were denied their own language, denied acknowledgment of their village, their family, their names—two issues come to mind that permeate this whole book: fear and shame. In the next chapter I will examine in greater detail gender aspects of the war in Sierra Leone. I do this by analyzing war rapes in a global as well as cultural context. I will also look at the figure of the female fighter and her resonance both in Sierra Leonean popular imagination and in the media, and I will track the journey from abductee to rebel fighter, from "victim" to "perpetrator."

4

FROM RAPE VICTIMS TO FEMALE FIGHTERS

Women's Participation in the War

A feminist curiosity leads one to be suspicious of a dependence only on
those categories that acknowledge women either as silently symbolic or as
silently victimized.

CYNTHIA ENLOE, "Demilitarization—or More of the Same? Feminist
Questions to Ask in the Postwar Moment"

As can be understood from the preceding discussion in chapter 3, rape
and sexual abuse were extremely common during the war in Sierra Leone.[1] Almost all girls and women I interviewed told of multiple rapes,
gang rapes, and continual sexual abuse during their time in "the bush."
It is just not possible to write about abducted women's experiences of war
without going into the issue of rape and sexual abuse, as this was part of
daily life for many women. In this chapter I will examine my informants'
accounts of rape and sexual abuse, and I will connect these to local notions
of rape and sexual morality and to a growing body of research on rape as a
"weapon of war." I will also describe how female abductees coped and the
strategies they used to maneuver in a very volatile situation, but I have also
tried to see how these strategies were bound to local moral imperatives.
Many of my informants described how they had to adapt to their new circumstances in order to survive; they talked about always being on guard,
never showing feelings or intent: "never cry," "don't talk," "go about your
business quietly," "you just have to bear it out." Some of them also became

adept at manipulating their environment, mostly to augment their position, their material wealth, and to protect the lives of their loved ones.

I will also discuss how many of my informants came to be female fighters, and how the notion of female fighters was interpreted by the local population as well as by international media. As I have described, quite a few abducted women became fighters with the very groups that abducted them. During the Sierra Leonean war, the RUF and the AFRC, but also government forces, and even the Civil Defense Forces, recruited girls and young women, who proved to be "highly effective combatants" (Abdullah and Muana 1998, 180).[2] About half of all the girls and women I talked to said that they had been trained as fighters during their time with the rebels, soldiers, or Civil Defense Forces, but many admitted to having fought only intermittently, in between serving as spies, laborers, bush wives, or sex slaves, making the definition of who was a fighter more complicated.[3] The presence of female fighters both disturbs and complicates conventional notions of war. The prevalent image of most conflicts is still that of "violent men and victimized women" (Aretxaga 1997, 4). Also, someone who has been raped is generally regarded as a victim and someone who has been a fighter is a perpetrator. In this chapter I will therefore examine the concept pair of "victims" and "perpetrators" often found in humanitarian discourse and I will discuss how the notion of agency relates to these concepts. This discussion is relevant to how female rebels were portrayed in the media and, as I will discuss in the next chapter, by DDR, the demilitarization, demobilization, and reintegration process.

War Rapes and Gendered Violence

"You will be with a friend, then suddenly you will see that person dead," Aminata said. "You will just hear a gun firing.... Where you will be, you won't be able to reject anything you are asked to do. You will just meet a fine, beautiful girl lying dead, then you will hear someone saying, 'She refused for me.' That means the girl refused to sex." The first experiences of rape and sexual abuse for my informants often coincided with the actual abduction, as has been illustrated in the previous chapter, and my informants often distinguished between these first rapes and the sexual abuse they later experienced by their bush husbands. When they talked about what happened, they would describe how the first rapes were often performed by several men and could go on for days. These rapes were then usually followed by the entrance of one man, often of higher command, claiming the woman as his "wife" and thereby "saving" her from future rapes and in turn making her feel loyal to him for having saved her life. As with young Kadi, who said, "To live in the bush, I also supported the men, because it was good for you. The one person that has captured you, protected your life, it is good to be with him only." As so many of my informants described similar events, it seems likely that this was not a random occurrence, but a strategy on the part of the rebels.

Rape of women in war has previously often been seen as an unavoidable by-product of war. Current research, however, has shown that sexual violence is often part of the strategies of war (see, e.g., Barstow 2000; Card 1996; Koeonig 1994; Moorehead 1995; Niarchos 1995; Swiss and Giller 1993; Turshen 2001). It has been argued that in Sierra Leone, rape was part of RUF's strategy for controlling the civilian population (Thompson 2006, 350), and it has also been speculated that men participated in rape as a form of male initiation into the rebel movement (Richards 1996, 30). I believe, however, that war rapes were not only about initiation into a violent male culture. War rapes in Sierra Leone also reflected the low status of rights for women in Sierra Leonean society, which was magnified by the war. The war rapes were not an isolated war phenomenon but had resonance within larger Sierra Leonean society. What war rapes do is to highlight "preexisting sociocultural dynamics" (Olujic 1998, 31). Therefore a concern with war rapes must resist reifying and objectifying women as victims (cf. Enloe 2000, 133). The ensuing reaction of families and communities to women who had been raped and sexually abused during the war also reflected local understandings of morality, as has been outlined in chapter 2 and as I will discuss further in chapter 7. The type of sexual abuse these women were subjected to, however, was a type that was unprecedented in rural Sierra Leone and has to be located in a global warscape where pornography often plays an important role (Enloe 1989, 196).

In my discussion of war rapes in this book, I initially had no intention of going into detail about the actual rapes. In most accounts of war rapes details are, for understandable reasons, often excluded. Instead it is often concluded that a certain number of women were raped, and context and detail are most often left unaccounted for, making rape victims the "faceless victims of war" (Enloe 2000, 108). Partly I was afraid of alienating readers with these disturbing narratives, yet, after going through a number of interviews, I came to see that to shy away from explicit descriptions of sexual violence is also a way of silencing and censoring women's experiences. Although relatively rare, detailed descriptions of sexual violence are not new to anthropology (see, e.g., Bourgois 2002). Rape during the Sierra Leonean war was so commonplace that if I had refrained from a detailed discussion of it, the many individual experiences of rape and sexual abuse would have to be collapsed into a collective and abstract "war rape."

If the war rapes are not contextualized, I believe important aspects are missed, such as the organized manner in which bush marriages followed multiple and gang rape, and the "pornographic" nature of the rapes. For example, much has been written about the influence of action films such as *Rambo* and *First Blood* on the formation of a rebel culture (Richards 1994, 1996; Utas 2006), and many informants also told of how they used to watch such videos. However, nothing has been mentioned about whether or to what extent pornography circulated during the war. At the time of fieldwork I did not think to ask; it was not until after fieldwork when I was transcribing interviews that the possibility of pornographic influence occurred to me. In postwar Sierra Leone, however, pornographic films and printed media, particularly from Nigeria, can be found almost everywhere (cf. Persson 2005, 40). Later, I found out that before the war, pornography was not widely distributed in rural areas as it was in the capital, and had been relatively unknown to young rural women and girls. It is well documented that pornography, sex trafficking, and prostitution are linked to the illicit economies of war (Enloe 1993; Kelly 2000; Nordstrom 2004), and seeing as other aspects of the war in Sierra Leone were closely interconnected to the global economy (diamonds, weapons, action films, etc.), it should be no surprise that pornography could also have been distributed and consumed by combatants during the war.[4]

In one interview, a young woman, Mateneh, whom we have already met in the previous chapter, told her story of abduction and rape under much duress and on the condition that she was guaranteed absolute anonymity. Her story is as follows. She was travelling on foot with her sister and a few other people in an area of Koinadugu District that they thought were safe from rebels, when they were caught in an ambush. Mateneh was separated from her sister and the others and was taken away by three men.

Immediately I was stripped naked and a young man, a Mende, put his fingers inside my vagina. After putting his fingers inside me, three of his companions came and said "Boh, if you not oh man, tell we" [Brother, if you are not a man, tell us]. One pushed that man and he started sexing me. After him the next one asked him, "Have you finished?" And he said, "I have spermed." So the other one said, "Get up and let me cool my own fire." So that man got up [pause]. Well, when he got up, instead of wiping his penis with cloth, he just put that penis with the sperm in my mouth. I was still lying in the veranda while the other has asked me to open my mouth to suck his penis. The second one was busy opening my legs to sex me. At this time one has a gun, the other a sharp knife, so what I was thinking of was 'next world'—death. So it happened while I was sucking the other's penis the next one was sexing me.

The rape was interrupted by the sound of a whistle calling everyone to gather for a meeting. Mateneh said she was very tired but she did not protest when they told her to dress and accompany them to the meeting. She said she was praying for them to spare her life. After the meeting, the group prepared to leave for Kabala. The third man, who had not participated in the rape, told Mateneh he wanted her to be his "wife," and like many women, she felt that he saved her life and that she was very fortunate. When Mateneh talked of the details of the rape she said, "I have never sexed like that. So I became tired." This statement was made in an interview characterized by openness and frank detail in terms of the sexual abuse. It seemed that Mateneh was as shocked by the type of sex she was subjected to as she was by being raped.

Although I am no expert on the sexual practices of people in Sierra Leone, what I was made to understand by various female informants was that this type of sex was unprecedented in most rural women's realm of experience. Fellatio, and having sex with more than one man at a time, were unheard of, and by many described as unthinkable. Many women also talked about the context of the rapes as violating taboos, as when women were stripped naked and raped in public view, or when they were raped in the daytime, or in the bush proper. This violation of social taboos seems to be a common feature for war rapes worldwide. Aminata said, when she reflected on what had happened to her, "they were not ashamed. Ten people will be on one veranda and there they will have sex with us. Those that are not married [i.e. those who were not bush wives], three to four men will have sex with her for a day. In fact, [she paused], it doesn't mean only at night. Even if it is during the day, if they feel like it, they will have sex with you." Most of the informants in Koinadugu District were from rural areas and had been abducted when very young. Some of those not yet married at the time of abduction had had sexual encounters before, but many had been virgins.

As a bush wife, Mateneh was exempt from household work, although she was encouraged to become a fighter. Nevertheless, her duty as a bush wife was to have sex with her bush husband whenever he wanted, which seemed to have been most of the time when he was not away on a mission. As has been described above, this aspect differed little from a traditional marriage, although the frequency with which she had to have sex was much higher than in a "normal" marriage and the constant consumption of drugs that played such a part in it had no part in "normal" marriage at all. She said, "If they didn't go anywhere for the whole day we will be sexing and the whole night. More especially when he has smoked jamba. That man is never tired of sexing. Also, that man was giving me cigarette to smoke, wine, and even jamba. And even I, if I smoke it, he will sex me for the rest of the day. I won't know anything."

Mateneh also explained what happened to girls and women who did not have the protection of a bush husband: "Like for the day, about five or six will use her for the day or night, if she refuse they kill her. If she is sick they take her to the hospital. You see, but, if you are lucky, like the commanders, the brigadiers will take you away you are free, you are a good woman." Notice here that a moral discourse on women's sexuality enters Mateneh's account: if a woman was taken by one of the leaders she becomes "a good woman." In what would seem to be extreme circumstances, this statement reflects a traditional discourse of morality concerning women. This is further emphasized when she continues, "So as I say, you don't have freedom of movement. If the men need you, if you are lucky some of the commanders, or brigadiers will have you as a wife, you are free. But if you are among those riff-raff women they want you in the day time, they will use you. At night they will use you, on the way, and not one, two, three."

In much humanitarian discourse, women like my informants were often referred to as "sex slaves" or "forced wives" (cf. Schroven 2005, 76). In these contexts their stories of war often focus on rape and sexual abuse. Mats Utas (2005) found during his work in war-torn Liberia that these types of "stories" told little about how the women he met in Liberia maneuvered, strategized, and planned their lives. This is consistent with what I described above, how in most war-torn settings the humanitarian community consistently characterizes abducted women as passive victims with no agency (cf. Shepler 2005, 156). The stories of rape take precedence over other war stories. However, although rape in Sierra Leone in general is seen as a stigma attached to the girl or woman, I found that many women were very direct with me when talking about having been raped during the war. Given the massive occurrence of war rapes, it was perhaps easier to talk about these particular rapes than about "peacetime" rapes. One report states that "the silence that often surrounds rape, in Sierra Leone and worldwide, was broken as women demanded peace and participated in recovery after the war" (Bambrick 2004, 10). In the case of Liberia, Utas considered the fact that since rape was so common and something that affected "all families and social networks," the sheer magnitude of it might actually help victims of rape to "mentally [be] able to leave a rape assault behind" (Utas 2003, 218). A Human Rights Watch report on Sierra Leone also pointed to this, arguing that because of its prevalence, rape became less stigmatizing (Human Rights Watch 2003, 52). I would argue that just because something bad happens often, does not necessarily mean that it is less bad. Susan McKay and Dyan Mazurana wrote, "Although we agree that many girls were (or will be) welcomed back to their communities' (if such still exist), the significant issue of stigma is being glossed over; indeed,...many girls felt intense personal shame and anger" (McKay and Mazurana 2004, 45).

But as there was such huge international attention in postwar Sierra Leone on rape and abductions, it is possible that these issues became less taboo for women to talk about with agencies and support groups. Still, rape was not an altogether uncomplicated topic in relation to raped women's families and husbands, as became obvious for many of my informants. In female-dominated contexts, rape and sexual violence were more openly debated, and even more so among women with similar backgrounds and experience, where the women felt safe and were encouraged to talk about these otherwise taboo aspects of their war experiences. Also, in discussion with Mary and me in private, many women would talk about the health problems they were still facing from the sexual abuse, something I will return to in a later chapter. War rape and sexual abuse became a "public secret." Everyone knows that most women were raped when they were abducted, but few women speak about it publicly, and given the types of attitudes and repercussions many might face if they did, why would they? In this cultural context, the trauma of rape appears not to be diminished by talking about it; on the contrary, those who do may face further stigmatization. I therefore never told "outsiders" that I was talking with my informants about war rapes. On the other hand, almost all women I talked to said that they wanted medical treatment for the effects of war-related rape and sexual abuse, but this meant that they would have to expose their secret, that they had been raped and sexually abused, and some girls and women were so afraid of this that they silently suffered their medical ailments instead.

Rape in war is something that has been, if not officially accepted, something that has not, at least not until recently, been condemned by soldiers or their superiors worldwide. Rape and sexual abuse appear always to have been a "weapon of war" (Ferris 1993; Höglund 2001; Seifert 1996). Unwritten rules have proclaimed enemy women of all ages fair game, implying that soldiers who commit rape in war should not be punished for these crimes. In fact, they have not even been conceived of as crimes among some soldiers. It was not until 1996, when eight male Bosnian Serb military and police officers were indicted in the International War Crimes Tribunal on charges of raping Bosnian Muslim women, that rape was treated separately as a crime of war (Enloe 2000, 135). As Robin Schott wrote, "Whatever account is given to explain sexual violence against women in wartime, the persistence of this violence is one indicator that gender identity is a pivotal factor in women's fates both during and after war" (1996, 23). Men also get raped in war, but it is assumed to a lesser degree. In most societies, including Sierra Leone, this is still not openly discussed and is often a source of great shame. Unfortunately little research has yet been done on effects, consequences, and cultural interpretations of male war rapes (see, e.g., Women's Commission for Refugee Women and Children 2002, 13).

Rape in war is frequently described not only as violence against women but as an act of aggression aimed at the nation or the group, and as a means of demoralizing and breaking down society. War rapes often take place in public and are used to break families or alliances, and to strengthen loyalty among those soldiers involved in the act, that is, the soldier/rapists (see, e.g., Barstow 2000; Byrne 1996; Card 1996; Höglund 2001; Koeonig

1994; Moorehead 1995; Nenadic 1996; Niarchos 1995; Sideris 2001). More rarely, but still common in certain contexts, rape in war is used as a form of genetic imperialism, to impregnate enemy women and thereby pollute the perceived purity of the group for generations to come, but also to undermine the solidarity of group members (see, e.g., Taylor 1999 on Rwanda), although this was not the case in Sierra Leone. However, when seen from a raped woman's perspective, it need not be obvious at all that it is her country that has been raped, or the sanctity of her group: it is she who was raped, it is *her body* that has been violated. When shifting the perspective from the woman who is raped to that of her husband, family, community, ethnic group, or nation, many seem to forget who the actual victim of a violent crime is. It is as if somehow the sufferings of the woman who was raped were diminished because the rape was not aimed at her personally but was an act targeting her group or her nation. In this mode of reasoning her body becomes immaterial, in more than one sense, as it is often transformed into a symbol of violated purity.

It is surprising, however, that given the frequency of war rapes in Sierra Leone, to my knowledge, no research has been done focusing on the rapists involved, on masculinity in general, and militarized masculinities in particular. What does this culture of rape and sexual abuse say about masculinity in Sierra Leone? And why is it that of all the humanitarian projects in postwar Sierra Leone, especially considering how much focus there has been on "changing" gender relations and pushing agendas to augment Sierra Leonean women's position in postwar society, none have focused on this part of a violent male culture? As far as I know, rape has only been addressed with a focus on the victims, the women. Obviously there is a huge gap in our knowledge of how masculinities are constructed and performed, not only in Sierra Leone, but in most other areas of conflict with high levels of rape and sexual abuse. Philippe Bourgois's study is an exception, although one can argue that even if they were living in a violent environment, his informants were not at war. Robert Connell (1992, 2000) has also focused on masculinity, war, and militarization, although with a heavy emphasis on the West. I argue that war rape was not an isolated war phenomenon, but part of a culture among the combatants that had resonance within the larger Sierra Leonean society, a setting in which masculinity, to some extent, was defined through multiple sexual relationships. Utas mentions that in Liberia, this type of masculine behavior had much to do with "a celebration of a hyper-masculine warrior identity" (Utas 2005, 418).[5]

War rapes in Sierra Leone have also been understood as part of a male initiation into male rebel life, which may to some extent be true. Yet this alone cannot explain the frequency of a phenomenon that seems to permeate most wars, although the effects of these are interpreted differently in different locales. In the words of Sierra Leonean lawyer Jamesina King: "The widespread acts of brutal and horrific forms of sexual violence committed against women during the conflict were a direct consequence of the culture of impunity and silence that existed prior to the conflict" (King n.d.). What becomes clear when comparing war rapes in various locations is that rape is a socially constructed experience, and although always traumatic, the "intensity of the trauma is partly dependent on the response of society" (Alidou and Turshen 2000).

In Sierra Leone, the cultural ground on which these rapes took place and through which they were subsequently interpreted varied immensely. For some families, the sexual violation of their daughter, especially if she had been a virgin prior to the rape, was a social disaster that meant she was "damaged goods," she was "spoilt," as one might suspect was the case for Aminata, while for other families, the actual sexual abuse was of less importance than the women's postwar behavior, as I will discuss later. And for the women themselves, added to the social stigma were often the long-term effects of rape and sexual abuse, sexually transmitted diseases, which in some cases led to infertility. War rapes thus etched everything from medical conditions to social stigma on their bodies. But a too exclusive focus on the body and its violation also, as Ross wrote, "fixes experience in time, in an event, and draws attention away from ways of understanding of that experience as a process that endures across bodies and through time" (2003, 49).

The stories I have collected thus tell not only of war rapes and sexual abuse, but also reflect local understandings of morality, the position of young women in the web of social relations. They tell of choices but also of factors beyond their control that delineated their possibilities to act. As I will discuss more in a later chapter, these stories were also told in a postwar context where their interpretations vary radically, from those of the benevolent and empathic NGO listener to the reproachful and judging family. Another phenomenon of the Sierra Leonean war that has received international attention, and which also relates to role reversals, is that of the female combatant. I have up to now discussed abducted women's experiences with a focus mainly on abduction, rape, and sexual abuse. However, as we know, many girls and women were also trained to use weapons and kill. How did such activities fit into the prevailing female gender ideology, and how were these women's stories articulated?

Female Fighters

As has already been mentioned, many abducted girls and women were trained to fight, although not all became fighters. Aminata said, "If you should have seen me with gun firing, you should have enjoyed me. Almost all of us were taught to fire in case enemy attack you." But like most female fighters, she never talked about specific incidents when she herself had killed; she would just say, "The commander or group leader will just tell you to kill so-and-so person. If you refuse they will kill you. So you just have to do it." However, she emphasized that in her group all women were trained. "No woman that had spent a year with them was not trained how to fix gun and fire. This was for protection, maybe even among ourselves, if your companion want to kill you and you also know how to fire, you can retaliate." Aminata said,

> Also, as I told you if you are not trained and you meet your enemy, how can you fight to rescue your life? Women were really fighting. If you see us entering Waterloo on the 5th of January [1999], to enter the city [Freetown], you won't be able to look at our faces. We were bloody....We were like slaves, very dirty. So to ask about women fighting! Some were even more brave than some men.

It was the same in Musu's group, and she said, "All the girls I met, all of them knew how to fire. All the girls are raw." According to Aminata, shooting was one of the first things they learned after being captured: "They teach us that first, because you can't go to the war zone without learning how to fire, or put cartridge in the gun." However, although all women were trained to use weapons, not all went to what Aminata called "the war zone." Often the younger girls and some bush wives would stay in the camp. But some bush wives would go on attacks to help their bush husbands to reload their weapons if they had no weapon of their own. Dyan Mazurana and Khristopher Carlson wrote,

> Captive "wives" of commanders exerted substantial power within the RUF compounds. These "wives" were predominately girls. When the commander was away, they were in charge of the compound. They kept in communication with the commander and would select and send troops, spies, and support when needed. These girls and young women decided on a daily basis who in the compound would fight, provide reconnaissance, and raid villages for food and loot. Some counseled their captor husbands on war strategies, troop movement, and upcoming attacks.
>
> (Mazurana and Carlson 2004, 14)

There were also cases in which women who had been sent to the front lines or to head particularly dangerous missions were bush wives who had been rejected by their bush husband commanders.[6] Aminata explained that it took her around three months to get used to "rebel life," to the guns firing and the killing. Kadi, whom I have mentioned before, had stayed with the rebels for six years. She told me that it took her only two months to get used to rebel life.

> It only took me two months to get used to it, because of the gun firings, because at that time when they were firing it would frighten me, but just after those two months I became used to the gun firing. It will resemble playing music. At that time [in the beginning] we were afraid, but then [after some time] when we were eating if firing started we will just look up to see if they were our enemies, the Kamajohs, the Tamaboros. So we were afraid of those people.

The life of a female fighter was far removed from a submissive feminine ideal. In Sierra Leone, during and after the war, stories of the brutality of rebel women became a popular theme. During my first fieldwork in 1998, I heard much about how "cold-blooded" and "cruel" female fighters were. Both "civilians" and fighters would frequently mention that the women had been even tougher than the men. "I said we were all trained but yet some were not brave because during the training, many died. But there were many brave girls, more than men. If you see some girls with guns, they were more brave than some men in fact," Aminata said. One male informant, John, who had been abducted and then joined the rebels, said that female fighters were "more wicked," and he claimed that abducted women had been given both more weapons and weapons training than many abducted men.

> When you reach there [the camp] they will give the weapons to the women. Then they will appoint a leader, a woman that has been with them for a long time, and count eight women and put that old rebel woman in charge of them. This is where the women will be wicked. When the commanders say, "Kill that person," the woman would kill. The commander will also say, "If anyone escapes, we will kill you." So this made the women to cause more danger and become wicked persons.

As I have described in the introduction, in places that are known to have female fighters, such as Sierra Leone, Liberia, Sri Lanka, and Peru, civilian populations often regard female fighters as monsters, barbarians, and frequently describe them as being more cold-blooded and cruel than male fighters (see, e.g., Bennett, Bexley, and Warnock 1995; E. Skinner 1999). This idea that female combatants are more evil and vicious than men is often attributed by researchers to female fighters' transgression of acceptable female behavior (see, e.g., Barth 2002; Farr 2002). In their work on girl soldiers, for example, McKay and Mazurana found that "girls in fighting forces have been forced to violate taboos more fully than boys" (McKay and Mazurana 2004, 44). Fighting is included in the moral universe of men in ways that it is not for women, and fighting women are frequently considered by their very existence to be transgressing accepted female behavior. Many of my informants, both ex-combatants and civilians, also stressed that female fighters had to "prove themselves" by becoming more violent than their male counterparts. In much research on gender and armed combat, women and men are positioned at opposite ends of a moral continuum. Women are generally considered peaceful and men aggressive (cf. Ferris 1993). But if women are regarded as inherently more peaceful than men, what do the images of women as soldiers/fighters/rebels convey?

In many societies, the violent practices of some women are often regarded as abnormal. The very act of fighting, if understood as a male preoccupation, by definition makes women and girls less feminine and by extension, "unnatural." Why is it that "the image of a gun-toting girl is more shocking than a small boy holding an AK47?"[7] Compounding the picture of the peaceful woman is the fact that in many wars and violent conflicts, women have shown themselves to be as capable as men in performing violent acts, something that has perhaps never been more obvious than in the case of the genocide in Rwanda (see, e.g., African Rights 1995). Although there are more and more women in armed forces, "the soldier" is still conceived of as a man. This idea of women as being more peaceful also fuels the perception that female fighters have to "become like men," that is, assume male roles and behavior, and also outdo men, in order to fit our notion of how real combatants should be.

A contextual analysis should be central in studying the participation of women in war, because issues of context are not secondary factors (cf. Bracken 1998, 55). This becomes apparent when comparing female fighters in Sierra Leone to those in the war of liberation in Mozambique. Here too West found that female fighters both behaved the same way as, and were considered to be, "men" (2000, 190). But in contrast to the female fighters in Sierra Leone, the female fighters in the *Destacamento Feminino* in Mozambique were ideologically empowered and motivated. The same has been said of women participating in the liberation movements in both Zimbabwe (Staunton 1990) and Eritrea (Bennett, Bexley, and Warnock 1995). These women were said to be motivated by a sense of freedom and camaraderie. The situation for women fighting in Sierra Leone and Liberia was very different. One important difference, for example, was the prohibition of sexual relations between male and female FRELIMO combatants, and male combatants and civilian women in Mozambique (West 2000, 190), whereas in Sierra Leone few female fighters had not experienced sexualized violence by the very force that recruited them.

Ideological motivation also had other, more long-term effects, and according to West, "Ideological involvement may in part determine why some people exposed to violence suffer traumatic effects while other do not" (2000, 181). Although contextually very different from my own field, West's analysis of the traumatic effects of violence on female combatants is of help in trying to understand the situation for female combatants in Sierra Leone. He writes in the case of the female fighters in Mozambique that "trauma is held at bay in the moment of the experience of violence by the force of narrative accounts that frame *violence as purposive and meaningful*" (2000, 182 my emphasis). It was only later, after the war, he writes, that female ex-combatants became "frustrated with the failures of the post-independence government to 'fulfil promises' made to them during the war" (ibid.). This was most definitely not the case for most female fighters in the Sierra Leonean war. The violence they committed was not emancipatory and in most cases was not perceived as meaningful in any ideological sense (although laden with *meaning*), nor were they motivated by any promises of improved status for women in postwar society.

Although female fighters in Sierra Leone did not fight to improve or empower their own or other women's lot in society, individual female fighters could definitely *feel* empowered when they had a gun. Aminata said that being able to fire a gun made her feel strong and fearless, which could have been her own motivation in order to keep going. Being a fighter could also improve bush life, and Mazurana and Carlson interviewed girls who claimed that it was "better to be a fighter and the 'wife' of a common soldier because you could protect yourself with your own weapon, you had access to food and loot, and your chances of escaping were greater, unlike captive 'wives' of commanders who were closely guarded with little chance of escape" (Mazurana and Carlson 2004, 12). Despite their bravery and toughness, however, the conditions of female combatants were very different from those of men, or even boys for that matter. If a female combatant hesitated when ordered to kill, her own group could later punish her, often through rape, and if she fell into enemy hands, she would also most likely be raped before being killed.

To describe female fighters as more terrifying than male fighters is the prerogative not only of the affected populations. Western media also frequently engage in and reproduce such images. Take, for example, the many descriptions in the media of the female Chechnyan or Palestinian terrorists.[8] In a byline to a close-up of one of the female Chechnyan terrorists covered in black, a BBC journalist wrote that "their female accomplices were almost *more terrifying,* covered from head to foot in black, their veils bearing Islamic slogans, their waists wrapped with belts full of explosives" (my emphasis).[9] Since many people perceive women as being more peaceful, any transgression from this moral code is seen as unnatural and incomprehensible. To transgress what is considered acceptable feminine behavior can be costly, and women with fighting experience often run the risk of being stigmatized. Also, female combatants are seldom seen as heroic, and their participation is rarely glorified.

Interestingly, female fighters in Sierra Leone and Liberia have been interpreted quite differently by Western media. In a BBC article, a female rebel commander and her female subordinates in Liberia are described like this: "'Black Diamond' and her comrades may look like any bunch of street-wise girls with attitude but they have the military hardware to back up the look."[10] The article is illustrated by a photograph in which Black Diamond and the other women are portrayed not as terrifying killers, but more along the lines of "sexy ghetto chicks." In another article illustrated by the same photograph, the byline reads: "Some of the fiercest warriors in Liberia wear tube tops and polished fingernails," followed by the body text, "Black Diamond could be the prototype for an action hero, a sort of African 'Lara Croft.' She's all sleek muscle and form-fitting clothes, with an AK-47 and red beret. She has a bevy of supporting beauties, equally stylish, who loiter nearby, polished fingernails clutching the cold steel of semi-automatic weapons."[11]

There is decidedly a sexualized language in Western media descriptions of West African female fighters, whereas veiled Muslim female fighters are only something frighteningly Other. This sexualized representation applies not only to fighting African women; media depictions of black women as sexually loose and accessible have been widely documented elsewhere (Kennedy 2002, 259). One of the more interesting works that deals at least cursorily with the image of women as fighters, is Mary Moran's "Warriors or Soldiers? Masculinity and Ritual Transvestism in the Liberian Civil War" (1995). Refraining from the sensationalist voyeurism of Western journalists, Moran instead situated her analysis of this phenomenon within the context of local gender constructions and argued that the phenomenon of the male transvestite soldier I discussed in the introduction was part of "an altogether more complex and multilayered identity," namely that of "the warrior" (1995, 75). The warrior image, she argues, also served as an "explicit critique and rejection of the state-identified soldier" (ibid.). There are obvious similarities with this and the Sierra Leonean situation. The warrior masculinity in this regional context gains its power and potency not from the opposition of masculinity and femininity. Rather, as Moran indicates, "In enacting their status as warriors, men incorporate items of feminine clothing to signify their transcendence of gender as an arbitrary and culturally located identity; *power is inherent in combination, not separation, in mixing rather than purifying an essential maleness*" (1995, 80 my emphasis). Also Mariane Ferme, in her work on the Mende noted that "at war, men appropriate transgressively feminine symbolic elements—from dress to wigs and makeup—that may appear grotesque. Indeed a feature of the grotesque is that it plays out the dramaturgy of power at the lowest bodily levels, the sites of sexuality and reproduction" (Ferme 2001; 178).

After analyzing the various ideals of masculinity in a number of local war figures—the soldier, the warrior, and the commando—Moran described one of the rebel leaders, Prince Johnson, and his two hundred female bodyguards, whom he also referred to as his "wives." She describes the women wearing tight-fitting army fatigues, with handbags to match (Moran 1995, 83) and conjures up an image reminiscent of the one of Black Diamond described earlier. However, her conclusions about this phenomenon are quite different from the BBC's. She writes, "As Western observers, we take it for granted that women will take on the clothing and accoutrements of men in times of war. This form of transvestism deemed acceptable and unremarkable in the West, is rarely commented upon. We assume that women entering formerly all-male domains...will dress 'like men'" (Moran 1995, 83). In contrast, Moran explains, in rural Liberia prior to the war, it was still quite shocking for women to wear trousers, and she speculates that people may have been more shocked by women in tight-fitting fatigues than by men wearing wigs and brassieres, which was conceived of as shocking to many Western readers. "To the participants...it may be the women's transvestism that is the most disruptive of expected gender norms" (Moran 1995, 84).

In postwar Kabala, I observed that many of the female ex-combatants often dressed in a very untraditional manner, favoring tight jeans and small tops more than traditional garb. However, many people, especially rural people, still felt that this was inappropriate for women, and some believed that those kinds of clothes were the very trademark of prostitution, they signaled sexual activity. As Moran wrote, "Rebel women are drawn into this mode of representation in a process that may 'liberate' them from feminine convention yet ironically emphasizes and commandeers their sexuality" (Moran 1995, 85). Richards, too, described how one young female combatant's appearance was given prominence in people's remarks on her violent death. "One of the cadres in charge of the RUF attack on Bo on 27 December 1994 was a young woman, Alice. Those who witnessed her being beaten to death by vengeful civilians later that day remarked on her personal smartness when preparing for the attack. The trouble taken to braid her hair drew particular wonder, as indicating youthful self-confidence and bravado, not the fear or despair women are popularly thought to experience at the thought of war" (Richards 2005a, 128–29).

Therefore, to analyze female combatants in Sierra Leone only in relation to the predominantly Western notion of the "peaceful woman" somehow misses the mark. In Sierra Leonean traditional culture, women are not believed to be inherently peaceful; on the contrary, women are wild and dangerous and therefore they need to be controlled (cf. Ferme 2001; Leach 1994). What life in the bush did, I argue, was to unleash their wild and unpredictable behavior. Perhaps this explains to some extent people's comments about female combatants as more wicked and brutal than men. It was not necessarily their transgression of gender roles that was shocking, as has been described by other researchers (see, e.g., Barth 2002; Farr 2002). Though women like Aminata were adamant that any woman who had spent over a year with the rebels had been trained in the use of a gun, it was obvious from the many interview situations that this was still a very sensitive topic to discuss. It became quite clear that some women had nothing to gain and everything to lose by admitting to having been a rebel fighter. But as I have noted earlier, not all women who were trained in how to use guns were in fact fighting.

I have described previously how most of my informants had been abducted during one of the many attacks on Kabala. I have also pointed out that this may not have been the case in other parts of the country, where women may have joined for a number of reasons. In their study of young soldiers, Rachel Brett and Irma Specht (2004, 87–90) noted that girls in fighting forces quite often stated their reason for joining as escaping domestic violence and abuse, and more rarely gave their motivation as religion or ethnicity, something that women involved in liberation struggles frequently said compelled them to fight. According to these authors, girls who volunteered to fight were often girls "who possess strength, independence, courage, persistence, and character. They are seeking a life of their own and behaving in ways that are contrary to social expectations as well as against the wishes of their family" (Brett and Specht 2004, 89). Interestingly these qualities—strength, independence, courage, persistence, and character—are not highly valued female characteristics in Kuranko culture, which rather promotes women's submission, servility, and willingness to endure and accept their subordinate position. Although Aminata had obviously felt empowered by carrying a gun, she explained that the actual killing of people did not make her feel good. In the context of postwar Sierra Leone, as I said above, only a few of the abducted women I came to know during my fieldwork discussed in any detail their experiences of armed combat. Aminata, Musu, and a few others eventually became very upfront with me about some of the things they had experienced during the war. Most other women talked of their experiences as bush wives, not as fighters, although some admitted that they knew how to fire a weapon. Those who did often just said that they were taught to use guns but never mentioned instances when they had to use them. Only a few admitted to having been forced to cut people's hands. But Aminata said,

> When they ask me to shoot or I see someone being shot, I always think if it happens to me I will die. Then at times I always feel that one day they will shoot at me and kill me. So I was not really happy…it is because of command. If you don't do it you also will be killed. No one will be happy to kill someone when you are normal. I always became afraid of guns even though I had one.

But while witnessing or participating in atrocities, Aminata said, she made sure never to reveal any emotions:

> If they see any sign of sorrow on your face, you also will be killed. Because either they kill us or we shed innocent blood. I always thought of the day they captured us. The first day, how you will sex and [be] used for work. Then, even though at times when we don't have a particular thing, then during attack we got them, like food, clothing. And burning houses, as my father's own was burnt. I even burnt one house when I knew we had gone to the Temne area. I will say, "These people burnt our town." But at times I was not happy. [On the other] hand, some will be happy because it was during this time we get things we don't have.

There were differences between my rural female informants and those from urban areas. Most of the young women I met had never been to a town bigger than Kabala before the war, and some entered Freetown for the first time during the rebel attack on 6 January 1999. They did not have that savvy and street-smart attitude Utas describes in his young female Liberian informants (2003, chapter 5). The abducted girls and women I met also had had no contact with their families during their time with the rebels and could not, as seems to have been the case in Liberia, negotiate their families' protection or provision of food. On the contrary, as I have explained earlier, family members pretended not to know each other or familiar villages, in order not to be killed. Also, the social organization of the rebel camps in northern Sierra Leone, where most of my informants were taken, more closely conformed to that of a rural village, making for a type of social control very difficult to maintain in an urban setting.[12]

From the stories I have related here emerges a picture of a life of constant tension, plagued by fear. Aminata and the other informants described a life in which they were always afraid, afraid of the enemy, afraid of the leaders of the group, afraid of their bush husbands or even co-wives; no one trusted anyone. During interviews it seemed difficult for women to talk about those moments when they had to put their faith in someone, when they had to trust someone. Occasionally someone would mention that only while she was doing the chores of everyday life, preparing food, washing clothes, even cleaning weapons, could the mind rest.

From Abductee to Fighter

Now I will turn to the very process by which abducted women, and men, ultimately became fighters. As I will show, this was a gendered process. It involved moving from complete alienation and loss, to integration and at least an illusion of control. Paul Richards writes, "If we want to understand the behaviour of wild RUF abductees we shall have to look at the way their social worlds were pulled apart by social exclusion and capture, and put together again through initiation and subsequent social control" (Richards 2005a, 125). In a particularly intense interview with a young man, John, whom we have met before, who had been captured by the rebels, this turning or reversal from abductee to fighter really comes to the fore. John was abducted by the rebels together with his mother, his mother's sister, and the sister's baby.

> When they took us to the road, the others we met there [the rebels], in my presence, [he pauses] sexed my mother and her sister. After that, we were

asked to carry loads on our heads.... When we have gone for about ten miles [pause] my mother and sister were not used to take heavy loads, so they said that they are tired. I told my mother to bear it up. But she can't, so about five or more of them lay mother [down], sexed her as they liked. Also her sister was laid down and sexed by another group. Not only them, but even the [other] women arrested were sexed frequently by them. If anyone shout they will knock you with the end of their gun. That weakened many of the women. And for the baby of my mother's sister, I don't know what was done to him but I know he was killed.

John said this all happened in his presence and that it hurt him immensely, but most of all, he said, he was "shamed" by the sexual violation of his mother in his presence; perhaps also he was ashamed on a more personal level as he could do nothing to protect her. He mentioned that the other abducted women were frequently raped during these first days, and how this continued sexual abuse weakened the women significantly. When, one day, a man again told his mother to lie down, John spoke out, saying, "This is enough!" He was told that he should "hold his words" unless he wanted to be killed. "So even though it was paining me in my heart there was nothing I could say." After this incident he was sent to another rebel group, under the command of Hold Mi Cap. The following day this group was sent after the first, and on the path he found his mother's mutilated body together with the bodies of many other women who had been killed. He said that his mother's feet had been cut off and that they had "done operation on one woman's vagina."

This was a turning point for John. In a form of revenge, he now joined the rebels and killed others as his own mother had been killed. He said that "I cried in my heart and from then on I became brave [fearless]. And so [when] they asked me to join them I said OK because I had planned to do what was done to my mother. So I joined them." John's mention of shame brings to mind a quote by Jackson, where "the loss of one's language, land, livelihood, and personal belongings, or belittlement and shaming of those with whom one most closely identifies, are readily experienced as assaults on one's own person" (1998, 17–18). As we will see more closely in later chapters, focusing on the postwar situation, shame played an important part in people's responses to the sexual violation of female relatives during the war.

My female informants did not in the same way express revenge as a motive for becoming a fighter. Musu, for example, had also witnessed the killing of a relative, her uncle. "Well, when they were killing him I had no way to talk. If I talk they will add me to him. That's why they took me to stand while killing my uncle. For me to see how they were dealing with my uncle. If I talk, they will kill me also." Still, Musu did not, like John, link this experience to the fact that she herself later became a fighter. Their motivations may have differed, and as I have tried to show, most strategies were also explicitly gendered. Musu was not, like John, shamed that her uncle was killed, because John's shame emanated from the fact that his mother had been sexually violated. What they shared was the experience of grief, fear, and perhaps anger.

Was there a point when John and Musu and others in similar situations stopped searching for, or could no longer find, purpose? In both cases it is possible to see how "without a sense of solidarity with others, one can find no meaning in oneself" (Jackson 1998, 10). For John and Musu, the reversion of their initial positions of vulnerability altered their position in the rebel hierarchy, which in a sense empowered them and gave them some sense of authority in the trajectory of their own lives, however illusory. Many informants described becoming a fighter as a difficult transition, but still, for some it was the only choice available, if the choice was between becoming a fighter and continuous sexual abuse, domestic slavery, or getting killed, a form of "choiceless decision." There were also those who saw becoming a fighter as their best option. Not only would they have a gun for protection, they would get more opportunities to loot and acquire resources. By becoming a perpetrator one perhaps also feels that one escapes being a victim, and perhaps the only way to gain even the least bit of control over one's own life in this milieu was to take up a weapon and assume the role of killer. "By transposing vulnerability to other places and other people we can arguably alter the structure. Through the control of violence we can also empower ourselves by inducing a sense, at least, of security," wrote Staffan Löfving (2005).

Seen from another perspective, this course can be perceived as part of a vicious circle, where violence becomes the condition of its own reproduction, and where "the destruction or the pushing back of what makes us vulnerable might fail," Löfving writes, going on to say that "the violence I use in order to escape my vulnerable position is in fact that which makes me most vulnerable" (2005). This was definitely true for many of my informants. If the condition of social existence for human beings is the quest for balance and control, for ontological security, for the "need to belong to and engage effectively in a world of others, having some say, some voice, some sense of making a difference" (Jackson 1998, 16), there were few alternative strategies for John, Musu, Aminata, and others; becoming a fighter was perhaps the only one. However, despite how fierce Musu became as a fighter, her experience was different from John's in one important respect; she was a woman, and as such she was continually sexually abused by her bush husband even after becoming a fighter. In John's case, although he did not mention it, it is likely that he eventually found a "wife" to cater to his sexual demands and reinforce his rebel masculinity. Remember the words of one of the men who raped Mateneh: "Boh, if you not oh man, tell we" (Brother, if you are not a man, tell us). The experience of war, and the experience of becoming an armed fighter during the war in Sierra Leone, was thus indisputably gendered.

When we were doing interviews, Mary and I usually asked our informants why they thought the rebels were fighting or what they thought the war was about, and most people would answer that they did not know. Some said that they were fighting against President Kabbah. Only a few were quite specific in explaining that they fought a war against corruption and inequality. In one interview, conducted by Mary, Musu positions the reasons for the war somewhere between discontent with the government and revenge by those individuals who witnessed the killing of their relatives.

MARY: But these people [the rebels], didn't they tell you any reason why they were fighting?

MUSU: Well, they didn't tell me the reason.

MARY: But in your own common understanding why was the war so severe?

MUSU: I don't know why the war was so severe because I was hearing some words I didn't understand. Some say they were fighting for power. Some are saying that they were fighting because they have killed his mother and father. Most of the fight reason, why it became worse, was because of advantage. They were seizing on the poor, the innocent one that didn't know nothing about the war. Those, they met and killed. So if that one's son was there, he also will revenge for his parents.

MARY: Were people joining them willingly?

MUSU: No, I don't think. When they have killed your parents then they will arrest you and when they go with you, you also won't spare anyone, because if you think of your mother and father you won't spare no one. So you will just do the same thing they did to your mother and father. So you won't spare no one.... When they killed people it seems as when they kill fowl, the way you will be happy. You don't get mind to talk even if it is your mother. If they meet you sitting crying in a corner, it will be problem for you.

With this in mind, the killings can be interpreted as a form of revenge that was not directed against the initial perpetrators, as there was no conceptual or symbolic space for this kind of action. Instead those who had been abducted and violently forced into the movement redirected their hurt, anger, and fear onto civilians and thereby perpetuated the cycle of violence (cf. Feldman 1991, 20). Löfving writes that "if the parameters for the definition of...social belonging are violently changed, then the Self—the individual's perception of the world and of his/her own role in it—is challenged and transformed" (2002, 3).

Throughout my fieldwork I found numerous examples of people who, faced with the threat of loss of life, would have resorted to almost anything in order to survive; children killed their mothers, brothers raped their sisters, fathers raped their daughters, and children cut off the hands of their parents. This leads me to believe that in these circumstances, the choice between life and death was not really a choice; the will to live and the fear of death were too strong. The fear and hurt channeled through the hardships of rebel life in war and the consumption of drugs became directed against civilians as there were no other paths of action, thereby perpetuating the spiral of violence. By becoming a fighter, one also to some extent escapes falling a victim to the violence of others. There seem to have been a number of reasons why women became fighters. Survival and control was an issue for some; for many others it was fear, anger, and even resignation; but there were some who mentioned the prestige and resources involved in being a fighter as their prime motivator. Many were constantly drugged and in hindsight could not recall having had any motivation whatsoever.

Of Victims and Perpetrators

In most aid discourse and conflict analyses on women and war, women are "located" primarily as refugees, displaced persons, or "victims" (cf. Thompson

2006, 348). This discourse of "victimhood," with its limited vocabulary for how victims of war can and should effectively articulate their experiences, also creates a certain kind of subject. In this discourse, a victim of a violent *event* becomes a victim as *a person*. It is in this power of naming that the development apparatus exerts its dominance (cf. Escobar 1995, xx). Rebecca Golden, an anthropologist with more than ten years of aid work experience in Africa, has argued that due to the enormous presence of aid agencies in Sierra Leone, "victims of the war were 'educated' about their suffering" (2004, 72). As I noted in the introduction, a similar argument was made by Alex Argenti-Pillen about the violence in Sri Lanka (2003). Impoverished populations in war-affected regions cannot wholly ignore this discourse, as the huge presence of humanitarian organizations in postwar societies is tied to material, and therefore also social, survival.

Although my informants have definitely been victims of violent events, bracketing them only as "victims," I argue, inadvertently conceals other roles they have played in the war. The notion of victim is also usually invested with connotations; it is feminized or alternatively infantilized: women and children are victims, men are not. The problem is even more multifaceted when *victim* becomes synonymous with *lack of agency* (see, e.g., Orford 2003, 179). The oppositional concepts of victim and perpetrator, and the attached notion of victims as having no agency, are so all-pervasive in humanitarian discourse and many conflict analyses that they are difficult to completely avoid.[13] However, the dichotomies of victim/perpetrator and passivity/agency are analytically inadequate in explaining my informants' experiences, or the attitudes of their communities. They can show on a more general level what women's status is in war, but they do not entertain any explanations of how these experiences might be interpreted.

As this victim/perpetrator dichotomy is so entrenched within much humanitarian discourse and conflict-related research, and given that these categories are by definition very narrow, it is not surprising that someone like Utas (2003, 2005), with experience of women in the Liberian war, would want to complicate the issue of women's agency in war. During his fieldwork, Utas found little resonance between the dominant discourse on women as powerless victims and the women he met. Therefore he strove to write against such stereotypes by emphasizing these women's agency and instead argued that the prevailing aid discourse encouraged war-affected women in Liberia to present themselves as victims (Utas 2005). However, he writes less about the structural constraints circumscribing their choices. In the most constraining of situations, one can, and indeed has to, act. As Rosalind Shaw pointed out, "It is, of course, crucial to recognize...that women inventively deploy patriarchal ideas and images for their own purposes, and that those who are subject to even the worst forms of oppression 'have agency too'. But if we stop there, we risk collapsing distinctions among contrasting kinds of agency that are associated with contrasting kinds of power" (Shaw 2002, 19). Whereas Utas wanted to problematize the predominant notion of women as victims in humanitarian discourse, I on the other hand have been more interested in examining local social relations and my informants' position in them. Although I do acknowledge that some of my informants may at times have chosen to become fighters or lovers to commanders, in my work I wanted to emphasize the structural constraints circumscribing those choices; sometimes the only choice was between becoming a fighter/lover or dying, which is not really much of a choice, more a matter of bare survival. Here, I find Aretxaga's concept of "choiceless decisions" useful precisely in its subtle double critique: it at once questions women's passivity and victimization while it also challenges the liberal belief of agents' free choice (Aretxaga 1997, 61). In interview after interview, women would tell me of almost indescribable pain and suffering, and I was given detailed descriptions of rape and humiliation. Indeed, most of my informants have been victims in any of the definitions of the word, but this does not mean that some of these women did not also at times loot, kill, and cut off hands, although these latter experiences have generally been more difficult to talk about in this particular postwar social context.

Although aid discourse had entered the language of everyday life in Sierra Leone, many of my informants were not considered by their communities to be "innocent" victims. Aminata's parents obviously did not see her as innocent, and even though these girls and women had been abducted and raped, for their families and communities this did not excuse, or even explain, the subsequent violence some of them committed as rebel fighters, or even their mere association with the rebels. The issue is therefore not about having or not having agency (which is a debate that has taken on almost absurd proportions of late).[14] My informants were neither ill-fated victims with no agency, nor ferocious perpetrators in command of their own destiny.[15] To rephrase my earlier statement, an understanding of Sierra Leonean women's war and postwar experiences is not augmented by positioning them in this dichotomy of victim/perpetrator, because, of course, all rebels were not evil, nor were all commanders rapists, and rebel base camps were not fenced death camps. While many girls and women managed to escape, others remained and made the best of the situation they found themselves in. One does not suddenly stop being a victim just by committing a violent act, just as one does not escape being a perpetrator just because one is also a victim. This is well illustrated by one woman, who had been abducted and forcefully conscripted by the RUF, in her statement to the TRC: "I was about to go to town, when suddenly four men appeared before us holding guns and knives in their hands. They said they were RUF from Kailahun...after a month we were taken to Kailahun to be trained. *Now I am a victim, a witness and a perpetrator*" (TRC 2004, 3b: chapter 3 § 217, my emphasis).

In the life worlds of rebel abductees there were some, although limited, spaces for negotiation. Even in the most constraining of circumstances, one has some degree of choice and some capability to act, but again as Shaw notes, the agency of those in power is very different from that of those subjugated to power and dominance. "The agency of those who deploy 'weapons of the weak,'" wrote Shaw, "is very different from the agency of those whose authority allows them to act upon the world through control of an apparatus of domination" (2002, 19). One needs to make a distinction, therefore, between different kinds and degrees of power and agency. Because even with a gun in hand, my informants' choices were circumscribed—by convention, tradition, morality, religion, family, or fear—in ways that were different from men's. Young men who were kidnapped and forcibly recruited as fighters were, of course, also victims. And although most of the girls and women were abducted, there were certainly cases where girls saw joining the rebels as a strategy of survival, or of opportunity. What becomes important is to relate these experiences, as narrated, to their position within a larger societal framework. As Nordstrom wrote, "Looking at the actual lives of girls, it becomes difficult to draw easy lines between wartime and peacetime. What people tolerate in peace shapes what they will tolerate in war" (Nordstrom 1997b, 1).

Concluding Remarks

In his book *Existential Anthropology,* Jackson argues that most violence is defensive and motivated by fear (Jackson 2005). I try to bear this in mind when I turn to the stories of my female informants, but when I try to understand the enormity of the brutal misogynous violence inflicted on all of them, I find that there is an important gender aspect missing in Jackson's analysis. What kind of fear could have instigated this gendered violence? As the cases of John and Musu reveal, fear was definitely a motivator in transforming victims into perpetrators after seeing family members killed, but the highly gendered violence speaks to something more. By contextualizing the war rapes, certain continuities of gendered violence emerged that transcend the neat peace-war dichotomy and challenge the assumption that the rapes were only horrifying acts of war. Obviously, in postwar Sierra Leone, the way people interpreted the war rapes was grounded in preexisting notions of rape and sexual morality. War rapes are effective precisely because they highlight dynamics that existed already before the war. Therefore it is necessary to examine how the act of rape is communicated and interpreted also in prewar and postwar society.

It is no easy task to understand why rape, sexual slavery, and forced marriage were so extremely frequent in the Sierra Leonean war. The high incidence of sexual abuse before the war certainly gives an indication but cannot alone explain the fact that almost all abducted women were raped. However, although I have argued that war rapes should not be viewed as an aberration, when attention to the war context is absent, war rapes are too often dismissed as by-products of war. Moreover, important aspects that differentiate war rapes from peacetime rapes will be missing, such as the organized manner in which they took place and their "pornographic" nature. Historically and in the present, in Africa and elsewhere, rape and sexual abuse seem commonplace in war; still, the level of rape during the Sierra Leonean war was remarkable. At certain times during the war, and in certain areas, sexual violence appeared endemic. Although violence cross-cut all social relations, there was, I argue, a type of violence directed specifically against girls and women.

The notion of female fighters also speaks to this issue, as these women were located as much in the dominant gender discourse as they were in the historical and cultural imaginary. For example, it is not irrelevant in the Sierra Leonean context that the rebels were spoken of as coming from "the bush," or that in postwar society female ex-fighters were accused of having "bushlike" behavior. Their war experiences in many ways severed my female informants from the conventional trajectories of Sierra Leonean womanhood, from their social and cultural ties, and from flows of reciprocity, something I will discuss more in a later chapter. What becomes apparent in my work is that the neat dichotomy of victim/perpetrator could explain neither the experiences of my informants nor those of their communities. I am not arguing whether or not abducted women and female fighters were victims; that is evident. I argue that the notion of victim has been appropriated by humanitarian agencies and quantitative conflict analyses in such a way as to make "victim" synonymous with "lack of agency," and so as such, the notion conceals, albeit unintentionally, other roles these victims might have played and how they have been interpreted by their local communities. In this chapter I have been occupied with the circumstances of my informants' experiences and choices. I have wanted to show how these were circumscribed by structural constraints and cultural convention at the same time that they also provided some women with an alternative to local feminine conventions. In this vein I have wanted to question notions of women's passivity and victimization, while also challenging the notion of belief of free choice.

Researching these phenomena was difficult already due to their subject matter, and it did not become easier, as these were topics that the women, in the postwar context, avoided talking about. In the next chapter I will discuss how the act of verbally narrating one's war experience of violence and humiliation in public was not a straightforward process in Sierra Leone but a culturally contested activity. The next chapter also concerns my informants' experiences of the demilitarization, demobilization, and reintegration process and how they interpreted institutionalized reconciliation, with an emphasis on the Truth and Reconciliation Commission and the Special Court.

5

RECONCILIATION OR REVENGE

Narratives of Fear and Shame

When the war was over, Aminata, who had been a fighter, wanted to register for disarmament. She said she wanted to disarm because she really "fought and suffered." But her bush husband had told her that if she did, "they" would take her picture and she would be sent to court. This made her afraid, which was why when he later asked her to give him her weapon, she did. "When my 'husband' told me that they will take our pictures and go to court and told me to give him the gun, I had to do it because he gave it to me.... But I was not afraid to disarm. I should have disarmed [if] I should have got a gun." My female informants had played many diverse roles in and had had many different experiences of the war. They had perhaps experienced being both victims and perpetrators. Some had been bush wives, others combatants, some by force, some for survival, and others by choice. In postwar society, many of these women were quite unsure of their legal and social status. Some of them had committed atrocities but may at other times have been victims of horrendous acts. Most of them kept quiet about what happened to them or what they had done in the war, for fear of stigmatization and revenge. In many ways, fear and shame shaped their responses to and their interpretations of the DDR process, the TRC, and the Special Court.

Female Fighters and Disarmament

Mary once asked Aminata what people in general thought of women who had joined the rebels. It was an innocent question, but the phrasing turned out to be all wrong and Aminata became very angry and upset and replied, "Don't say join! We didn't join them voluntarily, we were captured! So don't feel that we joined them! I will answer you, but we didn't join them. You know when we came back, people were afraid of us. They were afraid to even speak to us." In order to be registered in a DDR program, combatants had to hand in their weapons. Aminata wanted to disarm but had been persuaded to give her weapon to her bush husband, who in turn had given it to a boy so that he could disarm instead. This was quite a common scenario for female fighters during the period following the cease-fire, and as Aminata explained, "The men took the guns from we the women. But some only disarm with the woman they love, so they will take your own gun and give it to her." When the Sierra Leone DDR program ended in January 2002, a total of 72,500 combatants had demobilized, of whom 4,751 were women (6.5 percent) and 6,787 were children (9.4 percent), of whom 506 were girls (Mazurana and Carlson 2004, 6).[1] The framework for the DDR program in Sierra Leone was set in the Lomé Peace Accord in 1999.[2] The aims of the project were (1) to collect, register, and destroy all conventional weapons, (2) to demobilize approximately forty-five thousand combatants, and (3) to demobilize and reintegrate ex-combatants (McKay and Mazurana 2004, 98). Those who were enrolled in the DDR were provided with some monetary and material assistance and were also given three to six months of vocational training.[3] As I have described earlier, there were quite a few female fighters in the various fighting forces, although no one knows exactly how many. Most agree however, that the 4,751 women and 506 girls who entered the official DDR program are very low figures and do not accurately represent the number of actual female fighters. In theory, female fighters were included in the DDR process, but whereas the program was effective in reaching out to male combatants, female combatants were underserved (Mazurana and Carlson 2004, 2; see also Women's Commission for Refugee Women and Children 2002). One reason female combatants did not disarm, it has been argued, was because most DDR processes are planned and implemented by military officials who still *see* combatants as synonymous with men, which has "resulted in a bias against those the military does not consider 'real soldiers' (i.e. men with guns)" (McKay and Mazurana 2004, 114). In the Sierra Leone DDR, no specific measures were put in place to ensure that female fighters disarmed. In most DDR processes in countries with high numbers of women in fighting forces, the results are the same; there is a low turnout because, it is assumed, most women do not demobilize unless specific measures are made to include them in the process.[4]

Despite the low female turnout, the Sierra Leone DDR was considered a success by the UN, the Sierra Leone government, and many others, and a model for future DDR processes in other countries (see, e.g., Mazurana and Carlson 2004, 2). However, the low participation of female combatants despite existing knowledge of their presence has led some to question the design, implementation, and success of the DDR in Sierra Leone (e.g., Mazurana and Carlson 2004; McKay and Mazurana 2004; Shepler 2002). In general, the UN has been very aware of the shortcomings of DDR and other reconstruction and rehabilitation processes in terms of gender and has developed many tools to better serve women in war-torn societies. For example, in October 2000, the UN Security Council adopted Resolution 1325, "Women, Peace and Security." In this document, the UN "formally recognizes that achieving gender justice is as central to social transformation as any other form of reparations after war," and also urges "all those involved in the planning for disarmament, demobilization and reintegration to consider the different needs of female and male ex-combatants and to take into account the needs of their dependants."[5] However, this resolution was adopted prior to the UN mandated operation in Sierra Leone and seemed to have little effect on the design and implementation of the Sierra Leone DDR, which has been described as, if not gender discriminatory, then "definitely gender blind."[6] Considering the strong emphasis on gender mainstreaming that exists in the UN, the absence of a gender perspective in the Sierra Leone DDR was quite surprising, and given the gender mainstreaming process of all UN activities, women should, at least indirectly, have become "an integral part of all programming, excluding all potential discrimination" (Schroven 2005, 58).

The DDR is also a process aimed at adult combatants, but in Sierra Leone many fighters were under eighteen, and as such were categorized as child soldiers. With regard to the demobilization of child soldiers, The Cape Town Principles are a strong guiding policy document.[7] But again, as with Resolution 1325, these principles were not fully implemented in Sierra Leone.[8] A report on girls in armed conflicts concluded that "despite the explicit reference to girls in the Cape Town Principles, the international community has failed countless thousands of girls by consistently ignoring their particular needs" (Save the Children 2005, 8). What is interesting with this report is that it is one of few that explicitly directs criticism against itself, the international community. Girls in armed forces, it writes, "face discrimination on a daily basis—from their fellow soldiers, commanders, fellow citizens, governments and—perhaps most shocking of all—from the international community" (ibid., 1). The report's principal criticism was focused on the underfunding of projects aimed at girl soldiers, and the poor and inflexible planning and implementation of DDR processes. For example, in many UN policy documents, girl soldiers are mentioned as a priority target group, but in reality most reintegration programs tend to be one size fits all (Shepler 2002, 10). The reason for not working actively to include girls and women in institutionalized DDR programs could be that women are often not seen as real combatants, as was noted above. As I have described in a previous chapter, because most female fighters in Sierra Leone also performed additional roles—they were laborers, "wives," girlfriends, domestic workers, farmers—this could also have rendered the notion of who was a fighter and who was not unclear. Their different roles may have prevented the UN, aid organizations, and ordinary Sierra Leoneans from seeing girls and women as "real" fighters, thereby screening them out of the process of demobilization (cf. Brett and Specht 2004, 99).

I argue, as do others (Mazurana and Carlson 2004), that those women in Sierra Leone who were thought of as abducted women, or simply "camp followers," and who as such were excluded from formal demobilization, have actually formed the backbone of the rebel forces. Many of these women were actively involved in the planning and execution of attacks, they fought, and many were killed and wounded. Remember Aminata's comment from above: "No woman that had spent a year with them was not trained how to fix gun and fire." As I described in the previous chapter, women were also vital to the "war system." They served as spies and they produced, processed, and prepared food; they participated in looting expeditions and also nursed the wounded and sick. One difference between rebel groups and government troops is that the latter designate certain soldiers to carry out tasks such as laundry, cleaning, and cooking. One can belong to an armed force in many other capacities than that of combatant. An army battalion or a rebel group would not survive long without the logistical support that these people provide. The question is what happens to these auxiliary personnel in a DDR program. As Enloe notes, "In the late twentieth century, women who have been mobilized to serve the military's needs are still vulnerable to the stereotype of camp follower—dispensable, disreputable—no matter how professional their formal position is in the military" (2000, 40). In Sierra Leone it was evident that there was an over-classification of girls and young women as bush wives, camp followers, and sex slaves, which "prevented the establishment of DDR programs to address their actual lived experiences" (Mazurana and Carlson 2004, 21). It also became clear that both disarmament and reintegration were explic-itly gendered processes, something that was not addressed in Sierra Leone. The focus of the Sierra Leone DDR was on disarming male fighters, and as girls and women had played many different roles in the war, the narrow classification of them as dependants or "bush wives" effectively excluded them from the process.

More than half of all female ex-combatants I interviewed said that they had actually wanted to disarm, but only a handful did. It was unclear if this was what they had wanted during the time of registration, or if they had changed their minds in retrospect after seeing some of the benefits that were distributed in the DDR camps. Some of those who had wanted to disarm said that the reason they did not or could not was that they could not access a weapon.[9] One eighteen-year-old girl we met in Kono, Tina, said, "I had wanted to go but my husband had the gun and I was preg-nant. I was really eager to go, but no gun." After May 2001, however, it was also possible to register in groups and hand in a weapon together, but my informants seemed unaware of this, and the lack of a weapon was still seen by some as the main impediment. So why did female fighters not have weapons? This was partly a consequence of local rebel politics, where commanders were in charge of the distribution and ownership of guns. During the DDR, ex-combatants were also promised cash in exchange for their weapons; therefore commanders, who were in control of weapons and ammunition, quickly saw the opportunity to make money on the control of the distribution of these (Hoffman 2005; Women's Commission for Refugee Women and Children 2002, 3). Commanders provided mostly young men, sometimes relatives who had never fought in the war, with weapons in exchange for all or part of their "reinsertion package." In this way commanders could make more than US$100 per registered ex-combatant.[10] In this structure of informal social networks and the patronage of big men, young female ex-combatants had little leverage in an already corrupt disarmament program (cf. Hoffman 2005). Those who despite these constraints did manage to disarm often had the support of their husbands/commanders, who would provide them with the guns or ammunition to disarm. As Aminata said above, "Some only disarm with the woman they love, so they will take your own gun and give it to her." Another woman, twenty-year-old Hawa, who had fought with the rebels for two years, said, "I didn't disarm because...if your 'husband' didn't stand strong for you, you won't have gun to disarm."

It thus appears obvious that the Sierra Leone DDR did not incorporate the recommendations of either Resolution 1325 or the Cape Town Principles and thereby excluded many girls and women who had been eligible for registration. However, these were "programmatic errors" (Mazurana and Carlson 2004, 21); there were also other local and cultural reasons that made them choose not to disarm. Only about one-fifth of all the ex-combatant women interviewed said that it was actually the lack of a weapon that stopped them from registering. Many female fighters had been told by their bush husbands that DDR was "not good for women." Many felt that female fighters should not be in such a public place as a DDR camp. Aminata, for example, said, "We were threatened that it is good for men but [for] women it is not good to disarm," and this was something that was to be repeated in many interviews. It was perceived as negative for women to disarm, as it would make it more difficult for them to be accepted back into their communities, and it would also make it more difficult for them to get married, as they were told that no man wanted a "rebel woman." In conclusion, then, it seemed that combatant men were not eager to share the material benefits of the DDR with female fighters, and it was also seen as culturally inappropriate for women to publicly disarm.

It has been suggested that one reason many male commanders discouraged girls and women from registering for DDR was that bush husbands wanted to hold on to their bush wives, that it would have been in their best interest to keep them, as women's continued domestic work was still necessary (cf. Bennett 2002, 61; Brett and Specht 2004, 99). But it also became clear that it was first and foremost as bush wives that the girls and women were seen by the planners and implementers of the DDR process. Female ex-fighters thus became only "bush wives," and as bush wives they had no rights to disarm. This need not have been a problem, however, as Resolution 1325 clearly states that a DDR program is also to address the *needs of dependants* of ex-combatants. Yet it was not until quite late in the DDR process that a microcredit program was established to cater to "wives" of male ex-combatants. However, as McKay and Mazurana point out, "to qualify for the program, the girl or woman had to be accompanied by the male ex-combatant who would vouch she was his 'wife'" (2004, 102). This eventually resulted in some men abducting girls to pose as their wives and then abandoning them as soon as they got the money. None of the girls or women I interviewed mentioned having qualified for this program.

Not all women stayed with their bush husbands after the cease-fire; many were released and returned home. For these girls the possibility of disarming seemed even more remote. Many parents expressed feelings of shame at having daughters who were considered rebels, and according to many informants, parents frequently dissuaded them from registering in the DDR on these grounds. According to Schroven (2005, 74), who has done work on the subject of women in the Sierra Leone DDR process, if female fighters had associated with the DDR this would only have confirmed their already stigmatized relationship with the rebels and further decreased their chances of being well received by their communities. The prevailing sense of shame some of my informants felt about their rebel past often resulted in silence. This silence also became apparent in their responses to the TRC and the Special Court, as I will discuss later. At times and in certain contexts, it was very difficult or almost impossible for women to recount to me their wartime experiences as fighters or to talk about their reasons for not demobilizing. If and when they did speak, it was often in private and secluded spaces, and, as I have described in the introduction, with guarantees of absolute anonymity.

After the war, many of the women who had been associated with the rebels, whether or not they had been abducted, were viewed by civilians with much skepticism and also fear. Mariatu said that she was afraid of disarming but that hers had been a "fear of people's mouths"; she was afraid of what people would say. "I was thinking that when we disarm, then later, they will say, 'These were the rebels,' and then they'll kill us. So I was afraid to disarm. I was thinking that we would be involved in trouble.... I didn't aim for the money therefore I refused." This fear on the part of ex-rebels also applied, of course, to men, but there were differences. After demobilization, in which they received training, many male ex-combatants had been encouraged to enlist in the new national army. Kadi told me that her bush husband, a rebel commander, had enlisted in the army after DDR training. She said that the government had wanted the men in the army so that they could exert some degree of control over them, "so that they cannot go to the bush again." Aminata's bush husband also later became a soldier in the new Sierra Leone Army. Although the pay in the army is notoriously low, this still gave many male ex-combatants some form of official legitimacy and a small income. Female ex-combatants, on the other hand, had received no such legitimacy; and as I will discuss in a later chapter, many had neither formal nor vocational education and had very few means of earning a living. This, I argue, further increased their vulnerability to stigmatization by their families and communities in postwar society.

Many former abductees, female ex-fighters and bush wives, were afraid and ashamed to admit that they had stayed with the rebels, some for many years. For them to demobilize was seen as something inconceivable, since being a "rebel woman" was considered extremely shameful. Most of my informants felt that they had nothing to gain and much to lose by registering for the DDR. After the war many of my informants said that because rebel women were so badly treated and so disliked by "civilians," they became ashamed of having stayed for so long in the bush. The question of shame had to do with intimate personal as well as social relations, and included the feeling of shame at being called a rebel or having a rebel child (*rebel pikin*). It was not a personal sense of guilt, but rather a social shame, a shame emanating from their having *shamed* their families. Quite a few of my informants said that their reason for not wanting to register for the DDR was that they had "not willingly joined the fighters," and to disarm in this context would have been the same as admitting to having joined the rebels freely, something they felt was inconceivable in postwar society. Thus the power and status that some female fighters had accrued during the war did not translate into any culturally accepted prestige in postwar society. On the contrary, these qualities were the very opposite of socially accepted female behavior not only in northern Koinadugu but throughout most of Sierra Leone.

Later, as I have described, Aminata nevertheless regretted not disarming, and so did Mariatu. Mariatu said that she had not disarmed because she was afraid she would be arrested, and that later, when she saw her friends at the DDR camp with "blankets, buckets, plates and so many other things," she regretted her decision, but by then it was too late—DDR registration was closed. Aminata said that she had even provoked those of her female friends who had registered, thinking that in reality they had been arrested. Much later, when she saw the supplies, the vocational training, and the money they were receiving, she became bitter and blamed her husband for not letting her disarm. Finah, whom we met briefly in chapter 3, had been about seventeen when she was abducted from Tongo Fields, a diamond-rich area in the southeast where she lived with her parents. She said that she "entered [the war] when the fire was hot with flames, not like the others, when it was cool," meaning that she had been in the war from the beginning and stayed for a very long time. She was released in 2001 and had gone to Kabala, where her parents had relocated during the war. When I met her she was around twenty-six years old. Finah did not disarm after the war, which she regretted, especially after seeing those who got both benefits and training through the DDR. Many of those who disarmed, she claimed, were those who were abducted "when the fighting was cool." She said that some of them had only been with the rebels for a year or even a few months, and she felt that they were "enjoying the benefits, and they who were there when hot, did not." Young Kadi did disarm but complained that she had been given neither money nor supplies. She told me that at the time, many fighters from her group had been so disappointed with the DDR program that they had left the DDR camp and gone back to the bush.

> So some got discouraged and said that they are going back to the bush. But I said, "If you are planning to go back to the bush because of these things I'm not going again." Some were saying that they [the government] have disgraced them...and that the government lied to them, that when they come out of the bush they will give them money and supplies, but they didn't do as they promised, and therefore they will go back to the bush. The people [DDR] didn't do it, they didn't give them anything! So as for

me, whether they give me money now or if they don't pay me, I won't go again to the bush, so I sat down [stayed]. And it is the same seat I am sitting now.... Some went again in the bush and they went and took guns and went to Okra Hills, they fought there and [later] when in Freetown when they disarmed them, they gave them money. When they came now they met me, so they were telling me, "See, you refused to go back to the bush, now we have fought at Okra Hill and you didn't go and now they have paid us and now you don't have anything!" They were bluffing [showing off] with their money to me. They gave them money after disarming, they gave them clothes, so they were telling me, "Look how dirty you are. As for us, we have gone, we have fought, now they have given us clothes to wear, but you, you have remained like that, they didn't pay you. We told you to go but you didn't, look how dirty you are."

Despite being intimidated by her old fighting friends, Kadi never regretted her decision to leave the fighters, and she said, "Here is better than there, because there they were killing people a lot. That was a time of killing. They were just killing people. But here now, we live peacefully." In Kadi's story it becomes apparent that many fighters had expectations of the DDR and the government that were not fulfilled. Therefore many fighters saw little reason to disarm if they received no compensation. Instead, and as became clear in Kadi's narrative, they felt that they had been rewarded for continuing to fight. This speaks to the importance of both money and material assistance in Sierra Leone at large, but also specifically for the fighters who had managed to take whatever they wanted by violent means, and who during disarmament had been asked to disarm for nothing. While the fighters were disappointed with their level of compensation, many civilians were very upset that they received anything at all and felt that they were rewarded for the atrocities they had committed.

There were also other reasons female fighters did not disarm. One that was often mentioned had to do with the physical layout of DDR camps. It was the opinion of many informants that female fighters should not have been asked to disarm in such an open or public place as a DDR camp. This was also repeated in many interviews with family and community members, who voiced a wish for more private and secluded spaces in which women could have disarmed and demobilized. Some people said this was necessary because most Sierra Leonean women were afraid to be seen in such public places as DDR camps. I took this fear of the "public" to infer that both the women and their families were ashamed and would have preferred the whole DDR process to be done in "secret." Providing female fighters with safe, secure, and single-sex surroundings could, of course, have been a way of combating their fear and shame.[11] Tied to this, but perhaps more important, is the fact that many girls and young women had frequently been sexually and physically abused during their time with the fighters and continued to be so in the DDR camps. The incentive for those who had escaped or been released to go voluntarily to a camp where there were large numbers of male ex-combatants was not very high, and many of the interviewed girls and young women expressed fear of sexual and physical violence.[12] Seventeen-year-old Kadiatu, who had been abducted for ten months and had been sexually abused before being trained to fight, said that she did not want to demobilize as she was afraid that "if we all stay in one camp they will still do the same wickedness to me," and twenty-year-old Rugiatu, who had been a rebel fighter, said that she definitely had had no intention of demobilizing. "I didn't plan to join them, it was only because I was captured. So to say that I should be with those wicked people in a camp! No, I was afraid!"

The issue of sexual and physical abuse in the camps was a security issue that could have been dealt with relatively easily by DDR planners and implementers, and this makes it very clear that the DDR process in Sierra Leone did not have as its objective to demobilize the thousands of girls and young women associated in one way or another with the fighting forces. The issue of the suitability, or lack thereof, of the DDR camps in relation to pregnant and/or lactating mothers was also frequently raised.[13] The nature of the skills training provided by the DDR was also perceived as biased toward men, since training was geared toward traditional male activities such as carpentry, masonry, and mechanics (see also Shepler 2005). Again, it is clear that the camps and the activities were not designed for women and girls. At the time of the DDR registration, then, many of these girls and young women not only had no access to weapons, but they had left their commanders and groups and had little motivation to disarm. To disarm without the support of a bush husband or commander, as I have already mentioned, was almost impossible. Some of these impediments were of an organizational and logistical nature, but in addition to this there were other reasons having to do more with circumstance and bad timing. A few also said that they had been displaced or were refugees during the time of disarmament and therefore could not access DDR camps, and some said that at the time of disarmament they had just fled or been released from the fighting forces and did not want to disarm or could not, even if they had wanted. Although many girls and young women said they had stayed because they lived in marriagelike relationships with the man who abducted them, and might have spent many years together and even had children, like Aminata, the majority of those I interviewed escaped or left as soon as they were released.

Then there were the pictures. I have already described at the beginning of this chapter how my informants were terrified of having their pictures taken for the DDR identification card. The pictures were required for disarming combatants' identification cards and had no other purpose than to identify registered ex-combatants for the distribution of rations and benefits. Yet the fear of having their pictures taken was one of the reasons Aminata and so many other female ex-combatants never registered for disarmament. Aminata and many others said that "our pictures will be taken and later they will look for you and arrest you and you will appear in court," and believed that the Special Court would find them and kill them. This fear, of having their pictures taken and the consequences this could have for the girls and women, was widespread. The pictures, it was believed, would be "put in a computer" and circulated everywhere and to everyone, "shaming" them, and would also, they believed, effectively block them from ever getting a job or ever getting a travel visa to another country. The pictures thus became one of the strongest expressions of fear and social shame. The photographs were rather innocent in themselves, but they were taken in a context that was perceived as threatening and potentially harmful, a physical manifestation of their "shameful" behavior and of having "disgraced" their families. This held many girls and women back from registering for demobilization. One former female fighter, Mary, only fifteen years old, said that "some were afraid to join DDR because they were saying that your picture will be scattered everywhere. So after all, you will be arrested and sent to prison." Many female ex-combatants simply did not find the benefits of participating in DDR programs worth the risks involved in revealing their identities. Generally, female fighters "do not occupy a position that can be easily reconciled with predominant gender ideologies," noted Farr (2002, 8). Unlike male combatants, they are often excluded from the new army (thereby "remasculinizing" the army), from new political structures, and are also refused access to retraining or land. Many are also regarded with fear and suspicion when they attempt to return to the lives they lived before war broke out, as we have seen in Aminata's case. Judith Gardam and Hilary Charlesworth, for example, noted that the treatment of female combatants "by the military institution reflects the subordinate position of women in society generally" (2000, 152), and although this was quite well known, little was done during the DDR process in Sierra Leone to address it. So most girls and women quietly drifted back to their families or communities, but "while this secrecy protected them, it also concealed their need for support" (McKay and Mazurana 2004, 35).

Like countless girls and women I have interviewed, Aminata thought that the Special Court would send her to prison for what she had done during the war and then execute her. Aminata obviously had confidence in my assistant Mary. After our very first meeting Aminata had told Mary that she did not feel comfortable talking to anyone else but her, and that she was afraid of me. "You know the last time you brought that white woman [me], I talked to you but I was afraid to talk to her." Mary asked why she was afraid of me, and Aminata said that her father had told her not to talk to anyone about her wartime experiences, especially not white people, as they would send her to the Special Court. Although it was not always expressed as distinctly as Aminata put it, this was to become a common theme during my fieldwork. Next I will turn to the TRC and the Special Court.

Reconciling with a Violent Past: Narratives of War, the TRC, and the Special Court

> People are coming to listen to our stories, now they've done this to us and now we are going out struggling, to take up our own responsibilities, they are coming to ask ...but what are they doing for us in the future, what will help us? They are not giving us anything they just want us to talk, so I don't have to say anything.
>
> Interview, 11 May 2004

The establishment of a Truth and Reconciliation Commission (TRC) in Sierra Leone was already outlined in the Lomé Peace Accord of July 1999.

Its purpose was to "address impunity, break the cycle of violence, provide a forum for both the victims and perpetrators of human rights violations to tell their story, get a clear picture of the past in order to facilitate genuine healing and reconciliation."[14] The peace agreement stated that a TRC should be established within ninety days of the signing of the agreement and that its report should be submitted no later than twelve months after the commencement of its work. In reality it took much longer. There were initial difficulties, mainly with funding, and then the commission experienced managerial and staff problems (Kelsall 2005, 381). The report was released after much delay in October 2004.[15] The aim of the Special Court was quite different. In January 2002, after the official declaration of peace, the government and the UN signed an agreement creating a Special Court to try those ultimately responsible for the most atrocious crimes during the war (Cockayne 2005; Cryer et al. 2001; Malan 2003). Rebel fighters like Aminata and Musu were clearly not of interest to the Special Court, but they and other women like them did not know this and were genuinely afraid of what would happen to them if they talked to people from these institutions.

In Sierra Leone, the TRC stated in its report that "knowledge and understanding are the most powerful deterrents against conflict and war" and that "Sierra Leoneans had a *need* to express and acknowledge suffering, a *need* to relate their stories and experiences, a *need* to know who was behind the atrocities, a *need* to explain and contextualize decisions and conduct, a *need* to reconcile with former enemies, a *need* to begin personal and national healing and a *need* to build accountability in order to address impunity" (TRC 2004, vol. 1 § 3, my emphasis). Much human rights-related work operates on the basis of an assumed *need* for victims to "give voice" to pain inflicted by violence on the body, as I have discussed in the introduction. This is present, for example, in much of the work of Amnesty International and Human Rights Watch, and also in the Truth and Reconciliation Commissions in South Africa and Sierra Leone and elsewhere. In the South African TRC it was said that storytelling was the victims' chance to "set the record straight" and "reclaim their dignity," that it was meant to "empower" them (see Colvin 2004, 73). This need to publicly narrate their war experiences was not altogether obvious to many Sierra Leoneans, but through sensitization they were "educated" about the benefits and also necessity of this type of healing process (cf. Shaw 2005, 4).

In fact, it has been argued that to "give a voice" to people who have suffered violence and oppression is at once necessary and problematical (Handelman 2004; Linden 1993), and that the seemingly innocent claim, to "give voice," conceals both the identity and the agenda of the interviewer. Ruth Linden coined a term for the whole work of remembering, documenting, and commemorating the Holocaust, the producing of survivors' stories of war and terror, calling it "the remembrance industry" (1993, 73). She wanted to highlight the politico-economic nature of that undertaking, where survivors' memories have become "commodities." Following this, I endeavored not to commodify my informants' stories, not to treat them as "war texts" untethered from their local social and cultural landscape.

There was also another underlying need in Sierra Leone, not always explicitly stated, and that was the need of the international community to make records of atrocities, its need to create "justice," and its need to make the world never forget. "Truth commissions link together complex ideas about suffering, justice, human rights, accountability, history and witnessing," as anthropologist Fiona Ross (2003, 1) wrote in the introduction to her detailed gender analysis of the South African Truth Commission. From a human rights perspective, whether this perspective is applied by the UN, NGOs, or others dealing with reconciliation, Truth and Reconciliation Commissions are often seen as a necessary prelude to personal and national healing. It is also necessary, though this is not as clearly stated, to document atrocities for the world not to forget, and for the world not to let anything like this happen again. This was said after the Holocaust, after South African apartheid, and after the genocide in Rwanda. A TRC has a threefold agenda: first, to offer victims of atrocities a way to begin *personal* healing; second, to further *national* reconciliation; and third, and perhaps more theoretical, to make sure that these kinds of atrocities will not go unnoticed, that *the world is watching and will never forget.* These aims are thus compounded in the work of a TRC. Testifying is assumed to provide personal healing, and the published testimonies, for those who can read and have access to them, are meant to help the process of national healing. The reports are also the physical manifestation of the work of the TRC, and their distribution to the UN, various governments, NGOs, academics, and the like is the means by which the world will never forget.

In my work I did not focus on those who testified at the TRC hearings for the simple reason that none of my informants did. Therefore I am not in a position to discuss whether giving testimony was effective in personal healing. But public "truth telling" as a means of personal healing has been questioned, and Rosalind Shaw concluded that a "truth commission is not therapy" (2005, 7).[16] I can see parallels between the TRC in Sierra Leone and the one in South Africa, where Christopher Colvin (2004, 74) describes the narrative work of victims as "traumatic storytelling." It is traumatic in that, first, it is so defined by mainstream psychiatry, and second, it is framed by the language and practice of psychotherapy, and last, it is a storytelling that can be traumatizing to the teller.[17] It is also a storytelling that is founded on a model of memory that focuses on short stories of traumatic suffering, reduced to "the most important, shocking, and morally obvious details of harm," and which "does not easily admit the ambiguous and the unspectacular" (Colvin 2004, 74). This reminds me of what I have described earlier, of the short, condensed "war narratives" and how they too are focused on "recounting individual horror stories" at the expense of the structural violence of everyday life.[18] The idea of publicly sharing a story of personal experience of violence and trauma with the world, in the TRC or the Special Court, for example, was construed as a way also of reconciling the nation with its violent past, but whether it helped individual women to come to terms with and move on from their personal experiences of violence in the same way is questionable. On the issue of national healing, Shaw also noted that the idea of healing a nation that "is wounded or traumatized is primarily nation-building rhetoric that anthropomorphizes the nation as a feeling, suffering entity," and she writes, this is a notion derived from "nineteenth-century models of society as akin to an organism that can be healthy or sick" (Shaw 2005, 7). Shaw is skeptical of this biological model of the society and discredits the idea that mass violence can be conceptualized "in terms of a damaged collective national psyche that can be healed through a cathartic process of truth telling" (ibid.). This idea of healing a nation through a single collective memory, an official "truth about what happened," is problematic, as it implies that this "truth" is somehow something constant and unchanging, and not a contested process, and also something that is not always desired. In her recent work, Shaw argued that the Sierra Leone TRC engaged in a particular form of memory politics that "valorized a particular form of memory practice: 'truth telling,' the public recounting of memories of violence," and this valorization, she continues, "is based on deeply problematic assumptions about the purportedly universal benefits of the verbal recounting of past violence" (Shaw 2005, 2). Instead, Shaw argues, first, memory is not a specific and fixed set of facts but rather a process, and second, underlying the concept that truth telling creates healing and reconciliation are "ideas of the efficacy of recounting verbal memories of violence and trauma," and further, that these ideas are "the product of a culture of memory that arose from specific historical processes in North America and Europe" (2005, 7). It has also been argued that the "drama of healing through public confession and grief...enlists a number of tropes in the Christian imaginary, such as suffering, martyrdom, and resurrection, and explains in part the widespread fascination with truth commissions" (Kelsall 2005, 371). Participating in this drama seemed to have little appeal for people in Sierra Leone, however. Tim Kelsall (2005) and Shaw (2002, 2005) instead tried to analyze the memory politics specific to Sierra Leone and found that "truth telling" may not be the best way to heal trauma in this particular context, or as Kelsall has it, "public truth-telling—in the absence of strong ritual inducement—lacks deep roots in the local cultures of Sierra Leone" (2005, 363; see also Ferme 2001). Michael Jackson even went as far as questioning the very legitimacy of the TRC and argues that "Western rituals of reconciliation and renewal (The Truth Commission in Freetown) often outrage African conceptions of how best to create conciliation and peace."[19]

As I noted already in the introduction, my own field research was affected by rumors of TRC and the Special Court, and it took me quite some time to convince my informants that I had nothing to do with either. Only after establishing this fact did informants start to talk freely about their war experiences, but almost always in private conversations. Staff at an international NGO likewise said that the registration for one of their projects in Kono, targeting girls who had not disarmed, coincided with activities by Special Court and to some extent TRC in the area, and this had made the girls and young women afraid to identify themselves.[20] Shaw also noted that as "TRC's statement taking phase and hearings phase coincided with the Special Court's indictments," this resulted "in widespread ex-combatant fears that the TRC could be a covert conduit for the Special Court" (2005, 4), and she even mentions that in some towns, people were so afraid that they drove the TRC statement takers away. This could be interpreted as an expression of social control; people had tried to suppress certain aspects of social shame that the presence of the TRC would have unfolded and exposed. According to Shaw, however, their fears were not completely unfounded, as there were leakages of information between the institutions (2005, 4–5).[21] Most of my informants did not know that the Special Court tried only those who bore the greatest responsibility for the atrocities, and many expressed a fear of talking to the court's representatives. A twenty-two-year-old girl in Makeni said that the main reason she did not disarm was because she felt afraid of the Special Court, afraid of being "classed as RUF." Another nineteen-year-old girl, also from Makeni, said she was afraid that her name would be put in the "Special Court computer." It became clear quite early on in my fieldwork that my informants really had no idea what the TRC or the Special Court were about. They were not alone in this. In a survey of ex-combatants' views of the TRC and the Special Court by a Freetown based NGO, it was revealed that nearly half of the respondents felt that they did not understand the TRC (PRIDE 2002).[22] Once when I was talking to two of my informants, Finah and Aisha, I asked them what they thought about the Special Court. Aisha responded by saying that "Special Court is for those that did bad." But she also said that those who "did bad" to her had not been prosecuted, and that she found this problematic. When I then asked them about the TRC, Finah said she had never heard about it. So I explained what the TRC was, to which she replied, "We haven't met that here."[23] The TRC actually had been to Kabala, unbeknownst to most of my informants. I then asked them if they thought that people should "forget," and Finah said, "If it is for me, I will leave them [forget them] because they have done what they have done. Even if they put them in prison or do anything to them, that will not refund all that they have spoilt." Aisha, on the other hand, said that she thought those who had committed crimes should be sent to court and sentenced. When I said that this was difficult in practical terms because they had been so many, she relented but emphasized that "all those that are not arrested [by the Special Court], God will punish them," which was quite a common response (cf. Jackson 2004b).

Although the DDR, the TRC, and the Special Court were separate institutional bodies, they were often conflated for my informants. For example, as I have described above, having one's picture taken during demobilization, to ensure correct distribution of benefits, was believed to lead to incarceration and possible execution by the TRC and the Special Court. There seemed to be a lot of confusion among my informants about the nature and mandate of the DDR, the Special Court, and the TRC, and rumors abounded.[24] How is it possible that abducted girls were afraid of being judged, imprisoned, or killed by the government, the Special Court, and the TRC when they were being offered services and training that was meant to benefit them, emotionally, educationally, socially, and financially? What went wrong? I believe, first, that the DDR failed to provide accurate information about the nature and mandate of its work, and second, that neither the Special Court nor the TRC succeeded in explaining the nature of their work, at least not in northern Sierra Leone.[25] While there were differences between rural and urban areas, I have to maintain that the predominantly illiterate rural women whom I met in Koinadugu District had little or no comprehension about the actual work of the above-named institutions. Whether this was the result of a lack of information, the spread of rumors, an expression of gendered hierarchies in the transmission of knowledge, or all of these, is difficult to tell. The TRC, however, stated self-critically in its report that "the failure to clearly demarcate the roles and functions of the two bodies [TRC and Special Court], together with the highly uncertain nature of the relationship between them, led to a great deal of confusion in the minds of the public" (TRC 2004, 2: ch. 2 § 567). It also mentions that the "Commission finds that many Sierra Leoneans who might have wished to participate in the truth telling process stayed away for fear that their information may be turned over to the Special Court. This was particularly the case with regard to perpetrators" (ibid. § 658). Aminata is a case in point. Just after the war she had actually been asked to testify to the TRC. At that time she was still living with her bush husband and she believed that if she testified they would both be arrested, and so she refused. These institutions—the DDR, the TRC, and the Special Court— are international bodies, and are quite similarly planned and implemented wherever in the world they take place; they are part of a "global dynamic in post-conflict reconstruction efforts" (Hoffman 2004b, 326). It was apparent that the designers of these had little previous knowledge of the workings of the local politics of memory, justice, and reconciliation.

A local social worker in Kabala, who had worked as an interpreter for investigators from the Special Court in Koinadugu, told me of many cases where women who had initially volunteered to be interviewed later withdrew their statements. She also told me that girls and women frequently complained to her about their dealings with people from the Special Court and the TRC. Although some had initially been willing testifiers, many later started to feel singled out and were afraid of what the consequences of their testimonies would be. Others were just tired of talking about the war and wanted to move on. My friend Theresa, a local woman who had worked a lot with women who had been abducted, said that "they don't want to talk, because most of them have married, maybe to someone who is taking good care of them, and some are going to school. Like [one woman], the man is taking care of all her children. She's much happy now, so if you ask her she will say that she has forgotten about it." There was, for example, a case of one girl who had been interviewed by investigators from the Special Court. When the investigator came for a final assessment a year later for those going to testify at the Special Court, the girl had begun attending school. She was called to verify her testimony and make revisions if necessary. The social worker told me that,

> The girl was called for the last time to come and verify what she said before. After one year has passed, she has come into her senses, then the trauma is you know, giving her away, because she is going to school. Her parents are responsible for her, and when she was asked she said, "I was the one who said this but I am not ready to go and stand for Special Court, to say I was the one who said this. If you want to write, go ahead and write but I am not going to say anything again," and she didn't.

This girl had initially made a statement, whereas most of the girls and women I met would never have dreamed of doing even that. It was quite obvious that my informants believed that recounting their "trauma" would not "heal" them or "reconcile" them with their families and communities, but rather the opposite, that it would probably further stigmatize them and at worst "send them to court" or get them killed. Recall Aminata's initial response to me: "Do you want me to go to court!" Indeed, among the women I worked with it became very clear that the discourse of reconciliation favored by the TRC and the Special Court was in many ways, although probably unintentionally, inappropriate. From the point of view of local culture, coping with memories of pain, humiliation, and violence was often a private and not a public event, whereas the human rights style of coping with them was through public narration. The way my informants expressed their problems and concerns did not fit into the discursive style of the TRC. In her work on the South African TRC, Ross points out with respect to women's testimonies that personal as well as traditional narrative styles for talking about violence are difficult to include in "the crystallised forms generated by human rights discourses" (2005, 214). I think this a valid and important point for my female informants in Sierra Leone as well. To publicly express pain or shameful practices has negative connotations in local culture; it is in itself shameful, and silence and composure, or as Kelsall writes, "indirectness, evasiveness, and secrecy" (2005, 383), are the ideal. And Ferme, in her book on the hidden and the "underneath of things" in Sierra Leone culture (2001, 7), pointed out that only children or idiots will say straight out what they think. As I demonstrated previously, many parents went to quite some lengths to prevent their daughters from talking about their war experiences so that the families would not be shamed. Recall Aminata's comments above, where both her bush husband and her father warned her about giving a deposition to the TRC or the Special Court, or even of talking to white people, because she risked being arrested and executed. As Ross points out, "People do not necessarily want their activities and experiences to be widely known" (2003, 2), and this was definitely the case among my female informants in postwar Sierra Leone.

To suffer from "war trauma" or from post-traumatic stress disorder (PTSD) were concepts almost unheard of among my rural informants.[26] Such concepts had little meaning for them, and they were sometimes deeply skeptical about the diagnosis as well as the methods used by NGOs to heal this "trauma": giving testimony or in other ways verbally expressing their experiences of suffering in public. Instead of this therapeutic talking, many people in the communities, including some of the girls and women I worked with, believed that abducted women and female ex-combatants would be best served by forgetting the whole episode, never talking about it, and starting to behave in a culturally acceptable manner. I have already discussed in the introduction various aspects of narrating or talking about pain, violence, and suffering, and I have also noted that women rarely talk about pain and violence in public. For example, a common response to my questions about suffering was "You just have to bear it out." This discrepancy between a "trauma healing" discourse and local ways of healing and reconciliation was probably exacerbated by the way the TRC and the Special Court worked (cf. Jackson 2004b), as well as by people's lack of information about their mandates in the area. It thus became clear that the discourse of reconciliation favored by these institutions was in many ways unsuitable for my informants, because in publicly narrating their experiences they were further singled out and stigmatized.

Thus, in Sierra Leone there were tensions between the TRC on the one hand, which wanted to document "the truth" about the war in order to make sure it would never happen again, and on the other, the families and relatives of "victims" and "perpetrators" who wanted not a word uttered about the shameful experiences of war lest they be remembered, or worse, reproduced.[27] This was also noted by Shaw (2005, 9), who wrote that "speaking of the violence—especially in public—was (and is) viewed as encouraging its return, calling it forth when it is still very close and might at any moment erupt again," and, she continues, "social forgetting is a refusal to reproduce the violence by talking about it publicly." Kelsall also noted that "witnesses did not generally accept the idea that the Commission was a platform upon which to enact grief, catharsis and healing, either for their own benefit or for that of the nation" (2005, 371). I also found that the prescribed method of dealing with war trauma and for peace and reconciliation advocated by many Sierra Leoneans was one silence and social forgetting. This can also be related to why the DDR process contravened the notion of social forgetting. I support Anita Schroven's conclusion that participation in the DDR "would not allow forgetting; instead it would perpetuate remembering and therefore inhibit reintegration and social healing" (2005, 74). The kind of forgetting implied here, it has to be noted, is a form of social forgetting that needs to be distinguished from personal forgetting. Although social forgetting will affect the way personal memories of violence are articulated, people will never forget personal experiences of violence. One of my informants, Mariatu, whose father had been killed before she was abducted, vehemently emphasized that she would never forget or forgive those who killed her father. "The people that killed our father we knew. Will we forget that again? We won't forget that again until death!" Also Theresa said that "the amputees, they won't ever forget, ask them now, they will explain to you. They will say we forgive but we will never forget." Most of these sentiments of nonforgetting and nonforgiving were nevertheless often raised only in private. While talking about the war in general terms, people would quite often say that everyone should "forget and forgive," and that in fact they had been encouraged to do this by the president himself and the government. To "forget and forgive," then, was not only something that people had come up with on their own. In an interview with women from a women's group, I was told that they had heard it on the radio, in a speech by the president, where he had urged them to "forgive" all combatants. A Christian pastor I met a few times said that he had heard about it in town; "there were general meetings in town, we were told to forgive and embrace the ex-combatants."

People had been told to forget and forgive. Therefore, in public, people seemed to accept those rebels, men or women, who were able to adapt to the moral discourses of village or town life. Those young men and women who behaved well, made money, practiced their religion, worked hard, and did not use bad language, people generally thought better of. Of those, on the other hand, who continued to use drugs, who had difficulties in accepting their lower position in family and social hierarchies, and who drew attention to themselves by wearing certain types of clothing or by using a language people associated with the rebels, people were very suspicious. These feelings of suspicion were not always publicly expressed. Rather, many people would talk to each other, or to me, only in private, lest they be suspected of harboring ill feelings. Still, as I have mentioned, there was a very official discourse about reconciliation, and people were frequently reprimanded for using terms such as *rebel* or *combatant* and differentiating between fighters and civilians. Instead, people were encouraged to say "ex-combatants" if distinguishing them at all, or "citizens." "We are all citizens now," as one old man remarked. Still, I frequently got the feeling that when quarrels or disputes arose that involved ex-combatants, people were quick to condemn them due to their violent past.

Despite being told to, people did not easily forget, nor did some even pretend to forgive. Nevertheless, life went on and people struggled to make ends meet, to send their children to school, to rebuild their houses, "make their farms," "do their market." Both civilians and ex-combatants were war weary at the end of the war, and welcomed peace, at whatever price. In fact, keeping busy and occupied with making a living was often conceived of as the best way of healing from personal experiences of trauma, and also of reconciling with one's family and community. Like Finah, who said, "I am now trying to learn trading, God helps me to forget my sorrows." Interestingly, this is also where local notions of social forgetting were sometimes at odds with the practical realities of postwar survival strategies. Being inhabitants of a war-torn country, Sierra Leoneans were very dependent on aid, and any family member who could get accepted into one of the vocational programs implemented by NGOs was seen as a valuable asset to the family. However, most projects that were aimed at war-affected women did not exclusively provide for their material needs but also tried to cater to their psychosocial needs as well. To get accepted into such programs the telling of your "war story" was often mandatory. To put it simply, families had to negotiate between their wishes for the total obliteration of shameful war-time experiences on the one hand, and the material gain these narratives could produce through access to skills train-ing programs on the other. However, whereas I see the "war story" as focus-ing on "beneficiaries" as "victims of war-time violence," the "DDR story" focused on the "beneficiaries" as "fighters." When looking at some of these "war stories," it is easy to see how the very context of narration frames them and encourages some themes while suppressing others. In these narratives it was often women's experiences of victimhood that were emphasized, whereas other experiences were almost completely muted, because who would be accepted in fierce competition for a vocational program if they had not "suffered"? The production of these war stories thereby became one of the ways in which women were educated about their suffering.

There has been a lot of talk of local reconciliation alternatives to the TRC. In northern Uganda and also in Mozambique after the war, ritual cleans-ing ceremonies, old and new, to accept fighters back into their communities have been quite common (see, e.g., Finnström 2003; and Honwana 1997). In postwar Sierra Leone there has been some mention of "traditional rites of forgiveness" in relation to the public hearings held by the TRC (see, e.g., Dougherty 2004, 46; and Kelsall 2005), and I have heard of similar rites in parts of Temne-speaking areas.[28] But my informants never mentioned any "traditional" healing or cleansing rituals or ceremonies to further the rein-tegration of ex-combatants, young or old, men or women, into their origi-nal communities—to "rehumanize" them.[29] For most of my informants, disputes that arose between reunified girls and their families were dealt with in the manner usual for settling any kind of dispute, which is either by religious leaders, chiefs, or mamy queens. According to Kelsall, the TRC hearings did little in the way of reconciling victims and perpetrators, but the reconciliation ceremony following the hearing he attended, on the other hand, "had a remarkable impact...transforming the atmosphere from one of virtual crisis and farce, to one of emotional release and reconciliation"

(Kelsall 2005, 378). I did not attend any such ceremonies, but I observed instead how families could become reconciled with their ex-rebel children if the latter behaved in a morally respected manner and if they were able to contribute to the general welfare of the household, as I have described above. Healing and reconciliation then took place on a level that was much more social and material than individual and psychological.

Up to now I have focused on the different ways in which healing was organized and internalized at the level of community and the individual. When the gaze is shifted from the official discourse of healing and reconciliation of the TRC, other alternative stories emerge. By sharing with the world a story of personal experience of violence and trauma, a woman might help reconcile a nation with its violent past, but in view of my research, most of my informants did not believe that it could also help them come to terms with and move on from their personal experiences of violence.[30] This was especially true for those women who had experiences of both being abducted and being fighters, especially as many female fighters had not demobilized and had thereby not been able to utilize one of the formal avenues for reconciling their communities with their experiences. In telling their stories, many women expected not forgiveness and reconciliation, but disapproval and stigmatization.

Concluding Remarks

No particular measures were taken to encourage female combatants to demobilize in Sierra Leone by either the UN Assistance Mission to Sierra Leone (UNAMSIL) or the DDR. By all accounts it seems that the Sierra Leone DDR planners were gender blind, and thought that if women had fought with men, they could disarm with men. Although the DDR did not actively discourage women like Aminata from disarming, they did little to encourage them, and female combatants were seldom if ever allowed to formulate their own needs with regard to demobilization and reintegration processes. When we were discussing the disarmament process, Aminata was bitter and felt that a lot of men who had disarmed, whether RUF, AFRC, or CDF, had not been in combat to the extent that she had. Aminata's bush husband and also her parents had actively discouraged her from demobilizing, warning her of the social consequences. I believe that female fighters, in particular those with no weapons, were not seen as a threat to the peace process or the cease-fire and were therefore largely ignored. But considering that many women in fact constituted the rebel infrastructure, the question remains of what could happen after all combatants had demobilized and the infrastructure still remained, in case of renewed fighting.[31]

That the DDR program did not specifically focus on female fighters was one reason they did not disarm. Another reason for female fighters' reluctance to disarm, and one largely ignored by the DDR planners, was the position of these women in the local moral order. It was extremely shameful for women to be identified as fighters in postwar Sierra Leone. To disarm thus meant for them to publicly acknowledge that they had been willing participants and not only victims of the horrible circumstance of abduction. This was probably also why their attitude toward disarmament was so negative. Thus, although the lack of a weapon was seen as an impediment by many, I found that the major reason so many girls and women did not demobilize was not the lack of guns or ammunition, but rather that they felt shame or were too afraid. They were afraid of what would happen to them if they publicly identified as rebels, they were afraid of being stigmatized and ostracized, and they were afraid no one would ever marry them. This is not unique to Sierra Leone but has also been noted in many other demobilization schemes (cf. Brett and Specht 2004, 99).

My informants' unwillingness to disarm was also linked to the work of the DDR, Truth and Reconciliation Commission, and the Special Court. Although these three institutions were separate and had quite different mandates, my informants frequently confused them. They believed that if they had their pictures taken and if they disarmed, they would be sent to the TRC or the Special Court and there they would be judged and executed. Nothing could have been more mistaken. Still, this belief shaped their responses to the TRC and the Special Court. As they were not of concern to the Special Court, this was perhaps not an issue with which the court was overly concerned. The TRC, on the other hand, had reached out to many of my informants, asking for their testimonies of war. As I have described, it is generally believed within that diffuse entity we call the international humanitarian community that testifying about violence and humiliation, talking about what happened to them during the war, would be cathartic and healing for people. As I and many others have tried to show, in Sierra Leone, to publicly recount a "trauma" can actually be perceived as reproducing the hurt and shame associated with the original event in the present and into the future. For my informants it became quite clear that their social environment expected them to behave in a "normal" way if they were to be forgiven and their wrongs forgotten. This meant that they were encouraged to assume the ethics of the traditional female ideal of deference, to be hard working, and also to dress and speak "properly." In other words, to go on with life as if nothing had ever happened. This was not always easy, as I will discuss later. It was obvious that most of my informants had no desire to talk publicly about what had happened to them or what they had done during the war. Instead, healing for them, as well as for their families, was conceived of in terms of being able to procure a livelihood—to go to school, to trade, to get a job, to make a living—so that life could go on. Making a living and contributing to the family's welfare was something that could have ameliorated the reintegration of ex-fighters. As a matter of fact, material assets in many cases overcame shameful behavior. One might speculate that had Aminata gone through the DDR, received her "reinsertion package" and vocational training, her parents might perhaps have accepted her, despite the shame of her being known publicly as an ex-rebel. To be able to make a living was what most of my informants wanted, and this is what I will turn to next. Under all circumstances, making a living is often what counts.

6

Surviving the Postwar Economy

Female Livelihood Strategies

Sitting with a group of my informants in one of their compounds, I was talking with them about what working and having one's own income meant to women. As discussed in the previous chapter, working kept my informants from being "idle" and was, as I have noted, a recurring theme with many of them. They explained that it was very important for them to be able to contribute to the household, because this made them feel more respected, and this included the fact that having an income was seen as improving the relationships with their husbands. Aisha, Aminata's friend from the bush, said,

One of the things is this work, the [skills] training they have brought in the country. That is very good, because if you have learnt a skill, you are working, your husband is working, you won't quarrel a lot. Because the husband is not thinking that he is the only one bringing income in the house. The wife is also bringing income, so whatever thing you [the wife] say, he will support you!

Aisha also mentioned that since it is the responsibility of the husband to buy rice in bulk, if it used up before the end of the month he will often complain and accuse the wife of not being economical. But if a woman has her own money, "when it finishes, you buy...without asking," Aisha said and smiled. Finah also drew a parallel between women's making money and the way their families were treated by the husband.

> Another thing is, if your parents come, if you are working—let's say you are doing tailoring, or *gara* [tie dyeing]—you are bringing income in the house. If your husband sees your parents coming, or your brother, or your sister, the husband will welcome them warmly. But if you are not doing anything, when he sees your parents coming, he will take his bag and make as if he is going out.

In the case of Aminata, it was obvious that the way she was treated by her family forced her to seek other means of material and social survival. As this was the situation for many other young women, I will inquire here into what the cultural, social, and economic conditions of these other means were. I will examine the impact of these conditions on my informants' dreams for a better future. I will also look particularly at some generational differences in education and livelihood alternatives and the consequences of these differences on intergenerational relations.

Generational Dissonance

I often asked my young informants what they wanted to do in the future. The absolute majority said that they dreamed of becoming successful businesswomen. The next most popular choice was to become a skills training teacher. Perhaps this indicated the layout of the job market and the priorities of NGOs working in postwar settings, but whether this was a sign of the impact of skills training programs, and therefore a possible job opportunity, or a logical progression from skills training to skills training teacher was difficult to tell. In fact, only very few of my informants who had been trained in skills training programs actually managed to support themselves by practicing their new skills. Most of my informants were also illiterate; they had -missed out on school during the war years and were now reluctant to return to primary school because they were so much older than the other students. In Kabala there were no centers for adult education, and though there were a few vocational schools that provided lessons in basic literacy, these courses were often very brief and many women only learned how to write their names.

From reading regional ethnography and talking to many older men and women, I got the impression that there has been a substantial change in how young women today conceive of their life trajectories. Although these young women still did not have the tools and means to be able to really change their lives, young women today at least do not have to fear being called prostitutes by their own mothers if they want to go to school, as I described one of Morowa's wives telling me in chapter 2. I asked Aisha about this generational difference between mothers and daughters.

CHRIS: How do you see your mothers' life when compared to your own?

AISHA: Our mothers? One, they are not educated. They were not even thinking of education, they only know about marriage, and to give birth to many children. But nowadays, children want to be educated, they want to know something. So now, even two, three, four children is enough, for you to be able to educate your children. That is the difference.

This generational dissonance was also revealed each time I went to Kadi's house. Kadi's mother, Neneh, often complained about the behavior and attitude of young girls. "We expect most of the girls to know, not to be virgins, because, they know everything! Even in their mother's belly! They know it, about initiation, about delivery, about sexual intercourse, they know everything!" In a previous meeting, Neneh had said young girls today knew everything because they read it in books. Neneh herself was illiterate. Now I asked Kadi, Neneh's daughter, if it was really the same thing, to read it and to do it.

CHRIS: But you can read a book but you won't know everything until you do it [give birth], right?

KADI: I know everything that was in the book!

NENEH: "Economic," "biology" [she makes funny faces at Kadi and me].

CHRIS: Do you think that the real experience was like in the book?

KADI: Yes.

CHRIS: But can the book explain feelings or pain?

KADI: The book didn't tell us fully about the pain, but all they wrote in the book I saw them, I know everything from the book

CHRIS: What about sex?

KADI: Even that also, they taught us, even our teachers told us. Am I lying or is it true?

CHRIS: I don't know.... Your mother was saying that young people today do not respect elders, is it true?

KADI: It's true. Because most of the children know what their parents know, they know more than that, so they don't respect their elders.

CHRIS: What about experience, an old person has experienced more than a young person. An old person has *hankili* [sense].

KADI: That one has gone! But now presently we know more than the elders.

CHRIS: But how did this happen, what happened in Sierra Leone society that made this change?

KADI: Because of the hardship. [Mariatu, another of my key informants, who also lived in the house and was related to Kadi through marriage, sat next to us and nodded and hummed in agreement]. The hardship made us to go out. The reason why I said that the children know more than their parents, it is the hardship. If your father didn't take care of you, your mother didn't take care of you, they were not able to be responsible to buy cloth, food for you, you go out! You'll be in the street loving for money, for someone to give you food, for someone to buy clothes for you, for someone to buy shoes for you! So that has made the girls now to have more experience with these things.

CHRIS: But now you are a mother.

KADI: Yes, I must be a mother. I knew I must be a mother and now I have become a mother.

CHRIS: Is your way of being a mother much different than when your own mother was young?

KADI: The difference is now, my mother, when she was young, my mother's husband, my father, was giving everything to my mother. My mother was getting everything, but as for me now, my husband is not here, so unless my own mother gives to me.

Young women today, wives and mothers, seem to know that education and work can bring them many things in life that their mothers never dreamed of. On the other hand, young women today cannot count on the support that the old system guaranteed them. Husbands cannot or do not want to fulfill their "traditional" obligations, and women have not yet reached the position, in terms of education and work, that many of them strive for. Many of the younger women and girls had been with the rebels for many years and had completely missed out on education but most hoped that things will have improved by the time their own daughters are grown. I have described above how my informants felt that by contributing to the household economy, wives would be more respected by their husbands and there would be fewer marital disputes. It was similar with education.

Most informants believed, sometimes unrealistically, that education would solve many of their problems. This can perhaps be related to "the mystique of literacy" described earlier. Finah told me, "If you are educated, either in training or in book learning, the day the man doesn't have, you will bring! You feed the man, provide food for the house, you buy soap, take care of the children, you have some money, you are respected. At that time the man will say, Ah, anything! He won't decide anything. He'll say, 'Well, let's wait for my wife.' But if you don't have anything, he won't say it!" All the women sitting in the yard listening to Finah—there were about seven of us—laughed out loud at her last comment. However, given my informants' thirst for education, and what they believed education could provide, it was all the more disconcerting to hear them say that they were too old to go back to school. They were all in their late teens and early twenties. They complained that they would be ashamed to sit next to a small child in the second grade. Further, it is still quite unusual in Sierra Leone for girls and young women to continue school after having children.

Some of my informants also said that they were so ashamed about their past with the rebels that they did not want to expose themselves in a public space, such as a school. Although there was an emphasis in postwar Sierra Leone, by the government as well as the UN and associated organizations, on educating girls, most of the women I worked with were more interested in skills training than in formal education (cf. Bennett 2002, 59). This was because, they said, they realized that it was too late for them to be educated, and instead they wanted to invest in the education of their own children. NGOs often perceive literacy training as one way of improving the situation for these women, and most projects initially intended to offer basic literacy training. The official stance is that educating mothers will benefit their children also.[1] I have already mentioned the absence of adult education centers in Kabala and the limitations of the basic literacy courses offered at a few vocational schools. Still, in view of the already high level of vulnerability within this group of formerly abducted and ex-combatant women, they often perceived of nonformal literacy education as the only alternative, which perhaps held more promises than it could keep.

Vocational Training

In Sierra Leone after the war, hundreds of NGOs emerged to work with rehabilitation and reintegration projects. Many of these projects targeted young women with the intention of ameliorating their general situation, improving their economic and emotional status, and increasing their knowledge of health and reproductive issues. It took several years before the restoration of the country's basic infrastructure started up—roads, schools, hospitals, distribution of seeds and other agricultural extension services to farmers, for example—and in this setting NGOs became the major provider of both resources and activities, and their participatory projects were much coveted. One could speak of a new economy dictated by large-scale humanitarian interests. In this new postwar economy my informants had to navigate between agencies and projects created for their benefit.

When Aminata returned to Kabala after the war to live with her parents, as I described in the introduction, she was destitute and had few hopes of turning her situation around. In her father's household she was shunned and marginalized, and she described how her older brother was the only one who treated her well. After the war, providing for families was difficult for everyone; farmers had no seed rice, traders had lost their stocks, teachers were not paid, and those few people who actually had an income were forced to support an increasing number of family members. This was the case for Aminata's family. They were poor, and everyone depended on her brother's income. A few weeks after she returned, however, Aminata heard that a local NGO had started to register war-affected girls and women for vocational training. "When I came it didn't even take two weeks until I heard that [an NGO] is asking for women that have been captured. So I went and wrote my name, explained. Then after one month we started the training. That made all of them [her family] to love me more. But since that money finished, I have been hated again, only my brother loves me." In the vocational training project Aminata learned gara tie-dyeing, and she also went to class every day to learn basic literacy.[2] The NGO provided the women with one cooked meal a day during their training, and also childcare. Many of these women were single with children; some lived with their families and others with friends or boyfriends. Most of my informants felt insecure in their environments, and few could support themselves through work or other activities, and during the first few years after the war skills training projects were therefore seen by many as the only opportunity to improve their situation.

Over the years there has been a large number of projects all over Sierra Leone similar to the one Aminata attended, some more successful and better organized than others. What most of these projects share, however, is that they offered women training initiatives for a limited set of skills and were something of a quick-impact effort to solve a problem that is much more complex. The types of skills offered to women in these projects were mainly gara tie-dyeing, soap making, tailoring, hair dressing, and weaving. There were also trainings that taught different types of food processing and a few that taught women to improve their agricultural skills. As society in Sierra Leone has been characterized by the sexual division of labor, most of these skills were seen by the women participating in them, their communities, and the organizations implementing them as appropriate for women. The duration of the training projects varied from a few weeks to six months, during which time the women were supposed to learn skills that would enable them to support themselves after finishing their training. Many NGOs also emphasized that their objective was to make women independent and self-reliant.

As mentioned above, Aminata said that while she was in the vocational project and bringing home a small amount of money through the sale of her products, she was accepted and tolerated by her family. When the project finished, she did not have the resources, the support, or the drive to continue with the work on her own. And once she could no longer contribute to the household, she was again shunned and ostracized. Aminata was not alone in experiencing this relation between material provision and how she was treated. Mariatu confessed that she was afraid to return to her family because she did not have anything to bring home, neither skills nor money, and this, she believed, would fundamentally determine the way she would be treated. She felt that she could not return because people would not respect her, and that respect was intimately tied to the status with which she returned. If she were able to offer her relatives money or goods, she would be able to appease them and be forgiven. Another young woman in Kono District told me that her family had been happy to receive her because she had learned skills and could earn money, while her family had nothing. Most formerly abducted and ex-combatant women were afraid of returning empty handed (cf. Persson 2005, 33), and this was perhaps one of the main reasons most women, when asked, replied that they wanted to enroll in a skills training project.[3] Few, however, asked if the skills they were offered would lead to sustainable livelihoods.

Some of my informants were enrolled in vocational training projects at the time of my fieldwork, while others had already completed their training. But there were also those who had never participated in an organized project of any kind. I was told that to get accepted by an NGO for vocational training was not easy, and the right contacts and support from relatives was seen as essential. Many of those who were engaged in skills training projects were very hopeful about what their newly acquired skills would bring them in the future, while those who had completed their projects were generally more disillusioned. For one thing, there was not a lot of variation in the types of skills training offered to the women, as I have explained above, and second, these were also often skills that offered little economic gain if practiced. In fact, it seemed inconceivable that the Sierra Leone local economy could absorb all the gara tie-dyers, tailors, and soap makers being trained. Shepler noted that the enormous increase in similar skills training programs meant that such skills and products dramatically exceeded the demand (2005, 169), and Hoffman wrote of the vocational training provided under the demobilization program that "from the beginning it was clear that the country's ability to support newly minted welders, mechanics, and gara dyers was nowhere near the 77,000 who passed through the program" (2004b, 141–42). Still, in response to my questions at the time of my fieldwork, both organizations and the women they targeted could think of few alternatives to the skills already offered, although, their reasons varied.

When I once asked the managing director of an NGO why they had decided to work with such a limited set of skills, which were also the same skills that all the other organizations were offering, I was told that he had not really thought about it, but that all their projects were designed by "the ex-pats in Freetown." However, after asking around for a few days in the wider community for alternative suggestions to soap making and gara tie-dyeing, I found that people managed to come up with quite a number of alternatives, so there was nothing lacking in people's imagination.[4] Yet these were activities seldom mentioned in discussions with NGOs on skills training initiatives for women in Sierra Leone. Moreover, what most NGOs often referred to as "pre-skills training orientation" was not often implemented.[5] Very few female "beneficiaries" or NGO staff had reflected on these issues, and there was little or no critique of the basic principles guiding these projects, including the fact that extremely few who had graduated from a skills training program would actually be able to make a living from them. I will provide one example.

Weaving has previously been a male occupation in Sierra Leone (see, e.g., Ferme 2001), but since the war it has increasingly been made accessible to women through vocational training. After only the most basic inquiries, however, I found that it takes around three full working days to finish weaving a roll of "country cloth." The profit after deducting the cost of materials was not more than Le 4,000 in total, and provided that the weaver could sell it on the fourth day, which few could, this amounted to a profit of Le 1,000 a day (US$0.40). It was just not feasible that anyone could support herself, not to mention her children, on Le 1,000 a day. In comparison, women collecting and selling firewood could make between Le 1,500 and 2,000 per day.[6]

Although Aminata was happy that the project had made her parents tolerate her, she was still disappointed, for the gara tie-dyeing training she attended had lasted only three months, too short a time for her to really learn the technique. Unfortunately, this was quite common due to difficulties in finding funds for these types of projects, and many NGOs that had initially planned to have more extensive projects had to shorten the length of their training due to lack of funding. These perfunctory projects caused ill feeling and resentment among many women, who ended up thinking that it would have been better not to attend at all. Many of my informants who had finished their training complained that it had just been a waste of their time, and few managed to make a living by the skills they had learned (cf. Persson 2005, 29). There were also those who had difficulties completing their training. Amie, whom we have met before, lived with her mother. She had been a bush wife to a rebel during the war and they had one child, but she did not know what had happened to the man or where he was, if he was dead or alive. Like so many formerly abducted girls in Sierra Leone, she had missed out on schooling during the war and felt that she was too old to go back to school. Her father had died and no one, as she phrased it, was "responsible for" her. In the house where she lived everyone had to contribute food and other essentials. Amie had made a living by walking several miles each day in search of firewood to sell in town, but when we met she had just started to train as a tailor in a vocational institute. She had great faith in the material benefits her training would provide in the future. Still, she was very worried about her health, as she was suffering from incontinence due to the repeated sexual abuse she had experienced during the war, and she could not afford treatment. She felt ashamed of the way she smelled when she was in the training center, and the frequent vaginal pains she was experiencing also made her uneasy in the presence of others. Added to this was the problem of childcare. There was no one who could take care of her child while she was at the center, which did not provide childcare. Her mother was out collecting wood all day and the neighbors who had previously taken care of the child had started to complain. Another of her worries was the cost of the materials she needed to buy in order to pass the final exams. Also, her family at this time had started to threaten that if she did not get married soon they would throw her out of the house. She said that she did not oppose marriage as such but did not want to get married just now, because as she said, "I know the type of sickness I have." Amie had many concerns and problems interfering with her full concentration on the skills training, but her case was not rare. These were concerns shared by many of the women targeted by these types of projects. I found that many women wanted to participate in the projects to create a better future for themselves, but meanwhile, they also had to eat, take care of their children, and get medical attention for war-related afflictions.

For some of the women the situation was slightly better. I met a few industrious women who managed to make some money by their learned skills. Adama, one of my neighbors, had been abducted by the rebels and after the war lived alone with her two children. Her husband had died and she had been "inherited" by her husband's "brother." This man, however, never assumed responsibility for Adama and her children; as I have described in chapter 2, this is not uncommon in "inheritance marriages" (*key-aneh*). Adama therefore had to fend for herself. She had gone to one of the first vocational projects in Kabala, the same one as Aminata, where she had learned soap making. Soap making was one of the more popular skills in vocational projects, but very few managed to continue with the work after training. Adama, who was a very tenacious woman, strong and stubborn, and determined to make it on her own and not depend on a husband or lovers, could walk for days in the countryside in search of cheap nut-oil to lower the cost of her soap production. She also realized that if she only sold in town she would never make any money because of the competition. So she walked long distances to remote villages where perhaps soap was more difficult to come by and easier to sell. Because Adama was from another area of Koinadugu District and had moved to Kabala just after the war, she had no relatives and no social network in Kabala, and this might also have made it more difficult for her to sell in town. Another young woman, Jeneba, eighteen years old, proudly explained how she was able to make a living after attending vocational training. "The project has helped me because I didn't know gara [tie dye] but now I can make and sell and loan [to] people. At the end of the month they pay me and I buy another. Now I can earn my living without going to men or begging people. Now I am able to send [remittances] for my relatives. I am no longer mocked but respected by people because I don't go to men again to foolish me." Still, most women were not like Adama and Jeneba, most could not afford to invest and buy the materials necessary to perform the work. Some, in fact, had to sell the tools they had been given in order to survive. In some tailoring projects, for example, the women would be given a sewing machine on graduation, but since they could not afford to buy materials to start their businesses, many ended up hawking the machines for a few thousand leones just to get by.

Vocational Training as "Trauma Healing"?

Although few women could manage to make a living by the skills they had learned, many women explained that the projects had provided them with something else. For example, quite a few of my informants said that the projects had made them more self-confident, and some said that the projects had helped them to cope better socially. This is significant, as this is a category of women otherwise known to be marginalized and stigmatized in postwar Sierra Leone. Thus the projects, albeit unintentionally, operated as a form of "trauma healing." For example, after she returned from her bush husband to what she experienced as a hostile environment, the project Aminata enrolled in offered her a form of solace. She explained that while she was in the project she had started to deal with her emotions and experiences from the war, and it was also here that she realized she was not alone in having these feelings.

> It was [the project] that made me to feel that I am not lost. And it was [the project] that made my relatives to accept me. But when all has gone, I am not considered again as part of them. If I don't contribute for food, I won't eat. If I send any of my younger ones [siblings] now, compared to the time I was just from [the project], they won't even look at me.[7]...Even my mother is saying I should leave the house for me not to kill her children. That's why I am just moving from one place to another. After the war I was ashamed and afraid of people, more especially those that I knew. Because, even my closest friends were afraid of me. As for my parents, when I came from Makeni to meet them, instead of them to be happy to see me alive, they just started driving me, only my elder brother told them not to do that....I thank God for [the project] who made me to be recognized by even my friends.

This was repeated many times by other informants. It seemed that the projects were more successful as a "psychosocial" activity than they were in providing long-term economic benefits. Not only Aminata, but many women said that being part of a project made them come to terms with some of their more unpleasant wartime experiences. They had become less aggressive and less isolated from their communities, which I took as an indication that the projects might also have worked as a form of social training for women who had spent many years in rebel camps (see also Shepler 2005, 150, on the psychosocial impact of skills training). There were also those who said that they liked keeping busy, and that being enrolled in a skills training project had kept them "from idleness." And a few women said that they were very proud that they had mastered a skill. "Keeping busy" and not "being idle" thus connects the purely financial with more social aspects of making a living. In creating livelihood options for young women in postwar Sierra Leone, it is essential also to examine their social position and the links between being able to make a living and social well-being, between the economy and social life. I will provide two examples of women who went to the same vocational project but found themselves in very different circumstances after the war.

Kumba was twenty years old and had been abducted by the rebels in 1998 and held for three years. Like so many other women, she had been taken as a bush wife and had been continually raped and also beaten. She had also given birth to a child in the bush. She escaped with the child and returned to her father's house, where she had been warmly welcomed. But her widowed father was old and feeble, and she had to support him as well as her younger sisters. After some time, an NGO in town started a project for girls and women like her and she was very excited. Kumba had never been to school before and did not know how to read and write, and when I asked what she had expected of the project, she replied, "To learn to read and write, to do gara and batik. I was expecting happiness. I was expecting, after the learning, to stand on my own, and maybe even to teach others." In the project Kumba had learned basic literacy, she now knows the alphabet and can write her name. She was also taught how to make gara tie-dye. She said, "Now I say thanks to God, because at first I was just picking leaves to sell, but now I have learned this work and I can make it and sell, and get money. Also it made me to forget so many evil things." Kumba explained that when she had begun the training, "at first I didn't know how to talk to people, I was rude and hot tempered. But here I learned to be humble and friendly." Being part of a group, with women with similar experiences, and with teachers and counselors, helped her to cope better socially. She still had problems, though, and one of her biggest concerns was how she would be able to afford to buy new material to continue the work, because the costs were high. The profit she made from her sales often went to support her family, as she had to feed eight people. She wanted her sister to be trained as well so that she could help support the family. Still, Kumba could survive on the proceeds from her sales, and she said, "I can live fine, because now that I have been trained, I can make gara and sell and get money."

Mariama, twenty-two years old, had gone to the same project as Kumba but had chosen hairdressing instead of gara tie-dyeing. Mariama lived in her brother's household with her child. She too had been abducted and had become pregnant with her bush husband. She said that she had not been able to escape but after four years had been released following disarmament. Her family situation was much different from Kumba's. Mariama was constantly provoked and even beaten. "If I get into a quarrel they will call me a rebel and my child a rebel child," she said. She is also still suffering from a sexually transmitted disease and could not afford to pay for treatment. She had been happy when she was accepted for the vocational training program: "I expected to dance and enjoy, learn hairdressing and gara," she said. She did learn hairdressing, but more importantly, she said, "I learnt how to mingle with people, and to be gentle. Before, I was only idle, they were giving me medicines, I was very aggressive, but now I know how to be humble. They have removed wickedness from me." Mariama managed to make a little money through the skills she had learned, but mostly she had to depend on her brother, but as he had to support twelve other people as well, so she felt she was a burden to him. Her dream was to make money through hairdressing and be able to repair their house. In contrast to Kumba, Mariama's biggest obstacle in supporting herself by her skills was that no one in the family encouraged her but always berated her. Nevertheless, like so many other informants, Mariama said that she thought she could make it as long as she was "serious, hard working, and patient."

The two cases illustrate the relationship between material wealth and quality of social relations. Women who have nothing and can provide nothing are often stigmatized and marginalized in the family. A woman who has provisions, on the other hand, was more likely to be treated well. This was also the case for women who, like Musu, supported their families through "boyfriends," as I shall discuss below. However, Kumba and Mariama faced very different challenges due to their family situation and position in the social hierarchy. In Kumba's case her whole family depended on her, even her father, so she was never rebuked for having been with the rebels. Mariama, on the other hand, was constantly reminded of her rebel life though provocation and stigma. Due to circumstances beyond her control, the family situation Mariama found herself in was very different from Kumba's. As a provider, Kumba was respected and encouraged, but as a dependant, Mariama was not allowed to forget her past with the rebels.

Petty Trading

Despite the fact that many young women dreamed of a better life for themselves, and hoped that learning a skill would help them accomplish that dream, most of my informants had to find other ways to make a living. Many of the women who had been involved in vocational projects ended up doing petty trade. Like most women in West Africa, many Sierra Leonean women are engaged in one way or another in petty trading, often in agricultural products or cheap consumer goods (see, e.g., House-Midamba and Ekechi 1995; Little 1973; Ojukutu-Macauley 1997). Many young women who had just recently returned or moved to Kabala would start with going to the bush to collect firewood, stones for construction, or fruit, which they would then sell along the roads. If they managed to make a small profit from this venture many would try to buy and sell other products such as chewing gum, batteries, and candles. Not many, but a few women had risen from collecting firewood by the roadside to selling consumer goods in a rented stall in the market in just a year. These women were perhaps exceptional, as the general situation was one in which all profit went to the sustenance of their families.

As is the case for many female traders in rural West Africa, most of my informants were illiterate. Some had little or no knowledge of "Western" market economy, capitalism, of the principles of supply and demand, and of how they could best invest their surplus. To a Western visitor entering any of the markets in Sierra Leone, these markets might seem uniform, for most traders sell the exactly the same products at the exactly the same price. Setting prices according to supply and demand was not relevant at the Kabala market. Here, success in trade was based on the maintenance of personal relations. Lowering prices to attract new customers would be a violation of trust and communal rules of engagement, and such a trader would soon be ostracized from the market. Selling on credit to a customer was instead one of the more common ways of establishing a lasting relationship. Most women traders had a lot of customers with outstanding debts, something that at first glance might be seen as bad for business, but this system of credit was also a way of saving money. If traders were to receive a lot of money at once, it would soon be spent on the seemingly limitless needs of family and relatives. As I described in chapter 2, many wives were preoccupied with concealing from their husbands the true extent of their resources. By selling on credit they both "saved" their money for future use and concealed it from their husbands (cf. David 1997, 63, 150; Leach 1994, 187–89). This did involve some risk, however. During the time of my fieldwork there was a general increase in all prices, particularly on imported goods and fuel, and because of this many customers were unable to repay their outstanding debts when the women needed them most.

All activities in connection with trade, buying and selling food or other products, are referred to as "market" (in Krio *makit*). Many women in Kabala aimed to do business in the central market in town. The market is the center of trade, and people from the surrounding areas bring their produce there to sell. The food market is dominated by women traders and is separated from the trade in clothes, shoes, bags, and other nonfood commodities, where there are both male and female traders. The food market was also ethnically mixed, whereas the other market was dominated by Fula traders. However, for most of my informants, to be able to rent a stall at the market was difficult and to raise the money needed to invest was almost impossible. For example, even the price of a "table," a small lidded wooden box containing various merchandise, which people often place outside their houses or along the road, was prohibitive at Le 300,000 ($120) at the time of my fieldwork, and most of my informants lived on less than a dollar a day.

One of my informants, a young woman named Sirah, who had settled in Kabala after the war with her three children, younger sister, and two parents, supported her whole family by selling kerosene. With the help of a lover who was a driver, she was able to buy kerosene in bulk, in rubber drums, from Freetown at a much lower price than in Kabala. As a rule, all imported goods are much more expensive in Kabala than in Freetown, which is the main distribution point for imported goods. The further away from Freetown, the more expensive, as the cost of transport is added. Sirah then traded the kerosene either in old plastic water bottles (*tutik rubber*) or by the measure of an old tin of tomato paste (*tamatis cup*), which are common measurements in the area. Like most of my informants, Sirah was illiterate, which made her feel that she had little control over costs, expenses, and profits. When suddenly the retail price of kerosene went up in Freetown from Le 4,600 a gallon to Le 5,000 a gallon, Sirah became very worried that she would lose a lot of money. However, since the smallest denomination in the country is the fifty-Le coin, and as Sirah had to raise her price from Le 100 to Le 150 (US$ 0.04 to 0.06) per tomato cup of kerosene to cover the increase in expenses, in reality she would make much more money then she had before.[8] Still, my calculations did not ease her worries, as she was afraid that the increase in petrol and diesel would make the transport more expensive for her.

As I have described earlier, there has been a long tradition of female traders in the region, and being a successful market woman was also a feminine ideal, as well as one of the few ways women have been able to reach positions of wealth and authority in Sierra Leone society. But most of my informants were from rural farming backgrounds and were new to semiurban Kabala. Most of their parents had been subsistence farmers, and prior to the war many of these young women would not have had other livelihood options. Becoming a wife, a mother, and a farmer, and possibly getting a few years of education, was what most women expected and experienced. In postwar society, as Aminata's case so clearly illustrates, bush wives and female ex-combatants often found it difficult to marry because many men were afraid of them, and this traditional trajectory was thereby closed to them. Still, many women I talked to said that they had no wish to return to this kind of life but wanted something else, and many dreamed of becoming successful traders. For most of them, though, this would continue to be a dream, as they had few opportunities to realize it. These girls were not entrenched in the cultural feminine ideal of trading, and to make it in business often requires the support of a patron or sponsor, something most of these girls and women did not have, cut off as they were from social networks and the flows of reciprocity due to their vulnerable and often stigmatized position. Even becoming a petty trader was difficult, and not many women were able to advance from selling firewood or fruit by the roadside to having a stand of their own. Some of my informants would move from village to town to city in search of employment opportunities but would frequently return empty handed.

The reason petty trading and vocational training became so popular was that most girls and women who had spent many years with the rebels did not want to return to farming.[9] Most opportunities for trading and training were found in towns, which meant that increasingly these women migrated from their rural areas, believing that life in town would be easier and provide more opportunities. Many explained also that they were tired of the low standards of the rural areas with few educational and health care facilities. In Koinadugu, this process of urbanization, the transition from agriculture to commerce, from village to town, was something new for this generation of girls and women. In many cases, as became clear in the village, mothers and grandmothers had rarely travelled, but were born, raised, and married in the area.[10] Town life, however, often proved to be more difficult in ways they had not always anticipated. Persson describes how for her informants in Freetown daily life was one of struggle and hardship, how every day was a fight for survival, and each day they had to face the obstacles of poverty in cramped and overcrowded housing (2005, 18). In a village, though they were still poor, people would have farms and gardens which guaranteed some basic food supplies, while in a town this was often not the case.

To be able to make it either in petty trading or in marketing their skills, almost all my informants said they wanted microcredit. Microcredits are small, short-term loans taken either by individuals or by groups. However, the repayment rates for these loans were notoriously low, making donors hesitant to implement them. Some NGOs insisted that any microcredit scheme should always be preceded by "income-generating activities" (IGA)—another NGO buzz word—basic numeracy, or other such knowledge-based training. It was also communicated to me by various organizations that it was imperative that the "beneficiaries" understand that microcredit was a loan and not a donation. There was a local alternative to microcredit loans, however, one that has a long tradition in the region, Osusu (see, e.g., Ardener 1964). In general, and compared to men, women in Sierra Leone have faced limited access to formal credit facilities and have relied to a larger extent on informal networks. Briefly, Osusu is a system of revolving funds, where a group of women contribute a certain amount every week or month, which is then distributed to one member after another until everyone in the group has received her share and the circle is complete, where it can recommence or end. Sometimes this system is added to with repayment and interest rates, and the Osusu group itself may make a profit, which might then be used for group investments. In some projects, NGOs working with minor credit tapped into this local saving system, but most organizations were still hesitant in implementing microcredit programs in the somewhat unstable postwar period.

The "Girlfriend Business"

Despite most informants' wishes to learn a craft, to trade, and to read and write, quite a number of the girls and young women who had spent the war with the rebels chose strategies other than those to survive in postwar society. Some became "girlfriends," while others became prostitutes. After I left Kabala, Mary wrote to tell me that Aminata had gone to visit her bush husband at the military base where he was stationed. Apparently he had sent a message asking her to come. She stayed for a couple of months before returning to her parents in Kabala. The reason she went, she said, was that she was grateful that he had not forgotten her or their children. However, since she knew he did not have enough money to support them, she did not stay and had to continue to make a living by her own devices. When I once asked Aminata how she made a living, she became somewhat uneasy and answered defensively, "What else do you want me to tell you? Only God knows my situation now." Still, she went on to tell me that she had a boyfriend who would sometimes ask her to cook for him, which meant that she would also be fed. Aminata felt that her parents wanted her out of their house, and that the only way for her to manage this was to find someone who would marry her. But this was far from easy. She talked about having boyfriends, but no one who wanted to commit.

> I haven't got a lover that has told me to marry. We will be together peacefully, but all of a sudden, that person will neglect me...only God knows the way I am suffering. But now we are hearing about sickness [HIV/Aids]. How can I live only on loving? Also, the worst is, my parents are poor. We all lean on that of our elder brother. Most of the time we all contribute to buy food. How long can I live like this? Things are very stiff. Nowadays men have become very cunning. They won't count even Le 10,000 [US$4] to give you.

When the current boyfriend did not provide for her she would sometimes be helped by her elder brother, or she would collect and sell stones for construction.

> But even that, it will take one to two weeks before the stones are sold. And I am afraid to love because of sickness. But no way. At times, if it takes me two days without eating, I will go to people and help them in laundering

or cooking, just for me to eat, because my elder brother also has my father, mother, three sisters, and four brothers, his own three children and wife. I am the second child. I need soap, breakfast,…that's why I am praying to God to give me a husband to care for me. As I said, nowadays boys are very cunning in giving.

This particular boyfriend she had been seeing for about three months, but like her former boyfriends he eventually said he did not want to marry her. "I don't know why, when I love, the man will like me but when I told him to marry me he will leave me," she said. I believe Aminata's situation was representative of the situation of many bush wives who returned home after the war. For some of these women, although they were happy to be relieved of the pressures of everyday life in the bush, everyday postwar life posed new challenges. Still, there were those who seemed to have the wherewithal to deal even with these challenging and testing situations.

Of all the women I have met, Musu stands out as the one who least displayed her vulnerability or victimhood. She was proud, argumentative, and tough. Yet she too had suffered immensely during the war. She had lost family members, she had been abducted, raped, forced to marry, she had become a rebel fighter, and she had not disarmed. In contrast to others, though, she did not let it consume her with shame, and she did not even try to adapt to local ideals of femininity. When I met her she was supporting her entire household on what she was getting from her two boyfriends. Marriage was apparently not an option for Musu, and she explicitly said she would not marry. Another sign of Musu's break with conventional gender norms was the way she dressed. In contrast to those ex-rebel women who had adapted well back into society and who dressed in the traditional *lappa,* Musu often wore "Western" or "shop" clothes. In Freetown young women dressed in Western clothes were commonplace, but in Kabala, which is about as far as one can go from the capital, things were more traditional. Nevertheless, even in Kabala I observed that some women, female ex-combatants in particular, often dressed in a very untraditional manner, favoring tight jeans and small tops rather than traditional dress. This choice of Western clothes has larger cultural connotations than might first seem the case. In rural areas prior to the war, it was still quite shocking for women to wear trousers (cf. Moran 1995, 84). Here, many people felt that this kind of dress was inappropriate for women, and some even believed that these kinds of clothes were the very trademark of prostitution, as they signaled sexual activity (cf. Ferme 2001, 174–75). In other words, although Musu did not let herself be confined by conventional notions about women's proper behavior or manner of dress, and one could even say that in a way she was "liberated" from these cultural conventions, the only other option available to her, and many women like her, was to behave and dress in a way that "ironically emphasizes and commandeers their sexuality" (Moran 1995, 85). It was ironic in that it was the same behavior that constituted the reason for their stigmatization in the first place, immoral sexual and social behavior. However, I have to emphasize that as these Western clothes were very expensive and most of my informants poor, not many wore them. Most of the women I worked with in Kabala owned not more than one or two *lappa,* a couple of secondhand (*junks*) T-shirts, a handful of underwear, a torn bra, and one pair of slippers, that was all.

Musu's family, as far as I know, rarely commented on how Musu was able to support the whole household through her boyfriends. It was a public secret; everyone knew but said nothing. A frequent visitor to their household, I never observed even the slightest disapproval of her very atypical feminine behavior. Musu was most definitely not a prostitute but acted in the culturally approved, although conveniently less talked about, arena of the "girlfriend." The phenomenon of girlfriends is not new to this region; it has a long history (see, e.g., Bledsoe 1980; Little 1948). In the early twentieth century it was common, for example, for male Lebanese shopkeepers to have local girlfriends whom they would visit with gifts and money (Kaniki 1973, 105). To receive gifts, material or other, from a lover was conceived of as normal, and a lack of appreciation from a lover through the presentation of gifts would invariably end the relationship. Melissa Leach mentions how many women, both single and married, used these "covert" strategies to acquire resources; they subsisted partly on favors from lovers, but they also obtained and sold resources from their husbands and male kin without explicit authorization (see also Bledsoe 1980, 8; David 1997, 150; Leach 1994, 198).[11] Leach also describes how for the Mende, most young women "strongly associate 'loving' (extra-marital sex) with material gifts, so involvement in an affair offers a significant source of economic benefit to a single or married woman" (Leach 1994, 199). Many of the young women I met, whether single, divorced, or married, quite frequently engaged in relationships with men who would give them gifts, money, food, or clothes. It is also well known that schoolgirls may engage in sexual relationships for material benefits (cf. Bledsoe 1990; Gage and Bledsoe 1994). In a manner of speaking, then, Musu attained some degree of self-determination and independence within her own household. But this was a self-determination that was tied to her being the family provider, in the only way she could be, by having lovers. In other words, "to live on loving," as Aminata said above, was a strategy that Musu could pursue to some degree without being ostracized or stigmatized by her kin. Even Mariatu, who lived in the same household as Musu, and who did her utmost to conform to tradition, once told me that "now, thanks to God, my husband is not here but Musu is helping me for food. She is in love with one big man. When he comes with money, she uses that to feed us." Musu was thus in many ways considered a "big woman" with her many dependents, but her position was tenuous, should she fail to provide for her dependents, her downfall was a likely scenario.

> As a single person, a big woman is seen as a potential sexual threat to other women's husbands, with whom she might have affairs....However, the big woman's attributes go well beyond those of a sexually predatory person....a woman is called *kpako nyaha* [big woman] precisely because she has no husband or male patron taking care of her, and this demonstrates her ability to look after herself—to be "for herself" rather than someone else....However, she usually fulfills other criteria common to her male counterparts as well, such as supporting related and unrelated dependents of her own.
>
> (Ferme 2001, 174)

Aminata, on the other hand, although she engaged in the same kinds of relationships with men, was in such an inferior position in her own household that her behavior was condemned and punished. For Musu, her personality in conjunction with the composition of her household as well as the somewhat ambiguous status of "big woman" made it possible for her to choose this livelihood trajectory without being penalized (cf. Ferme 2001, 176). In contrast to Aminata's house, Musu's was occupied almost exclusively by women. All brothers, fathers, and husbands had either died or had migrated to bigger towns in search of jobs. So, whereas Aminata had to deal with the very traditional authority of her father, in Musu's house there was no male head of household. Another aspect which differentiated

Musu's household from Aminata's was that almost all the young women in Musu's house had been abducted during the war.

Women's sexual activities are still in many ways considered shameful, more so in rural areas, but in cases like Musu's, where the whole family depended on her, people closed their eyes to it. On the one hand, women are not supposed to get involved in extramarital sexual activities. On the other hand, many formerly abducted women and female ex-combatants, and sometimes their entire families, depended on "boyfriends" and lovers to support them, and in order to be attractive to existing and potential boyfriends they had to signal sexual activity. For a woman like Musu, who seemed to have little interest in conforming to tradition, unfortunately this was her only option, as she had few other means to support herself: she had no education, she had no skills she could put into practice, and she did not have the connections or social capital to engage in trading. Although both had to live on loving, Musu in contrast to Aminata conformed to local perceptions of a "big woman" by being a provider and having many dependents. In postwar Sierra Leone, there were few other livelihood options available for women like Musu and Aminata.

Musu was not considered a prostitute, she was a "girlfriend," and this is an important distinction to make. No one who has been to Freetown in recent years can possibly have failed to notice the prevalence of prostitution in and around the areas of recreation for international staff of the UN and other agencies, since most of it takes place in the open, but in Kabala, prostitution was much less visible. None of my informants engaged in this particular form of commercialized sexual activity, although many were involved, as I have described, in the "girlfriend business," in which a woman will stay with one man for a shorter or longer period of time in exchange for money, food, or material possessions. It is well known, though, that many of the "girlfriends" and prostitutes in urban areas are female ex-combatants, many of whom could not or would not return home, for various reasons, and who saw few other options for surviving in postwar society (see, e.g., Mazurana and Carlson 2004, 3). Some researchers (see, e.g., Higate 2004, 43) have distinguished between "survival" and "consumerist" prostitution. The former is more common in war-torn societies, and some have commented that "in a war-torn society, becoming a prostitute or a camp follower may be a woman's best economic option to support herself or her family" (Bennett, Bexley, and Warnock 1995, 8).

Prostitution as a survival strategy in postwar societies is quite common, and in war-torn countries with large resident peacekeeping or humanitarian aid interests, this prostitution is often described/acknowledged as such, a survival strategy in which "women and children offer the only material asset they have to trade, their bodies" (Martin 2005, 1). That there is an increase in prostitution wherever there are UN or other peacekeepers is well known and something that has been well documented all over the world, in Bosnia, in East Timor, in Ethiopia, in DR Congo, and definitely in Sierra Leone and neighboring Liberia.[12] In a war-torn context, where there are few other means for women to earn an income, UN peacekeepers, international aid workers, and other expatriates represent an economic opportunity for some girls and women, as these expatriates almost always are much better off than the local population they are there to assist. After a visit to Sierra Leone where he was offered an underage girl for the night (an offer he refused), anthropologist Richard Wilson concluded that "humanitarian intervention, however justified, creates all kinds of hidden social costs, including turning a sizeable part of the female population into prostitutes" (Wilson 2001, 21). This is well known by the UN and other humanitarian agencies, which have acknowledged that prostitution "continues to be a survival tactic, girls are all too ready to offer their services to generate paltry amounts of disposable income to support themselves and their families" (NCRRR & OCHA 2001, as quoted by Bennett 2002, 30), and to combat this, these organizations have "codes of conduct." According to these codes it is, for example, prohibited to buy sex. However, the codes of conduct do not prohibit men from having "bona fide [*sic!*] girlfriends."[13]

In a society where some young women have lovers or "sugar daddies," and where the exchange of sex for material benefits has been a practice, there is perhaps little difference between becoming a girlfriend to a local man or to a peacekeeper or an aid worker. Interestingly, some male peacekeepers and aid workers explained these relationships through this local idiom of "girlfriends" and saw these relationships as "a pattern of gift exchange" (Higate 2004, 43). Thus, in war-torn Sierra Leone, the hypermasculine culture of military peacekeepers in an uncanny way intersected with a local culture of "girlfriends."[14]

Some relationships between foreigners and Sierra Leonean women were of course legitimate, but still, many view these relationships as unequal and exploitative (see, e.g., Barth 2004; Higate 2004; Martin 2005), in that there is often a huge difference in economic power between the two and this "makes it unlikely that there is any real choice in the relationship for the women involved" (Martin 2005, 24). Paul Higate, for example, noted that "these relationships were exploitative in that they were characterized by sharp differentials of power between privileged male peacekeepers and local women" (2004, 43). The choice of words such as *unequal* and *exploitative* to describe relationships between local women and foreign men, and in this way to distinguish them from "normal" relationships, is not entirely unproblematic, however. Personally, I oppose both prostitution and sexual exploitation, and also see these as exploitative and unequal, but I am not sure that my informants would differentiate these types of relationships from "normal" relationships between men and women in the same way, in the way Martin does above, for example. On the basis of ethnographic experience in Sierra Leone I would have to conclude, although sadly, that for my informants, the majority of whom were neither girlfriends of peacekeepers nor prostitutes, the notion of an "equal" relationship is often a foreign concept. For most of them, many of their relationships were by definition unequal, whether they were between parents and children, husbands and wives, or older and younger siblings. Still, as I have noted above, what is often termed "gender equality" is improving in Sierra Leone, especially among the educated elite. Still, for the majority of rural women, not a lot has changed.

Concluding Remarks

In Sierra Leone, the absence of fighting did bring relative stability; at least women did not have to fear abductions by rebels or soldiers alike. However, peace also poses new problems for women. One of the great ironies of postwar peace, for example, is the sexual violation of women and girls by so-called peacekeeping forces as well as the increase in prostitution that always seems to accompany large military peacekeeping operations. The postwar situation for girls and women associated with the rebels was not unknown to the institutions dealing with national and international postwar rehabilitation. Girls and women have frequently been described as the most vulnerable group in war-torn societies. Yet, as we have also seen, they get the short end of the stick, as fewer funds have been allocated to projects targeting them, in particular female ex-combatants. Also, despite the good will of the UN and NGOs, I found that the types of vocational training offered to war-affected women were not successful in securing an income for girls and women. The training programs were often too short, and there was often a lack of training materials as well. The variety and differentiation in the types of training was also extremely limited and demonstrated perhaps a lack of vision more than anything. As I have shown, most programs in postwar projects targeting girls and women in Sierra Leone focused on soap making, gara tie-dyeing, hairdressing, and tailoring. As I have emphasized, this turned into a situation in which skills radically exceeded the demand, and in terms of economic viability these projects were less than successful. Many organizations seemed afraid of entertaining complexity and more often opted for quick-fix solutions to social problems rather than addressing fundamental structural concerns. Nevertheless, in a postwar society so infused with humanitarian aid, and practically governed by the "NGO dollar," many people have become dependent on this type of assistance. It is important to note just how economy and morality were inextricably linked in postwar society, and how economic prosperity could facilitate the integration of even the most morally wayward women.

One thing not fully addressed by organizations targeting these women was that the ability of abducted and ex-combatant women to reintegrate into postwar society was not only a question of their being able to generate an income but was also largely dependent on how they were viewed in postwar society. It matters little how many projects a female ex-combatant participates in if her ability to put her skills into practice is circumscribed by society's negative view of her. As I have described, becoming an actor in the local Sierra Leone economy depended on creating and upholding social relations. For many of my informants, these were social relations from which they had been cut off. If the principle for trade could be said to rest on mutual trust, they were given none. Their war and postwar experiences seemed to have much to do with a severed social reciprocity that was seldom addressed. For these and other reasons, my informants did not always view an NGO project as their best option. Some chose other ways to make a living, some became "girlfriends" and others prostitutes. In these contexts, "loving" or prostitution becomes a survival strategy, in which those who have nothing else trade the only thing they have, their bodies. The fact that women who had been subject to war-time rapes often turned to postwar prostitution also speaks to the continuation of structural violence.

What I have described above well reflects the situation for many young Sierra Leonean women today, not only of former abductees. The cases I have alluded to illustrate not only issues of livelihood, but also issues ranging from marital disharmony and the importance of affinal relationships, to married women's relationship to their natal home. In the next chapter, I will return to the case of Aminata and examine her return home to her parents after having stayed with the rebels for some years. I will discuss how families and communities responded to "rebel women" and will examine the social dilemmas that their return sometimes created.

7

Coming Home—Domesticating the Bush

Toward the end of the war many abducted girls and women were released, some escaped, and many were abandoned by their bush husbands. But there were also those who stayed with their bush husbands and commanders, some out of fear, others by choice, and those like Aminata, who had nowhere else to go. There were those who lived in informal conjugal relationships with their bush husbands, had children or were pregnant, and were reluctant to leave for an uncertain future with their natal families. They were also concerned for their "rebel children," fearing that the children would not be well treated. Others were hesitant about returning and being forced to marry men who had paid their bridewealth when they were young. A few women told me that they loved their bush husbands, or that they felt loyal to them for saving their lives, and for those reasons did not want to leave. A former human rights advisor to the UN Mission in Sierra Leone also speculated that the reason some bush wives did not return home was because they "knew of no other life" (O'Flaherty 2004, 58). Whatever their reasons, many were uncertain of what would happen to them in postwar society.

There is no easy way to generalize the position of abducted women in postwar society. Experiences and strategies were very personal and diverse. The purpose of this chapter is to account for both personal and structural dimensions of these diversities, but also to trace commonalities. Playing a huge part in abducted women's decision to stay with their bush husbands or to return to their families were attitudes of families and society.

Coming Home

A couple of years after the declaration of peace, many abducted women and female ex-combatants, including my informants, had eventually returned to their families. Most of my informants said that people had been very hostile toward them when they first returned. In postwar Sierra Leone it was not uncommon for "rebel women" to be stigmatized and verbally and physically abused by their families, husbands, and communities. Most of my informants feared that people would find out about their rebel past and tried hard to keep the full extent of their war experiences secret. That which was not "known" should not be socially articulated. By staying with the rebels for so many years, from the perspective of their families and communities, abducted girls and women had become rebels too, whatever the circumstances of their participation. The war the rebels waged in Sierra Leone, albeit not alone, had wreaked havoc on the country and its population. Many people had lost everything they owned, and everyone knew someone who had been killed or mutilated, raped or abducted. These were things that were not easily forgotten.

After the cease-fire Aminata stayed for a year in the northern town of Makeni with her bush husband. I have outlined Aminata's history of return in the introduction, so let me just briefly recapitulate. As I described, Aminata and her bush husband returned to her native Kabala when she found out that her parents had returned from exile in Guinea. But if Aminata had held any hopes of a warm welcome they soon came to nothing, as her parents vociferously rejected both her and her bush husband. Eventually, it was decided that Aminata could stay with her children, but the marriage proposal of her bush husband was rejected and he had to leave. As it happened, Aminata's elder brother was the only one who "spoke for her," and it was because of this that she was allowed to stay. I have already mentioned that Aminata's family at this time was entirely dependent on the income of her brother. This and the fact that he was the eldest son meant that he had some leverage in any family decisions. I have also previously indicated how strong the relationship between brothers and sisters of the same mother is in this region. "Only my brother loves me," Aminata said, and seen through this prism of local cultural notions of siblingship, one can understand Aminata's brother's will to support his sister. Still, Aminata was very lonely in her family's house. Her old friends, her neighbors, and even her own family were afraid of her, and she was often avoided. Even her younger siblings refused to run errands for her, which is highly uncharacteristic for Sierra Leonean society, where those who are younger almost have "a duty to serve" their elders. Aminata's story of return was not in any way unique. Eighteen-year-old Mameh had been abducted and spent two years with the rebels. Mameh described her life as very difficult when she returned to her village, and she told me that people in her village had said that she "had come with rebel blood," and despite her efforts to behave well, they had said that she could "change at any time." Mameh too felt lonely and outcast: "They were not mingling with me," she said. Throughout the research process I came to understand that people showed an enormous distrust of young women like Aminata and Mameh. People feared that rebel women could become violent and wreak havoc in the community. Another of my informants said, "They were afraid of me because they thought that the life we were living with the rebels will be the same I will do to them."

Many informants expressed similar feelings of being excluded and marginalized in their households and in the larger communities. I interpreted this fear of rebel women and the unwillingness to forgive and reintegrate them into society as a social inability to cope with women's deviant wartime and postwar behavior. It became clear that many families and local communities were not very eager to forgive girls and women who had been with the rebels, and sometimes they saw little difference between the abductees and the fighters who abducted them. This meant that for the majority of my informants, and many women like them, their fears about returning were realized. One young woman I met frankly stated that she had been anxious about going home "for them to maltreat me—and so it happened." Paul Richards tells of a woman who had escaped after more than two years with the rebels. This woman, Rose, "was unable to return home, since people vowed vengeance upon her, believing that in surviving she had somehow become a committed member of the RUF, rather than treating her as *a survivor of an experience they could not comprehend*" (Richards 2005a, 135, my emphasis). Returning bush wives also divided families; whereas some family members were happy about their return, others were more skeptical. There was twenty-four-year-old Isatah, for example, who had been abducted for three years. A commander had taken her as a bush wife and she had been trained to fight. She was actually one of the few I met who had disarmed. After disarming she stayed in Makeni with her bush husband, when one day she heard that her mother had been seen in a village nearby. She found her, and left her bush husband to go and live with her mother and stepfather in a village. Although she was happy that they had been reunited, life for Isatah became very difficult in her stepfather's house.

> My mother was happy to receive me, only my stepfather was provoking me. He said I am a rebel, my husband is a rebel. I was pregnant and gave birth to a child, but because I had no one to take care of us he died. Imams and some elders spoke to my stepfather for him to accept me but he refused. So I left there and came back to Makeni where I have now got a husband who met my mother and my uncle.

Despite being welcomed by her mother, and the urgings of the traditional and religious leaders, Isatah's stepfather refused to accept her. As I described in an earlier chapter, it was not unusual for the relationship between children and a mother's new husband to be strained, but in this case it was likely a result of the stepfather's attitude toward and interpretation of Isatah's rebel experience. Isatah became completely marginalized in the household, and as she describes, the situation became so severe that her newborn child died. I observed that many families were ashamed of having rebel children, and speculate that Isatah's stepfather, not being a close relative, felt even less morally obligated to take her in.

Notions of shame and shameful behavior played an important part in the reintegration of girls and women who had been abducted by rebels, whether they had been fighters or not. Women who had spent many years with the rebels were worse off and seemed more severely tainted by being associated with the rebels. As I have explained above, my informants said that they were not free to talk about their experiences of war in the context of postwar society. This meant in many cases that the presumptions their families and communities had of their experiences were based on rumors and notions of rebel brutality, not on conversations with them. These notions of "wicked" rebels were further reinforced if the girls and women behaved in a manner unacceptable to their families and communities, and if they had problems adapting to the more "traditional" feminine ideal of subservience and acquiescence, hard work and self-restraint.

After the war, many of my informants were regarded by their families and communities as having engaged in socially deviant behavior. This type of nonconformity to local social norms in some cases led to social disapproval, which was manifested in an experience of social exclusion, stigma, and shame. Many of my informants said that due to their war experiences they were excluded from participating fully in the life of the community; for example, some found it very difficult to get married. In a society where the opportunities for women are few beyond the role of wife and mother, these girls and women became a social dilemma. Parents did not want to exclude their daughters, they wanted them to become moral women, but the price of this morality was sometimes very high (cf. Bunting 2005: 26). Like many young women in her situation, Aminata was made to understand that she had "disgraced" her father and "shamed" her family (*I don shame*). Although Aminata's shame emanated from behavior associated with events outside the confines of her own moral community, when she returned home the relationships the war had severed could not be realigned in any conceivable way. The shaming of the family caused by Aminata's war experience and postwar behavior dishonored her father. However, Aminata's father's honor did not rest on the protection of her body in the same way as has been described, for example, by Maria Olujic (1998) for Bosnia. But, as the father of a rebel, her father's dignity and social standing had been violated. One might speculate that since her father had few material resources and depended on the income of his son, his social status was restricted, and his daughter's history with the rebels and her current behavior became a problem to him in upholding his status and reputation in society. Had he been the main household provider, perhaps he would have been able to be more generous toward Aminata.

Although most abducted and raped girls and women I interviewed said that they had been met with distrust by their families on returning home after the war, I also encountered some who received care and support from their families, had suffered no stigma, and had become happily married when they returned home after the war. This speaks perhaps to the diversity of Sierra Leone, where different religions, languages, cultural traditions, household compositions, and levels of education and income each intersect and create a variety of alternative actions within the same town or region. In the case of another young woman, Hawa, a welcome awaited her. "My parents were really happy to see me and even the man that married me at first was happy to see me. He said he loved me. It was not my will to follow them [the rebels], that's why I have managed to escape. So after two months I went to him. And from then on he is taking great care of me and I have got two children for him." There were also those who, like Ferma, a young woman who had been abducted while pregnant, told of welcoming parents but vengeful and unkind communities. She had not spent more than six months in the bush with the rebels before she managed to escape. Her husband had been happy to see her again, because, as she said, "he loves me." As it turned out, this was not enough, because people in her husband's village still distrusted her and often called her "a rebel woman." The neighbors were frightened of her, she said, and refused them food and assistance. The situation became so difficult in the village that they decided to move to live in Kabala. Life in the town was easier in many ways, Ferma explained, and at least they were left alone and she was not verbally abused, but town life provided other difficulties. Their problem here was more one of finding enough money to survive. Still, she was happy, she said. "My husband is not doing any evil thing to me, he is talking nicely to me."

In Koinadugu District most abducted girls and women I met had returned to their area of origin, or alternatively, had married and were now settled in their husbands' homes. When I later visited Koidu, I found that the situation in Kono District was quite different. There, abducted girls and women from all over the country had remained after the war, squatting in abandoned houses until they were evicted by returning landlords, turning to the streets and, not infrequently, to prostitution. Some of those who had been living here when they were abducted had also stayed with the rebels the longest, some up to ten years. The war was very intense in the Kono area. One explanation for this is that Kono is one of the most diamond-rich areas in the country. Although the urban center, the town of Koidu, was destroyed during the war, commercial interests in that region have made for quick postwar rehabilitation. Like any urban center, Koidu offers a wide range of livelihood alternatives not found in rural villages, and this may explain the presence of so many female ex-combatants and abductees. The same can be said for the capital, Freetown, which can provide even more of everything. In contrast to my informants, none of Persson's female ex-combatant informants in Freetown lived with their natal families and none were married. Instead they lived with friends or boyfriends, and many were still enmeshed in the same networks of social relations as during the war, networks that were based on the same wartime hierarchy, in which they were at the absolute bottom (Persson 2005: 20).

Domesticating the Bush

In Kabala and the surrounding villages, for people who had not participated actively in the war, the relationships between bush husbands and bush wives were seen, just as the people who had stayed with the rebels for a long time were seen, as "wild" and belonging to "the bush." The process of rehabilitation and reintegration was thus often framed in terms of taming or domesticating their bushlike behavior. Only those who managed to change their behavior, or people's impression of their behavior, were successfully reintegrated; for the rest, there was stigmatization or, at worst, social death. As I have described previously, in chapter 3, "the bush" is a serious matter. The bush is in a dialectical relationship with the town and the village; they are opposed yet define each other. Further, transformations from the wild to the domestic must be understood, according to Jackson, as "transformations of an even more fundamental opposition: self and other" (1977, 31). Formerly abducted women had no prestige or position of status in postwar society, and as has been noted before, stigma is the negative reciprocal of prestige.

The same mechanisms and behavior that enabled girls to survive the war, that made them independent and strong, often became a problem when they returned home, and therefore also often hindered their reintegration. Susan McKay, a psychologist with extensive experience in working with girls in war-torn societies, writes that abducted girls in Sierra Leone "learned how to survive during the conflict" but states that this same survival mechanism often interfered with their reintegration (2004, 25).

"Girls who were in a fighting force for a long time may deviate seriously from the norm in terms of their behavior: they may be aggressive and quarrelsome, use offensive language, abuse drugs, smoke, and kill and eat other people's animals" (ibid.), and in her work with female ex-combatants, Mariam Persson (2005, 38) found that many were suffering from behavioral problems, they would become aggressive and were often accused of "behaving like men."

In the area where I did most of my fieldwork, ideal female behavior included subservience to elders, being humble, refraining from shouting or using foul language, and showing restraint in the display of emotion, whether it be pain or anger. All these examples were key elements in the socialization of women in this setting. "Rebel behavior" contrasted with these "traditional" ideals, and female ex-combatants and abductees were made to understand that through their *abnormal,* bushlike, and antisocial behavior they shamed their families. This was communicated through physical and social isolation. My informants described situations that demonstrate how they were severed from the flows of social reciprocity, from information, and from participation in communal activities. In the introduction, I described how Aminata's mother got up and left as soon as Aminata sat down next to her, how her younger siblings refused to do errands for her, and how she was refused food. Other women described how they were treated like the children they had been when they left, not like the grown women they had become. For some female ex-fighters, it seemed that it did not matter what they did, they were always reminded by others of their rebel past. As one of Persson's informants expressed it, "In their eyes we will always be rebels" (2005, 33).

There was little doubt that these women's involvement with the rebels in general and as fighters in particular, constituted a break with the way they had been brought up, and with the values of their society and culture.[1] A prevalent attitude among people I met, whether in towns or in villages, was that "rebel women" were maltreated because they did not *behave* in a morally accepted manner. People would say that these women and girls were "not used to village life" but to "that free life with the rebels," and that "they don't know how to talk to people," or that "they don't know how to behave." There was also that lingering threat or suspicion that they, especially those who had been fighters, might do something rash or uncontrolled. Whenever there was an argument involving one of my informants,

I noticed that everyone was quick to condemn them for their "rebel behavior," whatever the nature of the argument.

Whereas humanitarians saw the abducted women as innocent victims, their families perceived them as potentially dangerous. The notion of "the innocent victim," then, in many ways challenged local idioms of shameful behavior. Many people associated the rebels with the bush, they were wild and sometimes seen as nonhuman. The people they abducted became, by association, wild and nonhuman too. This concerned not only their social behavior but also to some extent, at least implicitly, their having been sexually active; both were seen as a direct result of their having spent a long time in the bush. It was believed that this experience had changed them radically in ways not acceptable to families and communities. This seemed to be the case for Aminata, who could find no man who wanted to marry her. Still, although I believe that the fact that Aminata had lost her virginity was one reason it was difficult for her to get married, there were other reasons as well, namely, that she was considered wild, uncontrolled, and dangerous as a consequence of her time in the bush. So although the loss of virginity, the initial rapes almost all abducted women suffered, the type of sexual abuse many women were subjected to, which I have described earlier as being influenced by pornography, all had a bearing on how women like Aminata were viewed, these were matters that could be negotiated, suppressed, or "socially forgotten" had she only behaved in a culturally appropriate manner.

Women being seen as wild, uncontrolled, and unpredictable, however, has precedence in prewar society (cf. Ferme 2001, 62) and was one of the reasons women have to be "domesticated." Older women actually told me that the purpose of female circumcision was to calm and control women's wildness. There are few models against which to measure the status and position of female ex-fighters. Most of the women I met did not conform to the notion of "big women," with Musu being an exception as described in the preceding chapter. Still there are other variables that are comparable. Because just as big women have been described as morally ambivalent, uncontrollable, and as making difficult wives, so too are female ex-fighters and bush wives viewed as confounding norms of ideal feminine or wifely behavior. Although bush wives were not supposed to possess secret knowledge and practice as did traditional big women, one might assume that the experiences of the bush might in equal terms have elicited "an excess of respect and fear in others" (Ferme 2001, 160, on big women).

Although I have focused almost exclusively on women, it was apparent that there were differences in how female and male ex-combatants were received and reintegrated into postwar society. In Kabala where I lived, I did observe that although most people knew who had been a male combatant or not, such men were not ostracized in the same way as women. People might be frightened of them, and might talk about them when they were not present, but in general they were tolerated. One reason could be that, as opposed to most female fighters, most male fighters had demobilized and had been given vocational training, supplies, and money, and thereby respect and legitimacy. After the war, while returning boys and men seemed to be considered a valuable addition to the native household economy, women were perceived as unproductive and were not, like men, regarded as potential contributors. Male ex-combatants were also high on the priority lists of both government and aid agencies, as they were perceived to be a real threat to peace and stability, and therefore their containment and reintegration became a prime concern. However, another reason was definitely the issue of morality, as I have noted above. To quote Susan Shepler, "Girls face an explicitly *moral* discourse about their participation in war" (2002, 1; see also Persson 2005, 16) in ways much different from boys. As in prewar Sierra Leone, men's sexuality was never a sensitive issue in postwar society; on the contrary, it was to be expected, and it reinforced their masculinity. The moral discourse surrounding women's participation in the war was very different from that surrounding men's. In a study on child ex-combatants in Sierra Leone, it was noted that whereas almost all boys expected to be welcomed back by their families, only half of the girls thought that their families would be happy to have them back (Bennett 2002, 46).

Former bush wives were generally looked on with suspicion and distrust. Some women were nonetheless able to reverse their initial position of social uncertainty and ambiguity, and there were ways women could maneuver around these sentiments of suspicion. The most obvious was that many women (and their families) never openly admitted that they had been abducted, saying that they had been displaced or had become refugees, or downplayed the length of abduction. It seemed that people were generally more distrustful of a woman who had spent many years with the rebels. Many of my informants thus tried to keep their wartime experiences secret for fear of people's finding out about the full extent of their rebel past (see also Persson 2005, 21). By completely conforming to social rules and obligations, former bush wives and female ex-combatants could be accepted as full members of their communities. However, this did not apply to all women. Some informants said that even if they tried to conform to social and cultural norms, they were still socially excluded. In Kabala there were also a few women who could not or would not conform. According to informants, these women had been normal before the war but after they returned home behaved as if they were crazy (*dem craze*); they wore disheveled and unkempt clothes, had dirty and nappy hair, they drank alcohol, were aggressive, and cursed and insulted people. Women like this were not believed to be possessed, a condition which it was believed could be locally cured, but they had been "damaged" by the war in a way that people could not understand or explain. NGOs would say that they were traumatized, but this word meant little to the people I talked to.

In the early postwar period in Kabala, the hospital was run by Médecins Sans Frontièrs (MSF), and it distributed legal drugs that were sometimes used to control deviant behavior. In the previous chapter I described how one woman told how she had been helped during her vocational training with her behavioral problems. She said, "I was only idle, they were giving me medicines, I was very aggressive, but now I know how to be humble. They have removed wickedness from me." And a local NGO worker told me that in their project for war-affected women, some girls would suddenly start shouting in class, and "they will become crazy, so we will take them to hospital, where they sedate them." This excessive display of uncontrolled behavior was often seen as unnatural and something that was discouraged and, if necessary, controlled by medical substances.

There were those in the communities who were more tolerant, however, who saw this type of "wild" behavior among abducted girls as a result of the drug abuse they had been subjected to and of their experiences while with the rebels, and saw these emotional outbursts as something to be expected initially. But for those girls and women who, a couple of years after the end of the war, would still become aggressive and "quarrelsome," little tolerance was shown. Some women who had returned home eventually decided to leave, as life had become too difficult for them. Many lacked viable livelihood opportunities, as I have described in the previous chapter, and many others found that they had changed so profoundly that they could not or would not adapt to their communities (cf. McKay and Mazurana 2004, 37).

In some cases, it seemed that the past experiences of my informants could be, if not forgiven, then simply and conveniently "forgotten." It was not only the actual events and experiences of war per se that members of families and communities reacted against, it was their permutation into postwar life—their intrusion in the present—which was problematic. To some extent, then, as long as an abducted girl or woman, fighter or not, behaved well and complied with "traditional" norms, and the effects of her wartime experiences were not too obvious, people were more inclined to accept her. This is not uncommon in war-torn societies, and Schroven noted that "many people wish to return to 'traditional' notions of social interaction, opposing the war's chaos and instead seeking stability and a familiar order" (2005, 87). Getting married was often seen as a solution to many of the problems surrounding abducted young women and female ex-combatants in postwar society. For girls, marriage was seen as solving the problem of reintegration in a way that was unavailable to boys (Shepler 2002, 13). It was assumed that through marriage they would become more honorable and would be kept busy with the chores of domestic life. In other words, marriage was seen for many abducted girls and women as the only viable option and the only way to reintegrate, yet this proved to be difficult, as few families wanted "rebel women."[2] This may be related to the fact that men and their families knew that abducted women had been sexually active during the war; rebel women were "damaged goods," as I have discussed above. That marriage, and not other means, was the preferred solution to a social problem can most likely be related to the fact that marriage, not education or work, has been the dominant trajectory in the lives of girls and women. Shepler noted that some NGOs even "encouraged girls to marry their former commanders and captors" (2002, 14). To the Western observer this may seem absurd, but consider Aminata's case: she wanted to formalize the marriage with her bush husband, but her family refused.

As I have described above, although Aminata's parents refused to formalize her bush marriage, her father still desperately tried to get her married to other men, but all declined when they learned about her rebel past. These experiences of rejection as well as the way she was treated in her home, made Aminata reminisce about her bush husband. "They refused the [bush] marriage, and I haven't got another husband. That is really troubling me. Even if he doesn't have money, but if I should have been with him, it should have been better." Aminata was not alone in experiencing this; many women were so unhappy with their postwar lives that they often spoke of returning to their bush husbands. One young woman I met, Finda, continued to meet her bush husband in secret, as her parents had told him not to come to their house. When I asked her why she was still seeing him, she replied, "Because no one loves me again, and for the children." Like many others in similar situations, Aminata and Finda found that their parents and community did not accept their bush husbands and therefore they could not formalize these relationships. Although these women were called "wives" and their relationships with their men were called "marriages," these were prefixed by "bush" and as such were not culturally valid, since they had not been negotiated or sanctioned by family or community. The "transfer" of these girls and women to their so-called husbands had not been legitimate: they had been abducted, and remunerations to the girls' and women's families had been made neither for the emotional loss of a family member nor for their reproductive and productive labor, as is customary in "traditional" society. Schroven notes that the terms *bush wives* and *bush marriages,* "related the origin of the marriage to the bush, and were therefore 'uncivilized', 'unregulated' and also implied rebel associations. As such they had not been sanctioned and were therefore often considered 'un-approvable'" (2005, 76). The fact that bush marriages were neither socially nor culturally endorsed may explain why Aminata's father continually rejected the bush husband's marriage proposals, even though no other man wanted to marry her. Bush marriages were not proper marriages, as Mariatu so emphatically pointed out, somewhat upset by my question about it.

> Is that marriage? That type of marriage was to pass time. If it should have been me, as the country is cool [at peace], I should have said, "I don't love you any longer." This is because one day, as you were in the bush, one day he will treat you that way. In the bush, as I was with him, it was to save my life, [for him] not to kill me. But now, I know that when he kills me, they will kill him. So I will say, "I don't want you." But some [abducted women] are with them, giving birth to children for them. Some, up to now, they are not thinking of their relatives.

Mariatu on the other hand did not have to face Aminata's situation, as her bush husband had been killed during the war. When she returned to Kabala she met the man she had been engaged to before the war and married him. In a sense she was lucky that this man did not think her "spoilt" by her association with the rebels. Still, Mariatu had to live with the fact that other people, in particular her husband's kin, were suspicious of her for having been with the rebels for so long. She explained that she was worried that they were blaming his frequent bouts of illness on her. "I have just been married to this man and he is always sick. They will say I gave him these sicknesses. They will also say, 'This is not your lucky wife', more especially [when I have] come from the bush." At the time of my fieldwork Mariatu's husband lived and worked as a manual laborer in the diamond fields in Kono. Even so, the money he made was not enough to support his family in Kabala. Mariatu looked after his mother and kept him informed about what was happening in the house. As I described in the previous chapter, Mariatu lived in the same household as Musu, and was indirectly supported by Musu's lovers. In contrast to Musu, however, Mariatu was really working hard to become the perfect subservient wife; she was always humble, soft spoken, and never argumentative, she respected her mother-in-law and the other affines and contributed greatly to the domestic work of the household.

Despite the obvious brutalities of and suffering in war, some of my informants felt that life in the bush had not been that bad, especially favored wives of rebel commanders, who had lives of relative wealth during the war (cf. McKay and Mazurana 2004, 93). Looting also seemed to be a reason "why some women stayed in the movement: in a society which had so deprived them, they knew that they would never get the opportunity to earn legally a fraction of their gain from raiding and looting towns and villages" (Mansaray 2000, 146). These women often did not like the prospect of a return to impoverished communities. Their elevated status during the war did not translate into prestige in postwar society, and many were very disappointed with their situation. Not only did they not or could they not disarm, they were frequently abandoned by their bush husbands and ostracized in the communities they returned to. One of Persson's informants told her, "In a way life was easier in the bush, I was the wife of a commander and people respected me for that. Now I have to live with people calling me bad names and mistrusting me, I have to bear the shame of having been a rebel" (2005, 42). Considering the hardships many women experienced in postwar society, it is not surprising that some of them became nostalgic for, or idealized, the past. These feelings were also infused with ambiguity, as they were just as ashamed to admit having enjoyed the war as they were of having been in it. But there were also those like Musu who were happy that the war was over but still did not want to return to a "traditional" way of life.

Given the hardship many of my informants encountered when they returned home after the war, it is not surprising that some of them decided to leave. There were those who thought that it had not even been worth coming back. There were many instances where girls went back to their bush husbands after they had been reunited with their families.[3] For some it seems that leaving their village was less a choice than a necessity, and the return to a bush husband sometimes had less to do with love and loyalty to him, than that village life had been unbearable due to harassment and provocation, or sometimes just poverty. As I described above, Aminata saw returning to her bush husband as her best option. In Persson's words, "To stay meant to every day have to face those who knew their past and that blamed them for their losses and suffering. It meant constant stigmatization and rejection" (2005, 33). I have also mentioned Kadi, she who at the age of nine was abducted by the rebels and had stayed with them for six years. Kadi was her mother's youngest child, around sixteen years at the time of my fieldwork. She had a baby daughter with her bush husband, and she was waiting for him to send a message for her to join him in the soldiers' barracks in the town where he was stationed after being recruited by the new army. Kadi said she still loved her bush husband, although he had first deserted her when she became pregnant. Kadi's father had died, her brothers had all left Kabala to look for work in Freetown, and she lived with her mother, sisters, and other female in-laws. Kadi's mother had been dead set against the marriage between Kadi and her bush husband and made it clear that she had not accepted the marriage, but being poor and unable to provide for Kadi and her young child, she realized that she had little to bargain with, and silently but still reproachfully let Kadi leave for her husband when he finally sent for her. I drove Kadi myself to Makeni, where she was to take transport to the town where her bush husband lived. She wore her nicest clothes and seemed happy but also a little subdued; she talked little during the trip. Some time before her departure, I had arranged for her to go to school and had also given her a school uniform and some books. She had tried for a couple of months, and I believe she also really wanted to please me, but she found it hard to return to school and told me with some difficulty that she wanted to quit. In the circumstances she was facing, returning to her bush husband was one of the few options she could envisage, and she took it.

To sum up, some of the women I interviewed said that they loved their bush husbands and felt grateful to them for saving their lives during the war. Others said that they had few prospects of getting another husband and that at least the bush husband, if he had disarmed, had received some sort of vocational training with some hope of getting work and money. However, what of the case of Aminata and so many others who wanted to formalize their marriages with their bush husbands but had families that would not sanction this relationship? There are still many girls and young women who feel that these relationships should be formalized and accepted by their families, because the alternative, leaving parents and family to live with a man who has been rejected, has great social ramifications, especially if they live in the same community. Girls and women risk facing a complete break in social relations with their kin in such situations, thereby severely limiting their ability to negotiate their position in relation to a husband or, alternatively, his kin. They have nowhere to turn if the marriage fails, and the relationship for future generations is permanently severed. As I have mentioned, after marriage most women have frequent contact with their families. In most cases, the young women, their families, and also their former bush husbands would try to settle disputes by all possible means, through religious leaders, chiefs, and mamy queens, or through mediation by other relatives or family members, before resorting to actions that would, at worst, mean social exclusion. My research shows that it was not only the rebel abduction itself that defined the status of abducted women and female ex-combatants in postwar society but also *how* they behaved after returning to their communities. It was clear that in assuming traditional female behavior like subservience and humbleness, and in some cases religiosity, many formerly abducted women improved their status in postwar society and were less discriminated against in everyday social life. However, for some this came at a high cost and was far from easy.

Rape in War and Peace

As I discussed above, the notion of women's wartime sexual activity was not the only reason for their postwar dilemmas, and although the loss of virginity by war rape was often emphasized in interviews it did not seem to determine most of my informants' futures. However, I will not deny that the notion of lost virginity still had great social significance. War rapes are effective precisely because they highlight "preexisting sociocultural dynamics," argued Olujic (1998, 31), and therefore it is necessary to examine how the rape of virgins was communicated and interpreted in both prewar and postwar Sierra Leone society. The concept of shame was central in the moral universe surrounding girls and women who had spent time with the rebels, and shame had a great deal to do with women's bodies, and that this was a cultural logic that long preceded the war. Women's bodies were perceived as holding the future, and any breach of the conceived purity of women's bodies in this society could have far-reaching consequences. It is obvious that attitudes about young women's sexual activity, though not necessarily their actual sexual activities per se, were at the core of the way women were valued and esteemed, before, during, and after the war.

It was said that during the war, virgins, or young women who were thought to be virgins, had been especially targeted for rape. One report explains the high incidence of rape of virgins during the war with virginity's being seen as a sexual prize, and virgins being conceived of as sexually desirable (Bambrick 2004, 25). This report also notes that in Sierra Leone only the rape of a virgin is considered to be rape, and many people do not see the rape of a sexually active woman as a rape, although there was some indication that these attitudes were slowly changing, especially among young people. The rape of a virgin is seen in Sierra Leone as a serious crime, as it is believed that rape decreases girls' chances of marriage; they are seen as "spoilt." This notion relates to initiation practices in the region, where girls are expected to be virgins on entering marriage. It has been reported that girls were blamed for having been raped (cf. Shepler 2002), and McKay also found that virgins who had been raped were "considered 'spoiled goods' and targeted for sexual assault by male members of the community" (2004, 25). Generally, I found that people did not blame the girl, as though it had been her own fault that she had been raped, but that they did recognize that she was "damaged goods." Even though women of all ages were raped during the war, in my interviews many girls or very young women emphasized that they had been *virginated* (lost their virginity).[4]

Sometimes people had little tolerance or understanding for women with experiences similar to those of Aminata. There was Finah's husband, for instance, who every day told her, "You rebel woman, I don't want you!"

Before the war, Finah, whom we have met in the earlier chapters, had been engaged to a man who had paid for her initiation and bridewealth. When she came back after the war this man did not want her and threatened to take her parents to court if he did not get his bridewealth back. Finah knew that her parents could not possibly come up with the money, so the man was persuaded to take her and she married him, although this was something neither of them wanted.[5] She told me that she and her husband were not very close, and she felt that he did not trust her. Since they married she has had two children, but one died. She said her husband did not care for her or even for the children. She was also the third and most junior wife and did not have much say in household matters. She said she only accepted marrying him because her parents could not afford to refund the bridewealth. Initially she thought she could make it work, that if only her husband was patient with her, he would notice that her behavior was "not that of a rebel" and would treat her better, but now, "every day I think about leaving him," she said, but she would have to find another man who could reimburse the bridewealth. She said she behaved well but that her husband and his family still did not trust her. "My husband doesn't want me since I was abducted. Whatever I do, he says I was with the rebels." During her time in the bush Finah was never chosen as a bush wife, which means that she was continually abused by any number of men. Finah was not shy about talking about the sexual abuse she suffered during the war, as the following interview shows.

> CHRIS: Since all the women that were captured were raped, and everyone knows this, why are many women afraid or ashamed to talk of it?
>
> FINAH: I don't know, but I am not ashamed
>
> CHRIS: Why?
>
> FINAH: The reason why I am not ashamed is that because of what they did to me. I am not happy. I was a virgin, hoping to go to my husband a virgin. They virginated me and then I got sickness. Everyone was sexing me, up to the time I left them, and up to now, that has brought dispute in my family.
>
> CHRIS: So would you want the men that did this to you to be punished?
>
> FINAH: Yes, if the man is alive, I want them to punish that man, because the man has made me to be crying.
>
> CHRIS: Not only at that time but even now?

FINAH: Even right now, when I am saying it, I am crying inside my heart

CHRIS: Will you ever be happy again?

FINAH: I don't think I will be happy again, because the man I am married to is always provoking me.

CHRIS: But since divorce is so common here, many women will have married one or two or three times, so she'll only be a virgin at the first marriage?

FINAH: That one, the divorce case, then the man has known that he took her from another husband, this woman was married once. But this one, the man engaged me since I was small. So my own case is different from those.

As I have showed in a previous chapter, the divorce rates in the region were very high, so one can assume that virginity was not imperative for marriage in general, but even so, as Finah described, it was imperative to be known to be a virgin on entering the first marriage. At the initiation ceremony I attended, virginity was emphasized by the elders, but it was apparent that many young women already "knew" men, in a biblical sense.[6] What was important was who knew about the girls' premarital sexual affairs. Also, it has been noted elsewhere in Sierra Leone that premarital sex was not as big an issue as preinitiation sex (Gage and Bledsoe 1994, 155). Nevertheless, in many of my interviews, it was obvious that *virgination* had moral connotations, and the telling of such experiences was often accompanied by sentences such as "He disgraced me," "He spoilt me from my parents," or "I am spoilt." In a report this is interpreted as "if a girl has had sexual contact with a man outside marriage—voluntarily or not—she is considered to *no longer have value* in society" (Save the Children 2005, 12, my emphasis). I do not share this analysis. In fact, I did not find a strong emphasis on premarital or extramarital sexual relations; my sense was that they were rather commonplace. This is not to say that there are not exceptions. For example, Mary explained to me that for the Fula people in the area, the protection of virginity before marriage was more emphasized than among the other groups. As I noted above, most of my informants explained that many girls had sex before both initiation and marriage. For them, protecting their reputation was more important than protecting their actual virginity. Still, traditional and religious gender norms imply that a girl should be a virgin on entering her first marriage. This may explain why after the war, when everyone knew that most abducted girls and women had been raped, some girls faced negative attitudes from their families and communities when they returned home, as is illustrated by the cases of Aminata and Finah. The difference was that Finah's husband relented and agreed to marry her, whereas Aminata was rejected.

Virginity has a price, articulated through the exchange of bridewealth for the first marriage. This is another instance where morality and economy, in the social and cultural context of northern Sierra Leone, become intertwined and mutually imbricated. As I noted above, the women felt that they were spoilt or damaged goods; they were in a sense no longer marketable. This may also be why the girls and women themselves made a distinction between having been raped and having been violently virginated. Perhaps the fact that so many virgins were raped during the war, and that people knew this, was the reason for the strong emphasis placed on virginity in postwar marriage negotiations. It was not clear if this view—of damaging or spoiling—applied to all sexual relations with virgins, otherwise often described as playful and exciting encounters, or only to the violent sexual abuse of war rapes. In any case, this postwar emphasis on virginity did not translate into an increase in bridewealth at the time, rather the opposite.[7] In the fragile postwar economy, people had very few resources, and as I mentioned in chapter 2, one of Morowa's wives was very disappointed with the small bridewealth she received from her daughter's new in-laws. Informal bridewealth, such as later gifts and the bride service of the husbands, was difficult to realize as well, as I have also described, because people were poor and many men had left for an uncertain future in the diamond areas.

It is well known that all over Africa young girls who are raped face difficulties in finding someone willing to marry them, and they sometimes feel forced to marry the man who raped them out of fear of stigmatization (see, e.g., Amnesty International 2000; McKay 2004; Shepler 2002; Women's Commission for Refugee Women and Children 2002).[8] Although to most Western observers there is an abyss between consensual sex and rape, in Sierra Leone the divide is not that clear. Even if a woman has been raped it is not certain that her community would consider it a rape. As I mentioned above, abducted women often made a distinction between the initial rape and the sexual abuse they experienced in bush marriages.[9] As the idiom of marriage was applied to intimate relations between men and women in the bush, perhaps sexual coercion in this context was considered by the girls and women, if not normal, then to be expected. Whereas many NGOs in the area have focused on war rapes in general, I found, as I have described, that my informants and their families clearly distinguished between the rape of virgins and the rape of sexually active women, and that according to their interpretations of the initial sexual violence, only virgination was a "real" rape. Many of my informants had been girls when they were abducted, and had returned grown women. When they left their homes they had not been socially mature, and later, when they came back, they were not the virgins they had been, nor the married women they could have been. As they had not been ritually incorporated into society as moral women, they found themselves in limbo: they could not become social virgins again, nor could they get married. And as in the case of Aminata, the only man who wanted to marry her was rejected.

Rape of underage girls is a crime under Sierra Leone national legislation.[10] Sierra Leone has also signed and ratified the Convention on the Elimination of All Forms of Discrimination against Women (CEDAW), and the Additional Protocol to the African Charter but has failed to domesticate them into national law. Nevertheless, despite its prevalence, rape and sexual violence is not something that has been a priority in the Sierra Leone court system; in fact, there has been a culture of impunity surrounding rape and sexual abuse.[11] Marital rape, for example, was not recognized under Sierra Leone law until the passing of the Domestic Violence Act in 2007. The first successful prosecution of a rape case involving an adult woman in a Sierra Leone court took place only in 1999.[12] Issues of sexuality in general and rape in particular have been taboo to discuss publicly, and in much literature on this issue, the phrase "a culture of silence" is often invoked (see, e.g., Bambrick 2004; Women's Commission for Refugee Women and Children 2002). The tolerance for sexual violence in Sierra Leonean courts has generally been quite high, and communities have used other ways than the formal legal system to deal with accusations of rape.

With the establishment of the Family Support Unit (FSU) of the Sierra Leone Police after the war, the numbers of rape cases in the domestic setting to go to court have increased. The work of the FSU is not easy, however, and it is restrained both financially and to some extent culturally. Some of the rural women I interviewed said that they would never dream of taking a rape case to the FSU, as this would make members of their family and the family of the perpetrator enemies for life, which was perceived as potentially having far-reaching consequences in the tight-knit communities of small rural villages. Instead, cases of rape and sexual abuse in rural areas have more frequently been brought before the chief and settled in customary court, and have usually involved "damages" or fines to be paid by the perpetrator or his family to the family of the victim. This strategy has been favored by rural village people as it aims for a restoration of balance and mediation between both individuals and families in society. Taking a case to the police, on the other hand, is interpreted as the last resort, something you do if all else fails.

A police officer in an FSU in Kono was very critical of the "traditional" way of settling rape as a dispute between families. First of all, he said, although the victim's family might be remunerated for the shame imposed on them, the money will stay in the family, often with the father, and the girl will receive little or nothing. Second, and far worse according to him, was that in rape cases taken to traditional court, the girls are rarely if ever sent for medical examination. In the "traditional" way, then, the social shame of the act is dealt with, but the rape can have caused serious damage to a girl's health which, according to him, goes untreated. Thus taking a rape case to the FSU and later to court had social ramifications that seemed difficult to solve. Also, if a case were ever to have a chance of going to court, a medical examination was needed, and the cost of these examinations was borne solely by the victims. This, according to the police officer at the FSU in Kono, was the main reason most rape accusations were withdrawn by the victim or family.[13] Further, if a case ever went to court, the medical examiner was requested to testify, increasing the burden on the few medical doctors who worked in rural areas. Sometimes doctors had to travel to the capital to testify if the case went to a higher judicial level. Court cases have been known to drag on for a long time and may take months, if not years, to proceed. This was largely due to the lack of qualified magistrates in the country, particularly in the rural areas. In Koinadugu District, for example, the magistrate came only every fortnight, as he was also serving in a neighboring district. On his biweekly return to Kabala, the district capital, only the most urgent and critical cases were brought to trial and the others postponed indefinitely. It is difficult to see how the work of the newly established Family Support Unit, when it comes to rape and other forms of sexual and domestic abuse, which are also socially complicated, will progress under such harsh conditions. Police officers often said that their work would be easier if medical examinations in rape cases were free of charge and if there were more qualified magistrates working in the districts.

War rapes, however, are another matter altogether. Already in Article 3 of the 1949 Geneva Conventions, war rapes were a violation of international humanitarian law—in theory, though in practice we know that it was not until 1996 in the Hague War Crimes Tribunal that the first offenders were prosecuted and convicted.[14] In Sierra Leone, the Special Court is charging the leaders of the RUF with an eighteen-count indictment for crimes against humanity, of which four charges fall under the rubric of sexual violence and consist of (1) rape, (2) sexual slavery and any other form of sexual violence, (3) other inhumane acts, and (4) outrages upon personal dignity. The prosecutors will also, for the first time at a war crimes tribunal, try in court to show how acts of forced marriage "were and are inhumane acts and should forever be recognised as a crime against humanity."[15] As rape is one of the main reasons abducted women feel shame and are stigmatized by communities, many women's rights activists in Sierra Leone welcome these charges, hoping that public awareness and condemnation of these acts of sexualized violence will change the way people perceive rape victims. Because, as Binta Mansaray noted, "For some women, life [after the war] will never be the same; while men can move on, remarry and start new families, women victims of rape have no such chance. Although they are victims, their lives are forever marred by the social stigma associated with rape" (2000, 143). Persson too identified rape and sexual abuse as one "of the most important reasons for the shame and stigmatization attached to female ex-combatants" (2005, 35).

According to numerous reports, rape was so common in parts of Sierra Leone as to make it almost "normal." In certain areas that were especially hard hit, it is no exaggeration to say that almost every woman was raped, at least once. Abduction by rebels or soldiers and sexual slavery also existed to an unprecedented degree. Of the girls and young women I worked with, all but two had been raped at least once during their abduction. Yet this is still largely a taboo subject, rarely mentioned in public, or by representatives of the government, as a problem that needs to be dealt with. Although rape was a moral disgrace and the issue of shame loomed large in abducted girls' and women's postwar lives, there were also more tangible problems affecting their quality of life. Due to the sexual abuse she experienced during the war, Aminata suffered for a long time from vaginal pains and sexually transmitted diseases (STDs). This is very common in Sierra Leone, where many still suffer from STDs, which in some cases have led to infertility, and this is real social problem for many women in rural Sierra Leone. Eventually Aminata was treated, but many of the women I met were still suffering from the sexual abuse they experienced during the war: they complained of abdominal pains, vaginal problems (such as discharges), incontinence, and infertility. The majority of these girls do not have the funds to seek medical help for these ailments, and most emergency projects that addressed these needs without charging fees had left Sierra Leone, three years after the official declaration of peace.

That women and sexuality is a complicated issue was also reflected in how my informants viewed matrimonial sexual intercourse. Many of my older female informants, for example, explained that a wife could not easily reject a husband's demand for sex, while younger women were more divided on the subject. When I asked one young woman if a husband could demand sex even if the wife did not want it, she answered, "No, they are not allowed to do that. If you are in need of your wife you should kiss her, encourage her in love, so the woman also will know that this man is in need. She will be sorry for him and give herself. But if you bring it that forced way, I will show you that I also have small power. There is awareness. Most girls now have *awareness trousers*.[16] So for you to take that out, I won't allow." Most of the younger women I talked to agreed with this last statement, men should not be allowed to force their wives to have sex, and a few even said that it was tantamount to rape, although as mentioned above, marital rape was not a crime in Sierra Leone at that time. But there were also a few young women who felt that it was a husband's prerogative to have sex whenever he wanted, and that there was little they could do about it. Older women were still more likely to say that it was a wife's duty to have sex with her husband even if she did not want to.[17]

Under customary law a wife can refuse sex only if she is ill or breastfeeding, and for Muslims, during Ramadan (Human Rights Watch 2003, 18). According to some sources, these beliefs have "translated into a high rate of intimate partner violence and rape" (Bambrick 2004, 27; see also Human Rights Watch 2003; Physicians for Human Rights 2002). "Violence in sex is not questioned, but instead attributed to the evil sexuality of a woman," wrote Bambrick (2004, 26–27), who also argued that women's dangerous sexuality "is seen as an invitation to force." Apart from sexually transmitted diseases, there were, of course, other consequences of wartime rapes, namely pregnancy. Although some women had abortions and many more miscarried, there are still today many children who were the products of this sexualized violence, which I will turn to next.

Rebel Babies, ECOMOG Babies, and UN Babies

In postwar Sierra Leone it became obvious that many of the children born to abducted mothers were often stigmatized and sometimes even ostracized by their communities. People openly referred to them as "rebel babies." However, there were also many "ECOMOG babies" (after the West African peacekeeping soldiers) and "UN babies." All of these epithets have very negative connotations locally. In Kabala, where the UNAMSIL battalion was from Bangladesh, there were, for example, numerous light-skinned children between the ages of one and three named "Bangla." The attitudes in society surrounding children named Bangla or rebel children varied, naturally, and were often very complex. Some children were treated well, while others were constantly reminded of their paternal origin. In any event, these children not only face an uncertain future in society, but there is also the question of their legal position in postwar society. In traditional Sierra Leone society children belong to the father and the father's lineage, and perhaps because of this, the situation for rebel children who have no recognized fathers, or whose fathers are presumed to be "wicked" and "evil," is quite volatile (see, e.g., Bennett 2002, 50). Unfortunately, although most people—ordinary Sierra Leoneans, NGO workers, and international agencies—were aware of the precarious situation of rebel children in particular, little was done to address this, either on policy levels or in local projects.

I first met Kadiatu in 2001. She had been pregnant when she escaped from the rebels after many years in captivity. Nine months pregnant, she arrived in the capital with nowhere to go and she literally gave birth on the street. After some days she managed to get help and shelter from a Christian organization that had been active in her home region. Some of the women who were staying in the shelter told her that she should kill the child or leave him somewhere; they said it was a "bad child" and that it had "rebel blood." One day, she told me, she was sitting on a bridge, thinking about her life and the future of her children. She asked herself how she would raise this newborn child when she could hardly care for her older son. She was almost about to throw the baby in the river when a man approached her and said, "Don't even think about it!" She tells of this moment as something that changed her life, and she decided then and there to love and care for her child whatever happened.

The notion that rebel children have "bad blood" or are "wicked" was widespread. This became obvious to me when I met Kadiatu again three years later in Kabala, where she had resettled. The baby she had decided to love had now become a big and healthy boy. Yet everyone in the neighborhood knew that he was a rebel child and was not ashamed to point this out, especially if he got into trouble. The boy was said to have a bad temper and was also seemingly unafraid; without hesitation he would protect his older brother and throw stones at older children who were pestering them. Sadly, this behavior further marked him and reinforced people's prejudices about rebel children's behavior. This was quite a common phenomenon in Kabala. So-called rebel children were often identified as troublemakers and people had many preconceptions about their mentality and behavior. Only few women managed, through social skills, connections, and luck, to integrate their *rebel pikindem* into family and social networks. I met one such woman, Sita, who had a child born of a rebel father. During the first years after the war she too struggled to make ends meet and to care for her child. Since then she has since remarried, and her son, formerly named Savage (his father was the renowned rebel commander Savage), was doing well in this new milieu. Sita explained why her son was no longer singled out as a rebel child. She had quite quickly renamed him to the more inconspicuous Foday, and then she had been lucky in that her new husband did not discriminate against him. After a few months, the boy, who appeared to be around five or six years old, had also calmed down, she said; he no longer had aggressive fits or used foul language but had assimilated well into society. Sita's son was nevertheless one of the few positive examples; for the majority of rebel children the situation was not as encouraging. Some people I met in Sierra Leone seemed to fear these children, as if they were the embodiment of their rebel fathers, since they carried their "bad blood" and therefore could "become wicked." Something that caught my attention was the fact that I rarely encountered or heard of female rebel children. It was always boy children who were singled out, which indicated to me that perhaps mothers of female rebel children did more to protect their identity out of fear of future ramifications (cf. Nordstrom 1997b).

Having rebel children severely limited these women's prospects of finding new husbands. As Aminata reflected, "Maybe that's why up to now no man has ever told me to marry him, more especially when I have rebel children." After refusing to let Aminata marry her bush husband, her father tried to arrange for her to marry to a young man he knew. But as I have described above, this man rejected Aminata when he found out that she had been a rebel and had two rebel children. In Finah's case, the bush husband no longer felt obliged to provide for her or their children after her parents had rejected him. And another girl I met lamented, "One man had wanted to marry me, but people said, 'That captured woman is what you want?' So people were provoking us as that we went with them [the rebels] willingly. They were afraid of us. There was no encouragement." It is likely not only that the men feared marrying ex-rebel women, but that they were wary of the extra financial burden of supporting children who were not their own and had no fathers. Perhaps these men also feared for their reputation and social standing, afraid that the rebel children would affect them negatively.

Six-year-old Zainab had a father who had been a Nigerian ECOMOG peacekeeper. Since the war ended her mother, Sirah, has tried many times to contact him by the postal and e-mail addresses he left with her, with no success. There was no telecommunication in Kabala at the time, and the postal services were irregular and not very reliable; Sirah could not often afford to travel to the capital to have someone send an e-mail for her (she was illiterate), or to try calling the number he had given her. This is apparently not unusual; in Sierra Leone there are many UN/ECOMOG babies whose fathers left the country without making any provisions for them (Bennett 2002, 50).[18] It has been suggested in a recent UN policy report that DNA testing should be used to prove paternity and that peacekeepers should be made to provide child support for any children they father while on mission (Zeid al-Hussein 2005). Although left with sole responsibility for raising her daughter, Sirah has nevertheless managed to provide for her and her other children. Unlike most children of rebels, Zainab was not singled out or in any way stigmatized: her mother had been very particular in emphasizing that her relationship with Zainab's father had been of a more formal nature. She often told of how the man had come to see her parents when she was pregnant, and how he had offered some amount of money and kola nuts to them. Sirah had somehow also managed to legitimize the child by giving Zainab her father's surname.

These war children were living proof of their mothers' sexual activity during the war, but their position as outcasts in society was also in a sense a reflection of the cultural notion of women as "property," that they were not of and for themselves, that they and their children ideally should *belong to* someone. It seemed that many mothers appropriated and internalized to some extent the responses of their communities, and that for some, these children only reinforced their feelings of shame and stigma. Being single, many were also the sole providers for their children, and for some, unable to return to their families and abandoned by their bush husbands or boyfriends, there were few livelihood opportunities. It is not unusual that some of these women support themselves and their children through prostitution, particularly in the urban areas. A few are also still addicted to drugs, especially those who make a living through prostitution. It would not take a leap of the imagination to presume that some of these children, born under difficult circumstances, to mothers addicted to drugs with little or no means to support them, rejected by both their maternal and paternal kin, and by society at large, will face a rather grim future. Perhaps we are facing a situation where "the exclusion of single mothers means the exclusion of their children and thus another generation of unskilled, marginalized youth" (Mazurana and Carlson 2004, 5). This could imply that the notion of rebel children as inherently troublesome could become a self-fulfilling prophecy.

Concluding Remarks

In this chapter I have focused on issues concerning the relationships between abducted girls and the families and communities they returned to. In Sierra Leone, peace did not entail a return to normalcy, and although many had suffered throughout the war, peace did not necessarily mean the end of violence and abuse for many rebel women. Many were afraid to return home, fearing rejection by their families and communities. With good reason, they were afraid of being punished for returning with rebel children, for not being virgins, and for being called rebels. The women they had become were very different from the girls they had been when they were abducted. In postwar society many people were very suspicious of ex-rebels and distrusted them, and abducted women were not exempted.

Although many women were later stigmatized for having been raped, some were not, and although many women were viewed with suspicion for having fought with the rebels, again, others were not. Many people were disturbed by the fact that female fighters had killed and engaged in other brutal acts, and this characterized the way they viewed these women in postwar society, but others just shrugged and explained that a lot of bad things happened during the war, this was nothing exceptional. The postwar consequences of war rapes in Sierra Leone differed immensely from Bosnia, for example, where most families would shun their raped daughters because of permanent damage to the family honor (Olujic 1998). Even so, because rape was still seen in Sierra Leone as shameful for the victim, especially if she had been a virgin, most abducted women who tried to fit into society kept experiences of sexual abuse a secret. The way people in the communities interpreted war rapes, was grounded in preexisting notions of rape and sexual morality. As I have argued consistently, Sierra Leone is a country full of diversity and contradiction, and some of my informants who had been abducted, virginated, and had been fighters still managed to acclimatize well into postwar society, *if* they managed to conform to cultural conventions of feminine behavior, and *if* their social circumstances and the composition of their household were such as to make this change possible.

CONCLUSION

Life in a War-Torn Society

In the introduction I posed a series of specific questions after presenting the case of Aminata. I asked what had happened to Aminata during the war and why her return to her family after the war had been so difficult. I also asked why people were afraid of women like Aminata and why her parents were dismayed at her return. After trying unsuccessfully to get her married to other men, why could Aminata's father simply not legitimize her bush marriage? I also wondered why Aminata could not just leave her family and go to live with her bush husband anyway. Since she could not get married and had to stay in her family's compound, she had to find food and money for herself, and I inquired into what the options were for women like Aminata to make a living. Although these questions were specifically generated from the case of Aminata, they have wider relevance, and, as I have described throughout this book, these questions have no simple and straightforward answers. I have answered them to the extent it was possible, but I have also explored and discussed other aspects that they raised in relation to gender, kinship, and livelihood in a postwar setting.

The overall purpose of this book has been to examine war and postwar experiences of some young women in northern Sierra Leone who had been abducted by the rebels. More specifically, I focused on how these experiences were articulated and interpreted by the women themselves, their families, their communities, and to some extent the international humanitarian community, and on the relationships between stories of personal experience and cultural life. Of particular interest was how my informants expressed and coped with hardship on personal, social, and economic levels. In chapters 3 and 4 I focused on wartime issues such as abduction, rape, and female combat. I examined marriage, family and kinship relations, and livelihood options in chapters 2, 6, and 7, and in chapters 5 and 7 I discussed postwar issues such as reconciliation, demobilization, poverty, healing, and the women's strong feelings of fear and shame.

When most of my informants were abducted, or when they "met the war," as they would say, they were very young; some were only small girls. They were pulled away from their families, their communities, and from the only way of life they knew. Rebel life, or bush life, seemed at first like nothing they had ever experienced before. Most rebels were young; the majority was below thirty years of age. The rebel movement, as I described in chapter 1, was one that challenged conventional norms and traditions such as the rule of elders, chiefs, and big men; life in the bush was instead based on a violent meritocracy, where even young boys and girls could be commanders over their elders. Finally, in almost all cases, the rupture of being abducted from home and entering the bush was also marked by the violent assault of the social and physical body of my informants through war rapes.

The initial war rapes, which could go on for days and involve many different rapists, were almost all interrupted by an uninvolved bystander, often a commander claiming the girl or woman as his wife, thereby creating a sense of rescue and protection. As I have shown, it was not unusual for my informants to express a sense of loyalty and gratitude to these bush husbands who had rescued them and saved their lives. Thus began their socialization into rebel life. This was a life that for most entailed continual sexual abuse and forced labor, but for some also meant access to a material wealth they had never before experienced, and also for a few the possibility of exerting a type of authority over others hitherto unimaginable. It is necessary to bear this in mind. Although for most bush wives life in the bush was suffering from beginning to end, for a few women this life offered something that was not always easy to relinquish. For some, life in the bush turned out to be far more than just bare survival. Although all women strategized to improve their situation in the bush, some women succeeded better than others in their endeavors. What they shared was that their maneuvering capabilities were circumscribed in ways different from men's.

Although rebel life differed immensely from my informants' lives at home, there were also some significant similarities. These related in particular to the production of food, the sexual division of labor, and the composition of households. I have described how my informants became incorporated into pseudofamily-based domestic groups where the women were often one of several bush wives, which reflected the system of polygyny common to the region. My informants also described many elements of co-wife rivalry which were similar to prewar life, though in the bush, the stakes were decidedly much higher; a favorite wife could have a rival killed. In these domestic units there were also several dependents, children and sometimes even elders. I have also mentioned how in some rebel camps there were nurses, traditional midwives, teachers, and traditional figures of authority such as mamy queens. Each group was responsible for procuring and processing food and other necessities. Despite its youth bias, rebel hierarchy in a way resembled ordinary village hierarchies, with a senior commander instead of a chief, and junior commanders in place of compound heads.

In terms of food production, I have described how, although the rebels frequently looted towns and villages for supplies, they were also dependent on abducted women's labor in processing and preparing food left by fleeing villagers. Hence it is no exaggeration to say that abducted women's labor was in fact necessary for the maintenance of the rebel "war system," as I have described in chapter 3. There was no central distribution of food, so women's work upheld much of the rebel infrastructure. This meant that even though not all women became rebel fighters, they still constituted the backbone of the rebel movement. These aspects of rebel social life, however, did not strengthen the cohesion and structure of the groups. Rather, the constant power struggles—between commanders, between bush wives—and the constant threat of battle, the many escapes, and new abductions meant that the movement was fluctuating and fragile. Still, some of my informants stayed with the rebels for many years. They explained that this had less to do with ideological conviction or group solidarity than with fear. Fear of leaving and fear of returning home. There were many deterrents against leaving. Many were killed if they were caught escaping, and others had been forced to kill relatives and were afraid of reprisals if they returned home.

Another wartime issue that relates to preexisting notions in "traditional" society is that of virginity and marital sex. For example, the reason most of my informants so clearly differentiated between the initial abduction rapes and the later rapes and sexual abuse they suffered by their bush husbands, can be traced to how they conceive of marital sexual relations in general. Rape in marriage was not considered a crime by people in general, nor was it recognized as such under Sierra Leone legislation at the time. I also discussed how in Sierra Leonean gender ideology, wives are obliged to "serve" their husbands sexually and otherwise; women are not in control of their own sexuality. Although the bush marriages were not socially or culturally sanctioned, they were nevertheless conceived of as a form of marriage, and the sexual demands by bush husbands were inscribed in the familiar discourse of a matrimonial relations and obligations. Many informants also commented on the fact that the type of sexual violence they were subjected to during the war was something new and previously unknown to them. This was a sexual violence which effectively demoralized the women, their families, and their communities. It was a sexual violence that violated cultural taboos, such as being stripped naked in front of people, and having sex in public view and in public places. It was also a sexual violence with "pornographic" connotations completely foreign to most of my young rural informants. These are all issues similar to war rapes in many other war-torn and conflict-ridden societies. In this sense, the war rapes in Sierra Leone can be said to be part of a global warscape that intersects with the international trade in sex, drugs, and guns in the shadows of wars. Still, postwar interpretations of the wartime rapes in Sierra Leone made it clear that these rapes took place in a particular cultural landscape, making them subject to local understandings of morality.

It is also with these local notions of womanhood in mind that one has to approach the figure of the female fighter. Stories about the extreme brutality of female fighters proliferated during the war, stories that I had heard circulated by Western media even before visiting Sierra Leone for the first time in 1998. These female fighters were often described, both by locals and the media, as more cold blooded and vicious than male fighters. This notion of female fighters' cruelty was nothing unique to the Sierra Leonean war but can be found in most war zones with female combatants. As I discussed in the introduction and chapter 4, researchers on gender and war often interpret these notions as a consequence of the militarization of oppositional gender roles: women have to more fully transgress boundaries of acceptable female behavior when they become killers. Female fighters' behavior is thus understood as deviating more from ideal feminine behavior than the behavior of male fighters from ideal male behavior. And as this behavior of female fighters is in such stark contrast to feminine ideals, it is interpreted as being worse. In other words, their behavior need not always be worse to be interpreted as such. This has also been described as a typical feature of war-torn societies where women are also considered "by nature" to be more peaceful, maternal, and nurturing.

Judging by some of the peace movements in Freetown founded by women's organizations, it seems plausible that in Sierra Leone too, at least among the educated urban elite, these notions of women's inherent peacefulness prevailed. In rural Koinadugu, however, I found that many people spoke of the existence of an alternate femininity. In this particular rural context there was a notion of women as being by nature raw, wild, and dangerous, not at all inherently peaceful. Thus, in becoming fighters, some women did not necessarily transcend, but rather reinforced, certain aspects of femininity in Kuranko thought. The idiom of the "bush" further reinforced this view of "rebel women" as being "wild" and "bushlike." After the war, many people in Koinadugu stated that life in the bush had unleashed this destructive and uncontrolled femininity in bush wives in general and in female fighters in particular. Significantly, this perception came to affect the way many women were treated when they returned from the bush. In a sense, then, what the abduction of women into the bush did was to violently interrupt the continual social process of domesticating women. Therefore, their return to village and town from a life in the bush was often construed as a process of domestication, a process I have described in chapter 7.

Concomitantly, this view of women as inherently wild and dangerous did not fit well with international humanitarian discourse, with its emphasis on war-affected women as innocent victims. As I have described in chapter 4, this view of war-affected women as victims permeates much humanitarian work in war-torn countries. For example, this was why, although it was probably unintentional, nothing significant was done to include female combatants in the DDR process. Rebel women were simply not regarded as fighters; they were bush wives and sex slaves—that is, victims. Nevertheless, the lack of a gender perspective on the part of the DDR planners was perhaps not what excluded most female combatants from officially disarming. In their stories about the DDR, shame and fear of revenge often surfaced as reasons why my informants did not want to register for disarmament, and the dilemma some of these women faced, and the ambiguity of their position, were clearly expressed in how they interpreted and related to the DDR process.

At the time of registration, DDR was seen as something not only unsuitable and shameful for women, but also as potentially life threatening. First, most of my female ex-combatant informants explained that they had been dissuaded from registering for the DDR by bush husbands or by their families, for reasons I understood had to do with social shame. Women who had returned home had been made to understand that their rebel past and their present rebel behavior "shamed" their families. The DDR was also conceived of as a very public domain, in which women's shameful status would become even more exposed, for everyone to see. Some women also said that they did not disarm because it would have implied that they had joined the rebels willingly. This became particularly obvious in relation to the photographs that needed to be taken at the time of registration for identification purposes. Numerous informants said that they were afraid that their pictures would be circulated everywhere, "shaming" their families.

Second, for many, the reason why they did not disarm had to do with fear. Most believed that if they registered, they would be sent to court, arrested, and then executed. Rumors about the DDR and its collusion with the Truth and Reconciliation Commission and the Special Court flourished at this time. Some women explained that they had believed that the TRC would try them for war crimes and that the Special Court would execute them. The DDR finished its demobilization program in January 2002, and during my 2003–4 fieldwork, many women now expressed regret at their initial decision not to join. They had seen that their friends were not arrested or killed but had benefited.

Why was it that women and girls who had been abducted by the rebels were not welcomed back after the war? Why did their families not see them, as the international humanitarian community did, as innocent victims of terrible circumstances? The harsh reactions of the domestic and kinship group to former bush wives' inappropriate behavior draws attention to the importance of kinship for social relations in Sierra Leone. In Sierra Leone, kinship is a very important aspect of social organization, and one could even say that the individual is constituted through the kinship group and has been conceived of as having no social existence outside of this group. This system of social organization is also one that has emphasized hierarchy, gender, and generational difference. During the war, in the bush, my informants were cut off from their families, from an important source of authority in the kin group, and thus from the moral social control their community enforced.

The question of shame referred to above was to become a recurrent theme in my interviews with women about their postwar situation. Shame was an aspect of the social disapproval that the women had to cope with because of the rumors that circulated about their supposed transgressions during their time in the bush. In that precarious situation, abducted women's priority had been to survive. Later, when confronted with postwar local society—family members, neighbors, and representatives of local authorities—it was in terms of shame felt, manifested, and lived that returning female ex-fighters' moral standards were negotiated. Without any display of shame on their part, but through the fact of deviating moral behavior that clashed with current gender norms in a highly visible way, the women found themselves facing society's disapproval. This disapproval found different expressions, such as social stigmatization and social exclusion, and was often verbalized as the women's having "shamed" their families. Showing shame was in a sense necessary for women's reintegration into family and village life, besides other demands such as economic and social contributions to the maintenance of the local community.

For example, the rape of virgins held strong moral implications that were grounded in local notions of ideal femininity, and as I have described, were often expressed through marriage transactions and notions of female reputation. People in the community would often mention loss of virginity as one reason the women "shamed" their families, but many others pointed instead to the way these women behaved, dressed, and talked as the grounds for shame. It was also well known that most abducted women had been raped during the war, and many had also returned with "rebel children." As noted above, most of my informants had been very young and had not yet married when they were abducted. In this region there is a cultural ideal of female virginity before first marriage. Therefore some of these girls and women were seen as "damaged goods" when they returned from the bush, and thus found it difficult to get married. In a rural society where more or less the only female trajectory is marriage, the ambiguous position of these women—they were not girls, yet not "real women"—created many problems. For example, some men who had been engaged to these girls and women before the war now "refused the marriages" and demanded that their bridewealth be refunded. Despite the ideal of virginity, in reality girls and young women quite often have lovers before they marry, and sometimes even before initiation, which has been considered an even worse taboo. From this, it follows that virginity is a negotiable, not a physical, fact; what matters is what people know. On closer examination it seemed that the reason why some of these women became "unmarriageable" had more to do with how they behaved or how their behavior was interpreted rather than the actual loss of virginity. Potential husbands and affines sometimes expressed fear of these "rebel women"; they were afraid of their rebel behavior and suspected that they would never make good wives.

In contrast to many reports about the fate of abducted women in the aftermath of the Sierra Leonean war, I have shown that not all girls and women were stigmatized, shunned, or abused because they had been raped or lost their virginity. Postwar behavior in many cases proved to be more fundamental for how they would be treated. For example, it was often said of female ex-combatants that "they don't know how to behave" or "they don't know how to talk to people." In contrast to the feminine ideal of deference and servility, some of these women were aggressive, argumentative, used abusive language, did not respect elders, and in some cases also continued to use drugs.

In rural Koinadugu, some of these women challenged traditional gender norms by dressing in a culturally unconventional manner, in tight-fitting jeans and small tops. In Freetown this type of dress is quite common, but in rural Koinadugu it signaled both sexual activity and a rebel past. Because the women who returned from the bush sometimes behaved in a manner that clearly deviated from cultural norms, it was difficult for their families and communities to accept and reintegrate them. Whereas some women tried to conform to norms and conventions, to expected behavior, others said that they did not want to return to a "traditional" way of life. This was probably also one of the reasons why many ex-rebel women left their villages and small towns and went to live with friends, boyfriends, and even bush husbands in urban areas such as Freetown, Makeni, and Koidu.

Another reason for their precarious situation was the country's shattered postwar economy. Most people blamed this on the rebels (more rarely on decades of misrule and corruption), and in rural postwar Koinadugu everyone was poor. Most of the young women I worked with had returned to families who had lost everything. The lack of livelihood alternatives in the district had made many young men migrate to urban areas or the diamond district to try their luck; thereby many households became de facto female headed. Returning "rebel women" who could not get married were often seen as a burden on the already strained budgets of these families. After the war, women like my informants had few livelihood options at their disposal. Most girls and women said that they wanted to learn a skill such as hairdressing and soap making and then proceed to make money through this. Vocational training projects were meant to present women with alternatives to more traditional forms of livelihood, but unfortunately, most projects promised more than they could deliver. It was obvious that many projects failed as a means of making these young women self-reliant. Most women told me that they could make more money by selling firewood. However, many projects offered something else.

Given the insecure situation of many of these women in postwar society—they had "shamed" their families, they were dissuaded from demobilizing, and they were told not to talk to anyone about their wartime experiences—these projects managed to create a space in which some women were able to see that they were not alone in being excluded and stigmatized. Some projects hired counselors, who, the women told me, had encouraged and helped them to deal with their past, and who did not condemn or stigmatize them. Many women explained that the vocational training had kept them from being "idle," kept them from brooding over past experiences, and made them feel much better. Some projects offered medical services, which were appreciated, as quite a few women suffered from various sexually transmitted diseases and other ailments and infectious diseases from their time in the bush.

Most of my informants had dreams about what they wanted to do in the future. A good many said that they wanted to become successful traders and "big women" who would command respect and authority. Many also dreamt of being educated, becoming teachers or "learned people." For most women, however, these dreams will not be realized. For those of my informants who had neither moral nor economic standing, creating a position in society was very difficult. Instead, some women said that their only alternative was to become girlfriends. They would have one or two lovers who would give them money, clothes, and food. This "girlfriend business," as it has been called, was nothing new to postwar Sierra Leone, however, but had long been an established means for women to supplement their income.

Considering conventional norms about women's sexual activities and notions of shame, I found it interesting to see that those of my informants who supported their families by "loving" often were exempt from criticism and in fact sometimes had positions of authority within the household, as I described with Musu in chapter 6. Musu behaved in an untraditional manner but had a position of influence in her female-dominated domestic group because she was the main provider and supported the entire household through her two lovers. As I described above, in postwar Sierra Leone, most people were poor and it was not easy to find ways of making a living, so that people become increasingly dependent on those who could.

The initial response of fear and shame was thus mitigated and overcome by the young women's ability to provide for their families. Many informants explained that they believed that their families would accept them if only they could provide material and social resources. In other words, "keeping busy" meant not only that their emotional situation improved but also had to do with whether they were able to contribute to the household. This affected their general position positively, and in a way helped to reestablish them in the moral and social order. As I have explained in the preceding chapters, social relationships and material wealth, morality and economy, were inextricably linked. They operated within a system of mutual dependency, the one at once obfuscating and enhancing the other. The relationship between economy and morality created ways of overcoming social shame, and the social status created by economic resources could be projected onto, and improve, social relations.

Needless to say, "loving" as a livelihood strategy is a short-term solution. Women like Musu will get older and perhaps find it more difficult to attract wealthy patrons, and household composition and hierarchies might change over time. As Musu lived in a female-headed household, the appearance of a brother or a male affine as main provider might perhaps change her position in the family. It might also be a dangerous solution. With the rise of HIV and other sexually transmitted diseases in postwar Sierra Leone, women like Musu are also involved in a high-risk enterprise. But postwar culture had made socially marginalized women see their own loving strategy as something positive and beneficial. The "girlfriend business" seemed for many to lead to economic independence, and in Sierra Leone it did in a certain way also "liberate" women from conventional ideals of femininity. However, it did so by constantly stressing and even appropriating their sexuality, and thus came at a high cost. In this context, women were liberated from one convention only to be confined by another.

It is obvious that there have been profound changes in Sierra Leone in how young people conceive of their lives and their futures. Whether this is a result of the war or of longer processes of economic stagnation, corruption, and the structurally unjust world market is difficult to tell. What is clear in Sierra Leone is that these processes have made young people today, male and female, for reasons not of their own making, challenge the received wisdom of previous generations, creating what I refer to as a generational dissonance. As I described in chapter 6, when parents cannot provide and care for their children, and husbands cannot or will not support their wives, they will go out and "find it for themselves." In postwar Sierra Leone, the international community and their own society in a sense failed abducted girls and women. They could not count on the massive apparatus of humanitarian assistance nor could they rely on the comforts of tradition.

In a manner of speaking, it is possible to say that the war may have given many young women new opportunities and freedom. Some scholars have speculated that the participation of African women in combat might have emancipatory elements (see, e.g., Morris 1993). But in Sierra Leone, despite the fact that the social control of some girls and women lessened to some degree during the war, this did not translate into an increase in self-determination. Since the war ended, Sierra Leone has seen a gradual transference of rights and authority to women, legislation protecting women has been improved, the availability of social welfare has also increased, and the police have started to address rape and domestic abuse. Still, many of my informants, and many other women like them, were seldom in a position to directly profit from these incentives.

To sum up, during the war my informants were kidnapped, raped, drugged, and forcibly conscripted into fighting a war that promised them no improvements in terms of women's position or livelihood options. The violence these women experienced was also frequently sexualized. They could not disarm because the DDR had not taken into consideration women's special needs and because they were too afraid that their communities would condemn them. Having spent their formative years in "the bush" away from the authority of the family and the kin group, in a setting totally dominated by youth, it is little wonder that some of them displayed a type of behavior that was far removed from the "traditional" Kuranko feminine ideal. For this they were punished, ostracized, and even medicated when they returned home. Cultural idioms of femininity prevented ex-rebel women from being fully accepted in postwar society, and in contrast to many other war-torn societies, in northern Sierra Leone there were no rituals or reconciliatory ceremonies that could "wash" fighters from blood, death, and shame.

In the introduction I argued that it was necessary to take into account context, such as local notions of morality, gender, and kinship, in order to really understand my informants' war and postwar experiences and why these experiences were communicated in the way they were. Relationships between kin and affines constitute a large part of overall social organization in Sierra Leone. Therefore I argue that it is nearly impossible to understand some of the sentiments of families and communities surrounding former female combatants and their bush husbands without knowing how social relations between men and women are organized in Sierra Leonean society. Therefore, throughout the process of writing this book, my initial wish to explore the lives and experiences of abducted women became more and more an exploration of how my informants' lives and experiences were given shape and meaning in interactions with families, society, and the international humanitarian community. My informants' stories were not simple reflections of their experiences of life in the bush or of their situation in postwar society, for their stories reveal on a more general level something of how young women grew up during the war, about women's position in Sierra Leonean society, about gender and generations, about notions of morality, and about livelihood strategies.

Many of the themes I have worked with here emerged from my informants' stories. Prominent themes in our conversations were elements such as abduction, rape, and sexual abuse; surviving everyday life in the bush; drugs; violence; and killings. Their stories of life after the war dealt with their struggle to make a living and the difficulties of being accepted by family after returning from the bush. The importance of "keeping busy," not being "idle," and making a living came to the fore in the way they interpreted and related to NGO aid. Their stories about the DDR, the TRC, and the Special Court illustrated many aspects of these women's concerns in postwar society and also reflected local notions of morality and femininity. Conversations with a variety of people in Koinadugu and Freetown, observations of the activities of daily life, and reflections on the meaning of these provided other points of entry into these themes.

In this book I have privileged the stories of young women in Koinadugu District in northern Sierra Leone, but I have also related their stories to notions of culturally appropriate forms of expressions and behavior. I have given accounts of how the opinions and attitudes of people in their proximity, their families and communities, also shaped and influenced their stories as well as their futures. From the polarized position of local traditional norms and the story-based discourse of the international humanitarian community, the stories of my informants emerged, between the demands of their local communities to stay silent and the international community's emphasis on telling war stories. I have combined their narratives of war and violence with a description of their empirical reality and social positions. I argue that it is both the location of women's stories about their activities and position during the war in Sierra Leonean culture, and their postwar empirical reality that shaped the circumstances they had to relate to and act on.

Two distinct but interrelated themes can be discerned throughout this book: issues of morality and economy, often expressed as shame and livelihood. The reluctance many women expressed about publicly acknowledging their time in the bush was based largely on shame. It was just too shameful to talk about having participated in something that wrecked the whole country, displaced hundreds of thousands, and killed tens of thousands people. As I have shown, it was even more shameful because they were women. Through their participation the young women had brought shame on their families, and many had also wrecked any chances they had of a good marriage by coming back wild and unruly.

One way to handle postwar stigmatization for many of these girls and women was silence. Keeping quiet was also seen as the best way to move on in life and to forget the violent past. Many girls were encouraged by friends, family, counselors, and others to keep busy and refrain from being idle, and in this way it was believed that their emotional and behavioral problems would cease. To talk publicly about the past, it was understood, would only further reproduce the pain and suffering and the unconventional behavior that followed from their wartime experiences. In contrast, many actors in the international community worked with the notion that it was good to talk about traumatic events. It was good for the world to know what had happened so that we can work against its ever happening again. It was good for the nation to bring everything out in the open and deal with it to prevent it from happening again, and to create national healing and reconciliation. It was also conceived of as good for victims and perpetrators to testify about what they had experienced and what they had done, in order to heal their emotional and spiritual wounds.

As I have described earlier, many of my informants were quite skeptical about the public trauma-healing of international organizations. This was partly due to their fear of punishment but can also be related to local cultural notions about how pain and experiences of violence should and should not be communicated. My informants were thus located between two very different discourses for healing and reconciliation. Because of this divergence, I focused on the politics of memory and how different systems of thought sometimes clash. It is in relation to these two discourses that questions about culpability and agency surface. Were the girls bush wives or combatants, were they victims or perpetrators? I have argued that there are no easy answers to such questions, and as the ethnography shows, the oppositional categories victim and perpetrator were ill suited to explaining abducted Sierra Leonean women's postwar realities.

As I have indicated, I wanted to avoid opposing the generalized stereotypes of "victim" and "perpetrator," as many of my informants had indeed been both. Positing war rape and female fighters in the same chapter was a conscious move, as it draws attention to how women in war are portrayed in studies of conflict in general. I showed how the concepts of victims and perpetrators were problematic when analyzing the lives and experiences of the women I interviewed. As some of the women who had been abducted ended up being full-fledged rebel fighters, they had been both victims and perpetrators, but in the postwar context, narrating experiences of being the latter could be both shameful and dangerous. Therefore I moved from an analysis on the level of humanitarian discourse to experience grounded in local culture. In the postwar context, I have had to acknowledge that for many of my informants, to narrate their war stories from a position of "victim" was infinitely more acceptable than to confess experiences of being the perpetrator of violent acts. I have claimed that the context of narration was of great significance, and that women's narratives of war were dialectically shaped by cultural and social norms. Therefore, one could argue that their stories both broke with norms and conventions and also adapted to them, depending on context but also on differences of personality and circumstance.

Young women in Sierra Leone today have more or less come of age during a period of war and conflict. This has no doubt influenced their lives in a multitude of ways and can perhaps reveal something on a more general level about gender and war, and of how war affects gender relations in postwar society. The significance of this book is not limited to Sierra Leone, however, but is of wider relevance. To analyze women's war and postwar experiences provides new perspectives, new angles, and produces new knowledge in an area of research that has heretofore mostly been characterized by its male bias.

There is undoubtedly much we will never know or understand about what happened to bush wives and female combatants during and after the war in Sierra Leone. A colleague of mine once wrote that no honest ethnography claims to be exhaustive. This is also the case with the book at hand. There are still many other aspects of war and postwar society that need to be further explored and analyzed. Amina Mama wrote that for contemporary Africa in general, "changes in African gender relations have been so profound that they may well have been one of the most dramatic sites of struggle and change" (1997, 69). This is very likely true for Sierra Leone, but here it would be relevant as well to examine some of the ways that the war might have changed both gender and generational relations.

What my work indicates is that in terms of gender and generational *relations,* rural men and women, and parents and children, no longer really know what to expect from each other. This is a development that many rural Sierra Leonean people find exciting, as it opens up new possibilities and creates new ways in which to be a woman or a man. At the same time it is distressing, as this fluidity in some cases delegitimizes traditional knowledge and authority. A relevant future line of inquiry would be to see how these changes are articulated and communicated in postwar Sierra Leone.

There were certain things that I only glimpsed during fieldwork and could not pursue at the time. These had to do with topics related to more conventional anthropology, for example, divination and witchcraft. Considering the lack of traditional healing or reconciliation rituals or ceremonies, at least in Koinadugu, in would be very interesting to examine to what extent war-affected women consulted local diviners, *mori men,* or other ritual practitioners, as a means of emotional, physical, and social recovery. When I first went to Kabala in 2001, my friends in Freetown marveled at my decision to go to a place that in their eyes was the witch capital of Sierra Leone. Throughout my stay in Koinadugu District, I heard many rumors and whispers of witches, and my friend Pa Morowa once vociferously claimed, after I fell violently ill following a strange dream, that I had in fact been shot with a "witch gun." To be able to see if and how the articulation of witchcraft accusations has changed since the war, whether new themes and personas related to the war have emerged in the discourses of witchcraft, would provide unique insights if they are related to elements such as reconciliation and reintegration. It would be interesting to look at whether and to what extent people in this area regard and use witchcraft accusations as a means of war-related revenge.

Another aspect that has received far too little attention is the role of masculinities, specifically the hegemony of militarized masculinity in times of war, and how this type of masculinity works at the expense of alternative "civilian" masculinities. A lot has been written about the rebels, about the Civil Defense Forces, and about corrupt patrons and politicians, but very little of this writing has placed any emphasis on how these affect and are related to local cultural notions about masculinity. As I mentioned in chapter 4, it is quite surprising, given the frequency of rapes in war, and the focus that has been accorded women as victims in war in scholarly research, that militarized male cultures of rape and sexual abuse are so underresearched. One relevant issue, for example, could be to examine the relationship between war rapes and militarized masculinity in war-torn societies.

Considering that the large presence of male soldiers in a war-torn society increases the level of sexual exploitation, and coupled with the Sierra

Leonean cultural idiom of "girlfriends," perhaps it should not come as a surprise that these phenomena would intersect in a peculiarly unsettling way in postwar Sierra Leone. Further research should be encouraged on the relationship between peacekeepers and local populations, and on the relationship between and intersections of different notions of morality. The peacekeeping culture itself needs to be further examined as well. Why is it that there is still a hypermasculine culture among peacekeeping soldiers, and how does this relate to sexual exploitation and abuse?

I have already said that there were no easy answers to the questions I raised with regard to Aminata's case. Some of these questions have already been addressed throughout the chapters above. Below I will summarize a few of them and also try to give tentative answers to those I have not yet discussed. We know that Aminata was abducted during a rebel attack on Kabala in 1998, that she was raped, became a bush wife and later a rebel fighter. Her own wartime activities, widespread rebel atrocities in general, her loss of virginity, and her sullen mood and short temper were all factors that influenced the way she was treated by her family when she returned home after the war. She had "shamed" them. Still, as her brother was the main provider in the family at this time, his decision to let Aminata stay carried some weight and the others had to relent. After being accepted by a vocational training project that gave her the means to contribute to the household, Aminata found that she was treated better. But the training ended and she was unable to continue with the work and soon fell into disfavor with her parents again. Her low position in the family was also illustrated by the obvious disrespect with which her younger siblings and other children in the household treated her.

Aminata's father had rejected the marriage proposal of her bush husband, for reasons I do not know. One can speculate that such a marriage would make him lose face in the community, or that perhaps such a union would reinforce the associations people already had of Aminata as a rebel. Or perhaps it was the fact that the bush husband was a Christian and a Mende and Aminata's family Muslim and Kuranko, that made her father refuse. The importance of kinship and cultural notions of women's position in society—illustrated by the proverb "There is no such thing as an unmarried woman"—were factors that made it difficult for Aminata to leave her family. Aminata's marginal position in her household—she could not contribute financially and she was not married—forced her to seek other means of provision, which in her case amounted to "loving." She genuinely hoped that one of her lovers would want to marry her. But up until my departure, her hopes were to no avail. When I left she was getting increasingly worried about sexually transmitted diseases.

A year after I had returned home, Mary wrote to tell me that Aminata had visited her bush husband for a couple of months at the soldier camp where he was stationed but had since then returned to Kabala and continued with her loving business. Her situation with her family was still unresolved. Aminata's story is illustrative of the position in wartime and postwar Sierra Leone of abducted women, but it also speaks to many issues in contemporary Sierra Leone, such as the importance of kinship, the relevance of gender and generational hierarchies for social relations, and how important notions of shame and material wealth, morality, and economy are for women's life trajectories.

Mary called me on 20 May 2006 to tell me that at last Kabala had been connected to the world. A few weeks earlier, a mobile telephone network had been installed in town. People there still have no running water, no electricity, and the lowest literacy rate in the country, but now they have mobile phones. They are able to connect to friends and relatives in Freetown, the United States, and Europe. Mary was ecstatic. However, she did also mention that young women had already started to "love" to get money to buy mobile phones. The last I heard about Musu was that she had become pregnant with one of her lovers but that she was still not married, and of Aminata that she had left her family and gone to live in a rented room in town with a female friend. Aminata lived only on "loving"—until recently, that is. Just the week before completing this book, I called Mary, who told me that Aminata is now married.

Notes

Introduction

1. Aminata and the following names of female abductees are pseudonyms. To some extent I have also excluded references to place names. Names of rebel commanders are original.

2. For example, in Sierra Leone, war rapes did not affect the honor of male family members and affines in the same way that has been shown in Bosnia, for example (cf. Hughes and Foster 1996; Moorehead 1995; Olujic 1998).

3. Silje Lundgren, personal communication, September 2005.

4. Helle Rydstrøm, "From War to Reconciliation: Vulnerable Postwar Vietnam–U.S. Relations," paper presented at the conference "Structures of Vulnerability: Mobilisation and Resistance" in Stockholm, 14 January 2005.

5. However, the existence of these types of fighters should not lead anyone to believe that this was only a "tribal" or an "ethnic" war fought with "traditional" means. These armed factions often had access to the latest, most advanced weapons, they communicated by satellite telephones (see, e.g., Richards 2005c).

6. However, Moore also notes that, although of Western origin, this form of hegemonic masculinity is now more and more global, finding resonance in local and indigenous masculinities (1994, 63).

7. Lately, however, the interpretation of the black veil has reverted; it no longer signifies innocence or passivity but is frequently associated with terrorism. A veiled woman in a Moscow subway will now probably cause alarm and suspicion.

8. When discussing this with a UNAMSIL soldier working on a Military Observer team (MILOBS) in Sierra Leone, I was told that the similarities in training and organizational hierarchy, chain of command, etc. made cultural differences in a team with soldiers from seventeen different countries from all over the world a minor problem.

9. This has slowly changed in some countries, but in many others there are more or less pronounced taboos against women in the military.

10. One reviewer of Scarry's book concisely phrased it as a "mediation on the meaning of pain and the wide-ranging phenomenological consequences of the fact that we have bodies that can feel pain, and minds and spirits that usually try to avoid it" (J. E. Jackson 1990, 461). Nevertheless, Scarry has also been criticized (Amato and Monge 1990; Green 1995; J. E. Jackson 1990) for using exclusively Western texts in her quest to describe human realities, and for not acknowledging that there are other ways to interpret the meaning of pain and suffering.

11. This position bears some resemblance to Arendt's notion of "sheer happenings," which, in Linden's (1993, 11) words are "fragments of experience that refuse narrative forms—which literally cannot be talked about." However, Arendt herself emphasized that the story "reveals the meaning of what otherwise would remain an unbearable sequence of sheer happenings" (Arendt 1968, 104).

12. None perhaps has shown this more eloquently than Rosalind Shaw (2002) in her book about ritual and historical imagination in Sierra Leone with reference to the Atlantic slave trade.

13. Helle Rydstrøm, "From War to Reconciliation: Vulnerable Postwar Vietnam–U.S. Relations," paper presented at the conference "Structures of Vulnerability: Mobilisation and Resistance" in Stockholm, 14 January 2005.

14. By this she refers to the Special Court, which had only just started its work in Sierra Leone.

15. I was not alone in experiencing this. Persson's female ex-combatant informants were also initially worried that she might be an investigator of the Special Court sent out punish them (Persson 2005).

16. In this book I consistently speak of "the rebels." This is because most of my informants were abducted by the RUF and after 1998 some also by the AFRC junta, but more importantly, because all of my informants spoke of them as "rebels" whether they belonged to the RUF or the AFRC. This does not mean that I infer that other fighting forces, such as the CDF, the Sierra Leonean Army, and the various peacekeeping forces did not abduct people or commit atrocities.

1. A Decade of War—Centuries of Uncertainty

1. During the war Kabala was attacked thirteen times.

2. A prevalent attitude also among Jackson's informants (2004b, 47).

3. First British paratroopers and later soldiers from the British International Military Assistance Training Teams (IMATT).

4. Almost half of the population is under the age of fifteen. The infant and under-five mortality rates are one of the highest in the world at 165 and 282 per 1000 live births respectively; women give birth to an average of five children. Life expectancy at birth is forty years for men and forty-five for women. The literacy rate in 2007 was 46.7 percent for men and only 24.2 percent for women (UNDP 2007).

5. The Creoles, or later Krios, were actually quite a diverse category of people; some had been rescued from other West African regions before crossing the Atlantic, the so-called recaptives who came to be the largest group. Others came from Jamaica (the Maroons), Canada (The Nova Scotians), or elsewhere. Many were Christians but there were also many Muslims among them, most of Yoruba origin, also known as the Aku (see Bassir 1954).

6. Fyfe notes that the presence of these prostitutes was probably not sanctioned by Granville Sharp, who was "rabidly puritanical" (Fyfe 1962, 17). He also writes that some of the prostitutes later said that they had been, "made drunk, brought aboard, and married to settlers" (ibid).

7. People living in the area now called Sierra Leone of course have a history preceding that of European presence. Although little archaeological work has been done in the country, findings suggest that people have inhabited the area since at least 2500 BC (Alie 1990, 6).

8. Mainly in the south and southeast, as Islam was already so firmly entrenched in the north (see Ojukutu-Macauley 1997; D. E. Skinner 1978).

9. Although domestic slavery was widespread in the region and was documented by European travelers after the 16th century, there is little evidence that it existed prior to 1500 at least among the people along the coast, and may in fact have been a consequence of the Atlantic slave trade (Holsoe 1977, 292; MacCormack 1977, 182; and Nyerges 1992).

10. According to A. Zack-Williams "one immediate result of the penetration of capitalism into the Sierra Leone social formation was not the destruction of the pre-capitalist modes but, instead led to the intensification of the servile labor of the slave mode of production" (1995, 204).

11. This system, in which chiefs can amass wealth from rents and fees paid to them, by for example mining companies, is still present.

12. This style of colonial governing, also known as *laissez-faire* or *the model colony approach,* continued throughout the colonial period and meant that the colony should more or less pay for itself without subsidies from the colonizers. What this meant in reality was that there was no or few long-term plans or investments in colonial territories, the railway in Sierra Leone being an exception, but also one which greatly enhanced the monopoly of the European merchant houses on imports and exports (see A. Zack-Williams 1995, 44).

13. From 1892 to 1912 Krios lost more than 35 percent of the senior government posts. After the completion of the "white reserve" in Freetown, Hill Station, the number of Europeans increased from 210 to 351 in the last decade of the nineteenth century (Spitzer 1974).

14. The scarcity of rice was a result of a poor previous harvest, which in turn was partly caused by a lack of labor due to high mortality rates in the 1918–20 influenza pandemic known as the Spanish flu (Niall et al. 2002).

15. The Syrians, or Lebanese, were traders who had come to Sierra Leone and other West African countries during the end of the nineteenth century and early twentieth century (see van der Laan 1975).

16. In 1922 there were sixty-five primary and secondary schools in the colony, but only forty-six in the whole protectorate, and the majority of those were located in the Mende-dominated southern province, and in 1948, only thirteen years before independence, there were still no secondary schools in the northern province (Ojukutu-Macauley 1997, 96).

17. Tributing was something that began with the mining of gold in the 1930s where one person would have a license to mine and in turn "employ" other people to win gold within the lease. These tributors were organized in gangs under a headman and all winnings were sold to the owner of the lease at half price. This mode of production increased later with the increase in the mining of diamonds. According to Zack-Williams, tributing was a very exploitative system where the employer "was relieved of the burden of paying wages to laborers," and where the "tributors were induced to work as hard as possible, since earning depended on output and not on mere physical presence (*clocking*) on the working grounds" (Zack-Williams 1995, 48).

18. Also involved in this coup was the then young captain Hinga Norman who was subsequently imprisoned (Keen 2005, 111). He was joined later, after a failed coup attempt in 1971, by a young Foday Sankoh.

19. From RUF document *Footpaths to Democracy,* accessed 24 April 2006 at http://www.sierra-leone.org/footpaths.html.

20. The Green Book was Libya's Muammar Khadafy's political manifest, which forged together the ideas and values of Islam, socialism, and militarism. The Juche Idea was the revolutionist political philosophy of North Korea.

21. However, APC also successfully recruited marginalized young men to their youth wing, which became intimately associated with thug violence. For an in-depth analysis, see Abdullah (1998).

22. This has been confirmed by many of the conscripted school children and students within RUF ranks.

23. Cool was his nom de guerre.

24. There were a few women in the RUF leadership positions. According to Mansaray, "In the 1992–1994 war council, out of twenty-one members, five were women," among whom one, Memuna Sesay, "was appointed overall commander of the female combatants" (2000, 145).

25. Hinga Norman died in February of 2007 while awaiting verdict from the Special Court.

26. In fact, there have been extensive criticisms of the supposed fairness of the elections in 1996 in which the Sierra Leone People's Party (SLPP) won a landslide victory.

27. The NPRC were initially well received among the urban population, and Strasser was even compared by some to the Ghanaian "miracle" of Rawlings (Conteh-Morgan and Dixon-Fyle 1999, 131).

28. Other security companies were Gurkha Security Guards Ltd. and Sandline.

29. In a bid to work for gender equality, the new government established a Ministry of Gender and Children's Affairs, but despite intense lobbying by women's groups, only five out of eighty members of Parliament were women, and two out of twenty-five cabinet ministers (Mansaray 2000).

30. Aid has been given to Sierra Leone in unprecedented proportions, making some question the country's ability "to operate on a development choice of its own without the directives or sanctions from Western donors" (Conteh-Morgan and Dixon-Fyle 1999, 154). During the immediate postwar period an enormous amount of money poured into the country. The United Nations Mission in Sierra Leone (UNAMSIL) alone had a total budget of over US $2.8 billion between 2001 and 2005, UNDP and associated agencies had a budget of approximately $141 million between 2004 and 2007, and the International Committee of the Red Cross an impressive $14.5 million in 2002 alone.

31. Koroma had until then been serving a sentence in prison for an earlier coup attempt against the SLPP government (for more see Keen 2005, chap. 11).

32. James Jonah, former minister of finance (interview 10 March 1998).

33. This attack is also described in the TRC (2004, 3a: § 554) by one of the RUF fighters who attacked Kabala.

34. In 1997 a report estimated that 10,000 women were associated with the RUF (Conciliation Resources 1997), though considering that the war went on for another four years and that many of my informants were abducted after 1998, most by the RUF or the AFRC, it is possible that this figure may have been much higher. Another report estimated that the number of girls under eighteen in armed groups was greater than 12,000 (McKay and Mazurana 2004), and according to a Save the Children report, girls probably constituted over 40 percent of all child soldiers (2005).

35. This is an excerpt from an interview with a South African mercenary in a series of articles called "Dispatch from the Dark Continent," this article bearing the telling name of "Memorandum to a Cannibal," published by World Net Daily on 19 October 2004, http://www.worldnet daily.com/news/article.asp?ARTICLE_ID=40981.

36. See http://www.womanseelotofthings.com/

2. Gendered Lives in Rural Sierra Leone

1. Formal law comprises the Constitution, parliamentary laws, and Common law. Customary law is part of common law and is defined in the Sierra Leone Constitution of 1991, section 170 § 3 as "the rules of law which by custom are applicable to particular communities in Sierra Leone."

2. Formal law required that wives inherit 30 percent of their deceased husband's property, while husbands would receive 100 percent of a deceased wife's property. Under Muslim law women were not entitled to administer estates, and under customary law provisions have varied across the country, but in general marital property reverted to the husband's family. Widows were

sometimes ejected from their homes with their children unless they married a male relative of the husband, so called widow inheritance. Under the new law widows are entitled to remain in the family home until they die, and husbands and wives inherit property from each other equally, and daughters inherit on equal terms with sons.

3. *Segere* is the name of the women's society in Kuranko and is similar to *Sande* among the Mende, and *Bundu* among other ethnic groups.

4. As I noted in the introduction, in this book I consistently speak of "the rebels" as this was the term most used by my informants whether referring solely to the RUF or after 1997 also the AFRC.

5. Although this was only three decades ago, those in the village who still remember Jackson are few and very old. One old woman vividly recounted when he had taken her for her very first ride in a car, an event also described by Jackson in *The Kuranko* (1977, 19). Michael Jackson had for a month been a guest professor at my department in Uppsala before I went to the field, so when I came with greetings from him to the people in the village, and perhaps because I was a stranger and also white, he became my uncle (*mberi*), and I was thus positioned in a hierarchy of gender and age. Some old men complained that my Kuranko was not as good as my "uncle's" had been, and one of them sighed and said, "Ah, that one knew how to talk Kuranko clearly!"

6. A *lappa* is the traditional clothing for women, a cotton fabric wrapped around the waist, reaching to the calves.

7. For example, Jackson (1977) hardly mentions Islam in his work on Kamadugu Sokorala.

8. It is still mostly men who migrate to the diamond areas. Of all my informants, men and women, as many as 37 percent had brothers in the diamond districts. In comparison, only 11 percent had sisters in the diamond areas; most of these had relocated with their husbands.

9. Of the forty-eight men I interviewed in Kamadugu Sokorala, all but two had lived and worked in the diamond areas, some for a year or two but most for more than five, and a few for up to thirty years (the average was nine years).

10. The male to female ratio in Koinadugu District as a whole is 88.29 to 100, while in the diamond-rich district of Kono the male to female ratio is 106.05 to 100, according to the United Nations Common Country Assessment of Sierra Leone based on the 2004 Census. However, there has been some change since before the war, namely that the Northern Province, which traditionally was a sending area of internal migrants, became the highest receiver (2004 Population and Household Census, Republic of Sierra Leone, accessed at: http://www.statistics.sl/2004%20 Population%20and%20Housing%20Census%20Report%20on%20Poverty.pdf.

11. When I was in Kabala at the time of the district elections in May 2004, there was talk of a woman running for office in a neighboring chiefdom. This had never happened before. None of my informants knew this woman, and they were not eligible to vote in that area, but many young women nevertheless spoke with pride at the thought of having an elected female politician, in contrast to their mothers and grandmothers, who felt that politics was no place for a woman. Since then much has changed, and in the latest local elections in July 2008, my own assistant Mary ran for office in the chiefdom of her father and won.

12. The rural population of Koinadugu District at 80 percent is higher than the country average.

13. http://hdr.undp.org/reports/global/1999/en/pdf/hdr_1998_back2.pdf.

14. There are many factors that contribute to a successful harvest, including seed quality, soil fertility, protection of the sowed seeds and seedlings from birds, etc. Still, many agreed that if the seeds were of poor quality, nothing would help to create a good harvest.

15. At the time of fieldwork a cup of clean rice sold at 1,100 leones and seed rice at 350 leones (US$0.44 and 0.14 respectively in 2004).

16. It has been estimated that women also actually contribute around 20 percent of the production of cash crops and 5 percent of upland rice farming (Femmes Africa Solidarité 1997).

17. This may also have to do with a general decline in farming during the war, when 500,000 farm families were displaced and the production of rice dropped to some 80 percent of prewar levels (UNDP 2005).

18. Jackson noted that even after the Kabala road was built, vehicles seldom came to the village, and the cost of hiring transport to take rice to the Kabala market was prohibitive (1977, 19–20).

19. During my fieldwork the elders of the village decided to host a weekly market (*lumo*) to attract traders from afar to bring much-needed products such as salt, sugar, bouillon cubes (*maggi*), second-hand clothes and shoes, as well the occasional item of luxury such as cigarettes, cheap jewelry, medicines, and *pega pak* (small plastic containers of gin or vodka). These same traders would also buy the local agricultural products and transport them to town. After some weeks it was decided that the market was to be postponed until after the next harvest, as there was just nothing to trade.

20. Although prices fluctuated throughout my fieldwork depending on season and the price of the U.S. dollar, in November 2003, a bag of imported white rice (usually from China or Pakistan) was 42,000 leones (US$17), and in May the following year the same bag sold at 56,000 leones (US$23). One bag of rice is equivalent to 180 to 190 cups, and to buy by the cup is much more expensive.

21. In Koinadugu the female literacy rate is estimated at 14 percent and the male at 30 percent (The Sierra Leone Encyclopedia 2007, http://www.daco-sl.org/encyclopedia/3_dist/3_1g_ku.htm).

22. According to the United Nations Population Fund, education also not only increases women's income-earning potential but reduces maternal and infant mortality and improves reproductive health UNFPA (2005).

23. See Shepler (2005) for more on education in postwar Sierra Leone.

24. This event is described in *Reflections from the Field: A Girl's Initiation Ceremony in Northern Sierra Leone* (Coulter 2005).

25. This is also due in part to the fact that in town there are more school-going children, and parents are not as willing to let children miss out on months of schoolwork to be initiated.

26. However, even girls as young as seven were initiated during the ceremony I observed in Kamadugu Sokorala.

27. In reality, the amount of kola nut may vary, but the expression is still "four kola nut."

28. In God-gift marriages, bridewealth is not given by the future husband. Instead, the bride's family gives a dowry and the bride is given in marriage "in the name of God" (Jackson 1977, 95).

29. Jackson wrote that matrilateral cross-cousin marriages as well as the avunculate and sororate marriages all belong to what is referred to in Kuranko as "kinship marriages" (*nakelinyorgo fureh*) (1977, 114). Perhaps it is only a small shift in linguistic practice, but when referring to kinship marriages in conversations with me, people would always use the term *kebile fureh* instead of *nakelinyorgo fureh*. *Na keli nyorgo* translates literally as "mother one partners/relatives" and the use of this term in reference to marriage was because a man would traditionally and preferentially marry his mother's classificatory brother's daughter. The term *kebile*, on the other hand, indicates the more loosely defined concept of family or kin and is also used to refer to the compound. It is interesting that this shift in terminology occurs at a time when the bonds between sisters and brothers, the traditional custodians of their children's marriage, also seem to have changed.

30. According to my survey in Kamadugu Sokorala, among men aged 35–70, 73 percent of all marriages were engagement marriages (mabira yaneh), 9 percent inheritance marriages (keyaneh), 7 percent love marriages (dienye fureh), and 13 percent "wife stealing" (sumburi). For younger men up to 35, 60 percent were mabira yaneh, 4 percent keyaneh, 16 percent dienye fureh, and 20 percent sumburi.

31. I did encounter a few cases of patrilateral cross-cousin marriages, however, while there was no case of patrilateral parallel-cousin marriage in the village. This latter form is favored among Arab Muslims and the one advocated by some Islamic leaders in Sierra Leone, advice that

many older men in my area of research have had difficulties reconciling themselves with. They said it would be the same thing as marrying one's sister, which would be to violate the incest taboo (*tersan koe*).

32. In Kabala there were more than four times as many "love marriages" as in the village.

33. A note on methodology might also be in place here. Informants were asked to self-define their types of marriage and were not provided with preset alternatives. Therefore Christians would often answer that theirs was a "Christian marriage," while people in the village, although Muslim, would perhaps answer *mabira yaneh* or *keyaneh*.

34. In Kabala the average age of first marriage for men between the ages 35 and 80 was 26 years, and for men up to 35, 23 years. In Kamadugu Sokorala, the average age of first marriage for men between the ages 35 and 80 was 28 years, and up to 35, 24 years.

35. Average age 25.4 years.

36. Of 173 informants, 53 (31 percent) categorized their marriages as Muslim marriages (16 women, 37 men).

37. When this is compared with Jackson's material from Kamadugu Sokorala in 1970, for example, it becomes apparent that the divorce rate has increased substantially among male informants over a period of thirty-five years. In 2004, 41.3 percent of all marriages had ended in divorce, as compared to 18.3 percent in 1970 (Jackson 1977, 99).

38. Among male informants, in Kamadugu Sokorala, of 161 marriages, 41.3 percent had ended in divorce, whereas in Kabala, of 141 marriages, the figure was 29.8 percent.

39. Among female informants, the divorce rate in Kamadugu Sokorala was 16.7 percent, whereas among female informants in Kabala the number was 27.8 percent.

40. It remains to be seen how the new Gender Bills mentioned above regulating for example inheritance will affect these practices.

41. The situation for children of adulterous unions is another matter. There is seldom any stigma attached to those children, today or in the past, if the mother remains married to her husband. But, as Jackson also noted, and this still seemed to be the case today, "Should a woman marry her lover and bear a child before the refunding of bridewealth (*yilboi*) and the legal declaration of divorce, then that child will be in an invidious position. It will remain in the custody of the former husband but it will be motherless and therefore disadvantaged" (Jackson 1977, 101). Paternity is generally social, not genetic.

42. Many young unmarried women explained that the least attractive marriage proposals for them were those where they would be the last of several wives. They frequently stated that no one wanted to be "a slave to the head wife," and Leach wrote that "junior wives find independence from their senior co-wives as important as from their husband" (1994, 89).

43. Again, the new law, the Devolution of Estates Act (2007), is formulated to address exactly these issues.

3. Abduction and Everyday Rebel Life

1. Jackson too was struck by how Kuranko people were taught to endure pain and accept adversity. "Pain is an unavoidable part of life," he noted, "it can neither be abolished nor explained away; what matters most is how one suffers and withstands it" (2004b, 44).

2. This has historical precedents, where, as Ferme notes, "farms and work spaces hidden in the forest are the first temporary shelters for refugees from villages" (Ferme 2001, 14).

3. In the TRC report, Superman, aka Dennis Mingo, is held responsible for large-scale violence and abuse during Phase Two of the war, from 1994 onward. He is mentioned in this report as someone who was "one of the foremost perpetrators of abduction related crimes against children, including forced recruitment and drugging" (TRC 2004, 2: § 148).

4. Personal communication, Makeni, in August 2004.

5. This incident is also recorded in the TRC report and is dated to August 1998 (2004, 3a: § 110).

6. In the TRC report there are many references to the consumption of different kinds of drugs (TRC 2004, 3a: § 51 and § 52).

7. This same phenomenon is not unique to the war in Sierra Leone but has also been noted, for example, in war-torn northern Uganda (see, e.g., Finnström 2003, 258).

8. There is no easy way to estimate how many children were born under these circumstances during the war. In interviews made by the local organization CES, 20 percent state that they had become pregnant during the abduction. Still, in view of the social stigma, both I and the CES staff I have consulted believed this figure was much higher.

9. For example, Mazurana and Carlson found that 44 percent of abducted women were engaged in food production (2004, 12).

10. Women contribute about 55 percent to the production of rice, and 25 percent of the total GDP is through the contribution of female farmers. Despite the constant focus on diamonds and other natural resources as the means of enriching the country, agriculture is a substantial part of the country's GDP, at 45 percent (Femmes Africa Solidarité 1997).

11. Issa Sesay was later to step up and assume leadership in the RUF after the arrest of Foday Sankoh (see, e.g., Gberie 2005, 174).

12. *Virgination* or to be *virginated* means to lose one's virginity.

4. From Rape Victims to Female Fighters

1. It is assumed that a majority of abducted girls and women experienced some form of sexual violence, but any figures need to be treated with caution. Physicians for Human Rights (PHR) estimated that somewhere around 250,000 Sierra Leonean women and girls were subjected to sexual violence during the war (2002, 2), and former UN human rights adviser to the Sierra Leone Mission, Michael O'Flaherty, noted that in 1999–2000 "it became obvious that the incidence of sexual abuse of women abductees was at 100 per cent" (2004, 58). In one of my surveys in Bombali and Kono districts, as many as 68 percent said they had been raped at least once. An Amnesty report quotes sources estimating that between 70 and 90 percent of abducted girls were raped (Amnesty International 2000).

2. Save the Children estimates that as many as 40 percent of child soldiers are girls (Save the Children 2005). In reports from other African countries in armed conflict with a large population of abducted girls, the number of girls who identify themselves as fighters is almost the same or slightly more than in Sierra Leone (see Save the Children 2005, 11). It is considerably more difficult to find any figures on how many women over eighteen years were active in the various fighting forces in Sierra Leone. Estimates have varied from 10 percent (Richards 1996, 89) to 30 percent (Mazurana and Carlson 2004). There were more female fighters in the RUF, however, than in the various CDFs (Richards 2005b, 576). The difficulties in assessing numbers are due in part to the fact that most girls and women did not disarm and demobilize but drifted quietly back to their communities, and also that most NGO projects targeting female fighters have only sponsored those under eighteen years of age.

3. As I described in the introduction to this book, most of my informants rarely distinguished between different fighting factions; they simply called them "rebels," and for this reason I also use this term.

4. Mats Utas, personal communication, 16 February and 6 May 2005.

5. It has been noted that female fighters also participated in raping, and according to Mansaray, nearly 12 percent of rape cases were committed or assisted by female fighters (Mansaray 2000, 146). In my interviews, there is some mention of women inserting objects into other women's

vaginas, forcing boys and men to rape female family members, and assisting male fighters' rapes of women.

6. This has also been noted by Mazurana and Carlson (2004, 14) and by researcher Corinne Dufka (personal communication, August 2004) during her extensive work for Human Rights Watch in Sierra Leone.

7. Felicity Hill, personal communication, May 2005.

8. During the hostage situation at a Moscow theater in 2002 the female rebels/terrorists probably received more news coverage due to the fact that they were women. These women puzzled many, and the fact that they were obviously Muslim and wore veils further increased people's curiosity and also abhorrence. Experts, journalists, and others speculated on the motivation for the participation of these women: had they perhaps been raped, had their fathers or husbands or brothers been killed by the Russians? Perhaps this was the case, but what was striking was the fact that no one *ever* mentioned that the motivation behind the participation of these women could perhaps be political, such as, for instance, the liberation of Chechnya. The male Chechen rebels' motivations for the terror acts were interpreted only as political; they were simply Chechen rebels fighting against Russian dominance. In fact, the reason most young men joined the Chechnyan rebel forces was personal, often the death of a family member, writes Russian anthropologist Valery Tishkov (2004).

9. "Moscow Siege Leaves Dark Memories," by Caroline Wyatt, BBC Moscow correspondent Monday, 16 December 2002, 18:18 GMT, http://news.bbc.co.uk/1/hi/world/europe/2565585.stm.

10. "Liberia's Women Killers," BBC, Tuesday, 26 August 2003, 11:44 GMT 12:44 UK, http://news.bbc.co.uk/1/hi/world/africa/3181529.stm

11. See http://www.csmonitor.com/2003/0826/p07s01-woaf.html

12. It is likely that the situation in other parts of Sierra Leone during the war, such as the occupied town of Makeni or the diamond-rich areas in the eastern part of the country, displayed other characteristics. Another issue that also becomes clear is the difference between the two countries in terms of the important role ethnicity played in the Liberian war. The Sierra Leone war was not a war between different ethnic groups. This is not to say that there was no tension between various ethnic groups, in particular the Mende and the Temne, but it was not perceived by the informants as playing a part in the dynamics of the war. Rather, as I have shown above, ethnic belonging was downplayed for other reasons.

13. Still, although some women were combatants, the status of perpetrator is actually something that has not been widely researched or discussed when focusing on women in the Sierra Leone war, with a few exceptions (see e.g. Persson 2005, Coulter et al 2008).

14. Shaw convincingly summarized this debate: "At its most crude, this reaction takes the form of reiterations that people are not 'passive objects' but 'active subjects', are not 'victims' but 'agents', and are not 'subjugated' but 'authors of their own histories'. Such formulaic declarations are disturbingly resonant of a dominant North Atlantic discourse of unfettered individualism and freedom of choice" (2002, 19).

15. Several books have been published in the last decade concerning issues of gender and war and women's participation in war, e.g., Turshen and Twagiramariya (1998), Moser and Clark (2001), Bennett et al. (1995), and Jacobs et al. (2000), to name a few. Most have had as their aim to go beyond viewing women as passive *victims,* arguing instead that it is necessary to expand the inquiries of what women do in war and to critically analyse women's roles as perpetrators and perpetuators of war and conflict by focusing on *agency*. However, probably because many women in rebel and liberation movements are often forcefully conscripted or in other ways coerced, and because sexual violence in wartime is still widespread, few authors manage to completely circumvent the issue of women in war as victims. The lesson therefore seems to be that all women are not victims *all* the time, but still some of them some of the time become victims just because they are women (cf. Moore 1994, 17).

5. Reconciliation or Revenge

1. Mazurana and Carlson estimated that in the DDR program only 6.5 percent of all registered adults were women and that 7.4 percent of all children were girls (Mazurana and Carlson 2004).

2. The program was funded by a number of national and international actors such as the Sierra Leone government, donor governments, the UN, the World Bank, and various NGOs (see McKay and Mazurana 2004, 98). The program was divided into three phases. Phase one was conducted by the Economic Community of West African States Monitoring Group (ECOMOG) and the National Commission for Demilitarization, Demobilization and Reintegration (NCDDR); phase two was conducted by the UN Observer Mission to Sierra Leone (UNOMSIL); and the third and last phase jointly by the United Nations Mission in Sierra Leone (UNAMSIL) and the NCDDR.

3. There were some DDR programs which experienced difficulties in the payment to combatants and in organizing vocational projects, thereby delaying the process, or shortening the length of the training.

4. In the 1997 Liberian DDR program, for example, only very few women participated (Utas 2003, 178). On the other hand, in 2004, when gender mainstreaming was specifically incorporated into the United Nations mission to Liberia, over 17 percent of demobilized ex-combatants were women (Liberia Disarmament, Demobilization and Reintegration Program, Activity Report, UNDP 2004).

5. UN Security Council (2000).

6. UNIFEM Freetown, 27 July 2004, personal communication with staff.

7. The Cape Town Principles were adopted by international organizations in 1997 in recognition of the vulnerability of children in armed groups and explicitly state that child soldiers are all those who were part of any armed group—"not only in the capacity of fighter: child soldier means any person under eighteen years of age who is part of any kind of regular or irregular armed force or armed group in any capacity.... It includes girls recruited for sexual purposes and forced marriage. It does not, therefore, refer only to a child who is carrying or has carried arms" (Cape Town Principles 1997).

8. Shepler (2005) has also pointed to malfunctions in the programs aimed at reintegrating child ex-combatants.

9. In my survey of 111 girls and women in Kono and Bombali districts, 22 percent said that the main reason they did not demobilize was that they had no gun. However, it has to be noted that Mazurana and Carlson reached a much higher figure, 46 percent, in their survey (Mazurana and Carlson 2003).

10. A demobilized fighter was supposed to get three installments of 130,000 leones each, totaling 390,000 leones. At the time of fieldwork, US $1 was worth between 2,400 and 2,900 leones. Here I count 2,500 leones equaling $1 unless otherwise indicated.

11. During a UNICEF workshop in Freetown in August 2004, with many participants from local and international NGOs, representatives from the Liberian DDR, and NGOs working in Guinea and Côte d'Ivoire, this issue was raised and added to a list of recommendations on how to gender mainstream and improve DDR processes.

12. This is verified by McKay and Mazurana (2004), by Bennett (2002), and by the Women's Commission for Refugee Women and Children (2002).

13. This issue was also raised by Brett and Specht, who wrote that "rehabilitation programs need to be adapted to take into account the specific needs of... girl soldiers with babies, taking into account the sociocultural context" (Brett and Specht 2004, 100).

14. Peace Agreement between the Government of Sierra Leone and the Revolutionary United Front of Sierra Leone (1999).

15. Still, despite the lack of adequate funding and serious mismanagement problems, the TRC managed to collect more than eight thousand statements (Dougherty 2004, 47), some of which are quoted in its report.

16. See also Bronéus (2006) on "truth telling" and giving witness as increasing suffering rather than providing healing in the case of Rwanda.

17. Apparently, it was found that 60 percent of those who testified in the South African TRC felt worse after testifying (Shaw 2005, 7).

18. According to Colvin, there is also a tendency toward reifying as victims those who have experienced violence and also toward "obscuring the social and historical dynamics that produced that violence in the first place" (2004, 84), something that resonates with the Sierra Leonean context as well.

19. Personal communication. Whether there is or can be a specifically "African" way or an "African" solution to these problems, which are grounded on processes and injustices reaching far beyond both the Sierra Leone borders and the African continent, remains problematical. These are issues I will not discuss here, but for a recent discussion highlighting "Africa" and globalization, see Ferguson (2006).

20. Interview with COOPI staff, 14 August 2004, Koidu.

21. Which is not surprising, seeing that Sierra Leone is a small country, the capital even smaller, and the educated elite are often on a first-name basis with each other (see also Kelsall 2005, 381).

22. Considering the strong negative feelings my informants had towards the TRC, I was all the more surprised to see an opinion poll conducted by the Sierra Leone NGO, Campaign for Good Governance, in which 58 percent had said that they were "willing to testify" to the TRC. The poll was funded by the American Embassy and its purpose was to "conduct research measuring the extent to which Sierra Leoneans understand these institutions, whether or not they are willing to co-operate and how far they support the TRC and the Special Court" (Campaign for Good Governance 2005). This report did not, however, address how it could be that the most vulnerable, according to TRC's own definition—abducted women and female ex-combatants—were terrified of the TRC.

23. When I explained that the TRC recorded people's testimonies I said that it was in order for Sierra Leoneans "not to forget." I realized only when transcribing this interview the contradiction between this and the slogan that Sierra Leoneans should "forgive and forget." Unintentionally, I realized, I had reproduced the international humanitarian discourse that is so familiar to my generation of Western students, brought up as we are with the many narratives of the Holocaust, and the emphasis on "we must never forget," in contrast to Sierra Leone, where people were encouraged to do just that.

24. My findings are confirmed by other researchers and reports; see, e.g., Dougherty (2004, 48), O'Flaherty (2004) and the report from PRIDE in collaboration with the International Center for Transitional Justice (2002).

25. A UN Military Observer (MILOBS) serving in Moyamba later told me that in this district the Special Court had local staff who had toured the rural areas with a generator, TV, and VCR showing an informative video about their work. In Koinadugu, no such team existed.

26. Discussions on the meaning of trauma, and the suitability of PTSD for non-Western societies are not new and the concepts have been criticized widely (see, e.g., Argenti-Pillen 2003; Colvin 2004; Finnström 2003; Ross 2003; Sampson 2003; Shaw 2005).

27. It seems that the TRC constantly distinguished between victims on the one hand and perpetrators on the other, not recognizing that many were both (cf. Kelsall 2005). Ross (2005, 215) explains that in the setting of the Truth Commission in South Africa, "Violence was bifurcated into a concern with 'perpetrators' who committed acts of violence and 'victims' who suffered the consequences of violence," and says this is an approach that has been criticized both for obscuring the roles of beneficiaries and for not considering the structural components of South African apartheid.

28. Rosalind Shaw, personal communication, August 2004.

29. Also Shepler noted that her informants talked of no such rites or ceremonies (Shepler 2005, 144).

30. Kelsall also concluded, referencing two of the most renowned anthropological scholars on Sierra Leone, Shaw and Ferme, that "the practice of public confession and inquisitorial investigation may not be the most familiar vehicle by which to arrive at the truth in Sierra Leone" (Kelsall 2005, 384).

31. In fact, in the case of Sierra Leone and Liberia there are strong indications that the infrastructure and hierarchy of rebel organization remain even after war (Mynster Christensen 2007; Persson 2005; Utas 2003).

6. Surviving the Postwar Economy

1. "Ensuring that a woman is empowered, healthy and well educated—a good unto itself—can have a dramatic and positive effect on the well-being of her children." *The State of the World's Children* (UNICEF 2004, 46).

2. Tie-dyeing is also sometimes referred to as batik, but Sierra Leonean gara dyers distinguish between their technique and batik.

3. I did not quantify my information on this point, but I would say that an absolute majority of informants wanted skills training. Bennett states that 78 percent of the women she interviewed said they wanted skills training in order to improve their lives (Bennett 2002, 30).

4. Examples of these alternatives were, among others, electrical installations, driving instruction, auto mechanics, processing and trading of charcoal, specialized agricultural production, bamboo furniture construction, facilitating the creation of co-operatives, animal husbandry, poultry farming, and shoe making.

5. In the many projects I have visited, not once has skills training been preceded by preskills training orientation for the proposed beneficiaries, nor has any analysis or examination been performed on any level of the economic viability of these skills, which are provided by organizations to make girls and young women "more independent" and "self-reliant."

6. With regard to weaving, however, this was perhaps one instance where NGOs addressed issues of gender inequality in Sierra Leonean society, given that weaving has been a male occupation. This was most likely done unintentionally, however, although it might well reflect a gender bias within the predominantly "Western" international humanitarian community that sees weaving as women's work.

7. In Sierra Leone it is the custom and prerogative of someone older to send children on errands.

8. Sirah bought kerosene in rubber drums (1 drum = 5 gallons) for Le 4,600 per gallon, a total of Le 23,000. For every gallon there are 60 tomato cups, which she sold at Le 100, a total of Le 6,000 per gallon, and Le 30,000 per drum. She paid the driver Le 2,000 for every drum, which meant a total profit of no more than Le 5,000. With the new price, she had to pay Le 5,000 per gallon, which by the drum meant Le 25,000. But after raising the price to Le 150 for the smallest measurement, the tomato cup, she would in fact be able to sell for Le 9,000 per gallon (Le 45,000 leones per drum), and after deducting the cost of a drum and the driver's fee, she still had a profit of Le 13,000 compared to Le 5,000 before, and she would even be able to pay the driver more for transport and still make a bigger profit.

9. In Bennett's study as well, not one respondent expressed any interest in farming or animal husbandry (Bennett 2002, 66). This is not something new, however. Bledsoe (1990) describes, for example, how, before the war, formal schooling became a path for young girls to escape from the constraints of village life.

10. In my survey in Koinadugu District, I found that of 119 women, 58 (49 percent) had never been to Freetown, 11 (9 percent) had visited, while 50 (42 percent) had lived there between one and thirty years.

11. This illicit trade could be the sale of rice and palm oil (see, e.g., Ferme 2001, 108, on the trade of "night oil").

12. In 2002 in Sierra Leone and Liberia news hit the world about a "Sex for Food" scandal involving humanitarian staff as well as peacekeeping soldiers (UNHCR/Save the Children UK 2002). It was reported that girls and women had sex with peacekeepers in exchange for a piece of fruit or some food. There has also been a dramatic increase in prostitution in Freetown, often in close proximity to the expatriate recreation areas.

13. The UN Department of Peacekeeping Operations (DPKO) has worked a great deal on its codes of conduct in the past decade. It states, for example, that a peacekeeper should never "become involved in sexual liaisons which could affect impartiality, or the well-being of others," and the UN defines sexual exploitation as "any actual or attempted abuse of a position of vulnerability, differential power, or trust, for sexual purposes." http://ochaonline.un.org/GetBin.asp?DocID=1083

14. I was once told by a Scandinavian UNAMSIL officer, who had a wife and three children at home and several local girlfriends in Sierra Leone, that "what happens in the field, stays in the field." He did not respond kindly to my question whether that also applied to STDs and HIV/AIDS.

7. Coming Home—Domesticating the Bush

1. Cf. Barth (2002), on the similar situation for women after the war in Eritrea.

2. A Sierra Leonean friend of Shepler's told her that he definitely did not want such a girl married into his family and suggested instead that "rebel boys and girls should be married to each other, then there would be no stigma" (as quoted by Shepler 2002, 14).

3. In a reunification program in the district of Kono, the organization International Rescue Committee (IRC) reported that it had reunited 196 girls and young women with their families. They had been provided with a "reunification package" consisting of blankets, buckets, and other household utensils, and the families and the returning girls had been "sensitized" to ameliorate the process. Despite this, after a few months, as many as 157 girls had left their families and either returned to a bush husband or gone to live with friends in urban areas. According to IRC social workers, many of these girls and young women "just couldn't cope with the family situation or village life" (Interview with IRC Child Protection Unit, Kono, 11 August 2004).

4. In Kabala, during the war, there had been rumors of rebels capturing a whole set of newly initiated girls and raping them. Stories like this seemed particularly upsetting to people, as it was understood that those girls had all been "spoilt."

5. That women are tied to marriage by the inability of their poor parents to repay bridewealth is not uncommon in Sierra Leone (cf. Richards 2005b, 584).

6. After an initiation ceremony I attended, a male elder proudly announced before the whole village that all girls had been virgins, for which they thanked God. I knew for a fact that this was not the case, and so I asked the older women about it. They told me that the girl's parents usually confronted the girl before initiation, asking her to confess if she had had sex, with the threat of sickness and possible death during the initiation if she lied. If she admitted, a sacrifice of rice flour was made and the girl was officially a virgin again, although parents would keep the whole affair a secret.

7. The situation is very different from, for example, Islamic countries such as Morocco and Senegal, where the cost of bridewealth has gone up substantially and where virginity is of increasing importance. Personal communication, Eva Evers Rosander, 10 June 2006.

8. Although the level of sexual abuse reached enormous proportions during the war, experiences of sexual abuse and forced sex were common even before the war. Physicians for Human

Rights estimated that 9 percent of Sierra Leonean women have at some time in their lives experienced nonwar-related sexual violence, which is almost the same level of sexual abuse as during the war (2002, 2–3).

9. Swedish gynecologist Margareta Sidenwall, who has worked with internally displaced people in neighboring Liberia, also noticed that her female patients differentiated between rape and involuntary sex in a way that is perhaps surprising to a Western audience. Personal communication, 25 November 2005.

10. The 1960 Protection of Girls and Women Act, and also the 1960 Prevention of Cruelty to Children Act.

11. See, e.g., reports from HRW (2003), Bambrick (2004), and Physicians for Human Rights (2002).

12. Interview with police officer at the Family Support Unit, Koidu police station, 6 August 2004; also noted by Physicians for Human Rights (Physicians for Human Rights 2002).

13. After some questioning, it turned out that the cost of medical examinations could be anywhere from Le 5,000 to Le 20,000 (around US$2 to $8 in 2004), a lot of money for most rural Sierra Leoneans.

14. It was not until 1996, when eight male Bosnian Serb military and police officers were indicted in the International War Crimes Tribunal on charges of raping Bosnian Muslim women, that rape was treated separately as a crime of war (see Enloe 2000, 135).

15. Transcript of case number SCSL-04-15-T from 5 July 2004.

16. The "awareness trousers" of which she speaks refer to a wartime phenomenon that became quite widespread throughout the country. Often it is simply called "awareness" and means that a person, man or woman, will wear several pairs of trousers on top of each other. This became a habit during the war when people felt that they had to be ready to escape at any time if attacked. Women would often have skirts or the traditional *lappa* on top of their trousers. Awareness trousers were also seen as a form of protection from rape, as it was more difficult to undress. This war term has subsequently entered everyday language.

17. For example, in the Physicians for Human Rights' study, 60 percent of the women surveyed believed that a wife had to obey her husband and succumb to his demands for sex (Physicians for Human Rights 2002, 55).

18. Bennett cites a source in Tikonko chiefdom who mentioned 10 children of ECOMOG and UN peacekeepers born to single mothers only in that small area (Bennett 2002, 50).

REFERENCES

Abdullah, Ibrahim, ed. 2004. *Between Democracy and Terror: The Sierra Leone Civil War.* Dakar, Senegal: CODESRIA, Council for the Development of Social Science Research in Africa.

———. 1998. "Bush Path to Destruction: The Origin and Character of the Revolutionary United Front/Sierra Leone." *The Journal of Modern African Studies* 36, 2: 203–35.

———. 1995. "Liberty or Death: Working-Class Agitation and the Labour Question in Colonial Freetown, 1938–39." *International Review of Social History* 40: 195–221.

———. 1994. "Rethinking the Freetown Crowd: The Moral Economy of the 1919 Strikes and Riot in Sierra Leone." *Canadian Journal of African Studies* 28, 2: 197–218.

Abdullah, Ibrahim, and Patrick Muana. 1998. "The Revolutionary United Front of Sierra Leone." In *African Guerrillas,* edited by C. Clapham, 170–93. London: James Currey.

Abrahams, R. G. 1973. "Some Aspects of the Levirate." In *The Character of Kinship,* edited by J. Goody, 163–74. Cambridge: Cambridge University Press.

Adams, Abigail E. 1993. "Dyke to Dyke: Ritual Reproduction at a U.S. Men's Military College." *Anthropology Today* 9, 5: 3–6.

African Rights. 1995. *Rwanda, Not So Innocent: When Women Become Killers.* London: African Rights.

Alidou, Ousseina, and Meredeth Turshen. 2000. "Africa: Women in the Aftermath of Civil War." *Race and Class* 4, 1: 81–92.

Alie, Joe A.D. 2005. "The Kamajor Militia in Sierra Leone: Liberators or Nihilists?" In *Civil Militia: Africa's Intractable Security Menace*, edited by D. J. Francis, 51–70. Aldershot, UK: Ashgate.

———. 1990. *A New History of Sierra Leone*. London: Macmillan.

Amato, Joseph Anthony, and David Monge. 1990. *Victims and Values: A History and a Theory of Suffering*. Contributions in Philosophy, No. 42. New York: Greenwood Press.

Amnesty International. 2006. "Sierra Leone: Women Face Human Rights Abuses in the Informal Legal Sector." New York: Amnesty International.

———. 2000. "Sierra Leone: Rape and Other Forms of Sexual Violence against Girls and Women." New York: Amnesty International.

Andreas, Carol. 1990–91. "Women at War." *NACLA Report on the Americas* 24, 4: 20–27.

Archibald, Stephen, and Paul Richards. 2002. "Converts to Human Rights? Popular Debate about War and Justice in Rural Central Sierra Leone." *Africa* 72, 3: 339–67.

Ardener, Shirley. 1964. "The Comparative Study of Rotating Credit Associations." *Journal of the Royal Anthropological Institute of Great Britain and Ireland* 94, 2: 201–29.

Arendt, Hannah. 1968. *Men in Dark Times*. New York: Harcourt Brace and World.

Aretxaga, Begoña. 1997. *Shattering Silence: Women, Nationalism, and Political Subjectivity in Northern Ireland*. Princeton, NJ: Princeton University Press.

Argenti-Pillen, Alex. 2003. *Masking Terror: How Women Contain Violence in Southern Sri Lanka*. Philadelphia: University of Pennsylvania Press.

Bambrick, Kati. 2004. "Silent Victims, Young Girls at Risk: An Evaluation of Post-War Rape and the Response to Rape in the Provinces of Sierra Leone." Freetown, Sierra Leone: Campaign for Good Governance.

Barstow, Anne Llewellyn. 2000. *War's Dirty Secret: Rape, Prostitution, and Other Crimes against Women*. Cleveland, OH: Pilgrim Press.

Barth, Elise F. 2004. "The United Nations Mission in Eritrea/Ethiopia: Gender(Ed) Effects." In *Gender Aspects of Conflict Interventions: Intended and Unintended Consequences*, edited by L. Olsson, I. Skjelsbæk, E. F. Barth, and K. Hostens, 9–24. Oslo: PRIO.

———. 2002. "Peace as Disappointment: The Reintegration of Female Soldiers in Post-Conflict Societies, a Comparative Study from Africa." Oslo: International Peace Research Institute (PRIO).

Bassir, Olumbe. 1954. "Marriage Rites among the Aku (Yoruba) of Freetown." *Africa: Journal of the International African Institute* 24, 3: 251–56.

Beattie, Kenneth James. 1978. *Human Leopards: An Account of the Trials of Human Leopards before the Special Commission Court: With a Note on Sierra Leone, Past and Present*. 1915; Reprint New York: AMS Press.

Ben-Ari, Eyal. 1998. *Mastering Soldiers: Conflict, Emotions, and the Enemy in an Israeli Military Unit*. New York: Berghahn.

Bennett, Allison. 2002. "The Reintegration of Child Ex-Combatants in Sierra Leone with a Particular Focus on the Needs of Females." MA diss., University of East London.

Bennett, Olivia, Jo Bexley, and Kitty Warnock, eds. 1995. *Arms to Fight—Arms to Protect: Women Speak out About Conflict*. London: Panos.

Besteman, Catherine, and Hugh Gusterson, eds. 2005. *Why America's Top Pundits Are Wrong: Anthropologists Talking Back.* Berkeley: University of California Press.

Bledsoe, Caroline H. 1992. "The Cultural Transformation of Western Education in Sierra Leone." *Africa* 62, 2: 182–202.

———. 1990. "School Fees and the Marriage Process for Mende Girls in Sierra Leone." In *Beyond the Second Sex: New Directions in the Anthropology of Gender,* edited by P. R. Sanday and R. G. Goodenough, 283–309. Philadelphia: University of Pennsylvania Press.

———. 1987. "Side-Stepping the Postpartum Sex Taboo: Mende Cultural Perceptions of Tinned Milk in Sierra Leone." In *The Cultural Roots of African Fertility Regimes,* edited by E. v. d. Walle and J. A. Ebigola, 101–24. Ile-Ife, Nigeria: Obafemi Awolowo University.

———. 1980. *Women and Marriage in Kpelle Society.* Stanford: Stanford University Press.

Bøås, Morten. 1997. "Rebuilding Social Capital in the Line of Fire: The Reinvention of Civil Society in Sierra Leone." Paper presented at the Africa Days: Poverty and Prosperity in the African Context, Nordiska Afrikainstitutet, Uppsala, 19–21 September 1997.

Bott, David, and Matthew Hodes. 1989. "Structural Therapy for a West African Family." *Journal of Family Therapy* 11, 2: 169–79.

Bourgois, Philippe I. 2002. *In Search of Respect: Selling Crack in El Barrio.* Cambridge: Cambridge University Press.

Bracken, Patrick J. 1998. "Hidden Agendas: Deconstructing Post Traumatic Stress Disorder." In *Rethinking the Trauma of War,* edited by P. J. Bracken and C. Petty, 38–59. London: Free Association Books.

Braidwood, Stephen J. 1994. *Black Poor and White Philanthropists: London's Blacks and the Foundation of the Sierra Leone Settlement, 1786–91.* Liverpool: Liverpool University Press.

Brett, Rachel, and Irma Specht. 2004. *Young Soldiers: Why They Choose to Fight.* Boulder, CO: Lynne Rienner.

Bruner, Edward M. 1986. "Experience and Its Expressions." In *The Anthropology of Experience,* edited by V. W. Turner and E. M. Bruner, 3–30. Chicago: University of Illinois Press.

Bunting, Annie. 2005. "Stages of Development: Marriage of Girls and Teens as an International Human Rights Issue." *Social and Legal Studies* 14, 1: 17–38.

Byrne, Bridget. 1996. "Towards a Gendered Understanding of Conflict." *IDS Bulletin* 27, 3: 31–40.

Campaign for Good Governance. 2005. "Opinion Poll Report on the TRC and Special Court." Freetown: Campaign for Good Governance.

Cape Town Principles. 1997. "Annotated Principles and Best Practices: On the Prevention of Recruitment of Children into the Armed Forces and Demobilization and Social Reintegration of Child Soldiers in Africa." Cape Town: UNICEF, Working Group on the Convention on the Rights of the Child.

Card, Claudia. 1996. "Rape as a Weapon of War." *Hypatia* 11, 4: 5–18.

Caulker, Patrick S. 1981. "Legitimate Commerce and Statecraft: A Study of the Hinterland Adjacent to Nineteenth-Century Sierra Leone." *Journal of Black Studies* 11, 4: 397–419.

Clark, Suzanne. 2000. *Cold Warriors: Manliness on Trial in the Rhetoric of the West.* Carbondale: Southern Illinois University Press.

Cockayne, James. 2005. "Hybrids or Mongrels? Internationalized War Crimes Trials as Unsuccessful Degradation Ceremonies." *Journal of Human Rights* 4: 455–73.

Cockburn, Cynthia, and Dubravka Zarkov. 2002. *The Postwar Moment: Militaries, Masculinities, and International Peacekeeping.* London: Lawrence and Wishart.

Cohn, Carol. 1993. "Wars, Wimps, and Women: Talking Gender and Thinking War." In *Gendering War Talk,* edited by M. Cooke and A. Woollacott, 227–46. Princeton, NJ: Princeton University Press.

Colvin, Christopher J. 2004. "Ambivalent Narrations: Pursuing the Political through Traumatic Storytelling." *PoLAR* 27, 1: 72–89.

Conciliation Resources. 1997. "Gender and Conflict in Sierra Leone." London, UK: Conciliation Resources.

Connell, Robert W. 2000. *The Men and the Boys.* Cambridge: Polity.

——. 1992. "Masculinity, Violence, and War." In *Men's Lives,* edited by M. S. Kimmel and M. A. Messner, 176–83. New York: Macmillan.

Conteh-Morgan, Earl, and Mac Dixon-Fyle. 1999. *Sierra Leone at the End of the Twentieth Century: History, Politics, and Society.* New York: P. Lang.

Coulter, Chris. 2008. "Female Fighters in the Sierra Leone War: Challenging the Assumptions?" *Feminist Review* 88: 54–73.

——. 2005. "Reflections from the Field: A Girl's Initiation Ceremony in Northern Sierra Leone." *Anthropological Quarterly* 78, 2: 431–42.

——. 2001. "Organizing People and Places: Humanitarian Discourse and Sierra Leonean Refugees." Working Papers in Cultural Anthropology no. 10. Uppsala: Department of Cultural Anthropology and Ethnology.

Coulter, Chris, Mariam Persson, and Mats Utas. 2008. "Young Female Fighters in African Wars: Conflict and Its Consequences." The Nordic Africa Institute Policy Dialogue 3.

Cowan, Jane K., Marie-Bénédicte Dembour, and Richard A. Wilson, eds. 2001. *Culture and Rights: Anthropological Perspectives.* Cambridge: Cambridge University Press, 2001.

Cruise O'Brien, Donal B. 1996. "A Lost Generation? Youth Identity and State Decay in West Africa." In *Postcolonial Identities in Africa,* edited by R. Werbner and T. Ranger, 55–74. London: Zed Books.

Cryer, Robert, Colin Warbrick, and Dominic McGoldrick. 2001. "A 'Special Court' for Sierra Leone?" *The International and Comparative Law Quarterly* 50, 2: 435–46.

Daniel, E. Valentine. 1996. *Charred Lullabies: Chapters in an Anthropography of Violence.* Princeton, NJ: Princeton University Press.

Das, Veena. 1996. "Language and Body: Transactions in the Construction of Pain." *Daedalus* 125, 1: 67–91.

——. 1995. *Critical Events: An Anthropological Perspective on Contemporary India.* New Delhi: Oxford University Press.

Das, Veena, Arthur Kleinman, Margaret Lock, Mamphela Ramphele, and Pamela Reynolds eds. 2001. *Remaking a World: Violence, Social Suffering, and Recovery.* Berkeley: University of California Press, 2001.

David, Soniia. 1997. "'You Become One in Marriage': Domestic Budgeting among the Kpelle of Liberia." *Canadian Journal of African Studies* 31, 1: 144–69.

Dawson, Graham. 1994. *Soldier Heroes: British Adventure, Empire, and the Imagining of Masculinities.* London: Routledge.

Day, Lynda R. 1994. *The Female Chiefs of the Mende, 1885–1977: Tracing the Evolution of an Indigenous Political Institution.* Madison: University Press of Wisconsin.

Denov, Myriam, and Richard Maclure. 2007. "Turnings and Epiphanies: Militarization, Life Histories, and the Making and Unmaking of Two Child Soldiers in Sierra Leone." *Journal of Youth Studies* 10, 2: 243–61.

Dolan, Chris. 2002. "Collapsing Masculinities and Weak States—A Case Study of Northern Uganda." In *Masculinities Matter! Men, Gender, and Development,* edited by F. Cleaver, 57–83. London: Zed Books.

Dorjahn, V. R., and Christopher Fyfe. 1962. "Landlord and Stranger: Change in Tenancy Relations in Sierra Leone." *Journal of African History* 3, 3: 391–97.

Dougherty, Beth K. 2004. "Searching for Answers: Sierra Leone's Truth and Reconciliation Commission." *African Studies Quarterly* 8, 1: 39–56.

Ellis, Stephen. 1999. *The Mask of Anarchy: The Destruction of Liberia and the Religious Dimension of an African Civil War.* New York: New York University Press.

Englund, Harri. 2006. *Prisoners of Freedom: Human Rights and the African Poor.* Berkeley: University of California Press.

——. 2000a. "The Dead Hand of Human Rights: Contrasting Christianities in Post-Transition Malawi." *The Journal of Modern African Studies* 38, 4: 579–603.

——. 2000b. "(Wo)Man in War." *Antropologiska Studier* 66–67: 61–73.

Enloe, Cynthia. 2002. "Demilitarization—Or More of the Same? Feminist Questions to Ask in the Postwar Moment." In *The Postwar Moment: Militaries, Masculinities, and International Peacekeeping,* edited by C. Cockburn and D. Zarkov, 22–32. London: Lawrence and Wishart.

——. 2000. *Maneuvers: The International Politics of Militarizing Women's Lives.* Berkeley: University of California Press.

——. 1993. *The Morning After: Sexual Politics at the End of the Cold War.* Berkeley: University of California Press.

——. 1991. "The Implications of Militarism." *Outlook* 13 (summer): 22.

——. 1989. *Bananas, Beaches, and Bases: Making Feminist Sense of International Politics.* Berkeley: University of California Press.

Escobar, Arturo. 1995. *Encountering Development: The Making and Unmaking of the Third World.* Princeton, NJ: Princeton University Press.

Fanthorpe, Richard. 1998. "Locating the Politics of a Sierra Leonean Chiefdom." *Africa* 68, 4: 558–84.

Farr, Vanessa. 2002. "Gendering Demilitarization as a Peacebuilding Tool." Bonn: Bonn International Center for Conversion.

Feldman, Allen. 1991. *Formations of Violence: The Narrative of Body and Political Terror in Northern Ireland.* Chicago: University of Chicago Press.

Femmes Africa Solidarité. 1997. "Women's Participation in the Peace Process in Sierra Leone." Freetown: Femmes Africa Solidarité.

Ferguson, James. 2006. *Global Shadows: Africa in the Neoliberal World Order.* Durham, NC: Duke University Press.

Ferme, Mariane C. 2001. *The Underneath of Things: Violence, History, and the Everyday in Sierra Leone.* Berkeley: University of California Press.

Ferme, Mariane C., and Danny Hoffman. 2004. "Hunter Militias and the International Human Rights Discourse in Sierra Leone and Beyond." *Africa Today* 50, 4: 73–95.

Ferris, Elizabeth. 1993. "Women, War, and Peace." Uppsala: Life and Peace Institute.

Finnström, Sverker. 2003. *Living with Bad Surroundings: War and Existential Uncertainty in Acholiland, Northern Uganda.* Vol. 35. Uppsala Studies in Cultural Anthropology. Uppsala, Sweden: Acta Universitatis Upsaliensis.

Fithen, Caspar, and Paul Richards. 2005. "Making War, Crafting Peace: Militia Solidarities and Demobilisation in Sierra Leone." In *No Peace, No War: An Anthropology of Contemporary Armed Conflicts,* edited by P. Richards, 117–36. Oxford: James Currey.

Forna, Aminatta. 2002. *The Devil that Danced on the Water: A Daughter's Memoir of Her Father, Her Family, Her Country, and a Continent.* London: HarperCollins.

Fyfe, Christopher. 1962. *A History of Sierra Leone.* Oxford: Oxford University Press.

Gage, Anastasia J., and Caroline Bledsoe. 1994. "The Effects of Education and Social Stratification on Marriage and the Transition to Parenthood in Freetown, Sierra Leone." In *Nuptiality in Sub-Saharan Africa,* edited by C. Bledsoe and G. Pison, 148–64. Oxford: Clarendon Press.

Gardam, Judith, and Hilary Charlesworth. 2000. "Protection of Women in Armed Conflict." *Human Rights Quarterly* 22, 1: 148–66.

Gberie, Lansana. 2005. *A Dirty War in West Africa: The RUF and the Destruction of Sierra Leone.* London: C. Hurst.

———. 2003. "Ecomog: The History of an Heroic Failure." *African Affairs* 102, 406: 147–54.

Geiger, Susan. 1999. "Women and Gender in African Studies." *African Studies Review* 42, 3: 21–33.

Golden, Rebecca. 2004. "Sobels, Ogas, and Green Beans. Language as Representations of Violence: The Language Diary of an Aid Worker in Africa." In *Representations of Violence: Art about the Sierra Leone Civil War,* edited by P. K. Muana and C. Corcoran, 71–77. Madison, WI: 21st Century African Youth Movement.

Good, Mary-Jo Delvecchio, Paul E. Brodwin, Byron J. Good, and Arthur Kleinman, eds. 1992. *Pain as Human Experience: An Anthropological Perspective.* Berkeley: University of California Press.

Goody, Jack. 1973. "Polygyny, Economy, and the Role of Women." In *The Character of Kinship,* edited by J. Goody, 175–90. Cambridge: Cambridge University Press.

Grace, John J. 1977. "Slavery and Emancipation among the Mende in Sierra Leone, 1896–1928." In *Slavery in Africa: Historical and Anthropological Perspectives,* edited by S. Miers and I. Kopytoff, 415–34. Madison: The University of Wisconsin Press.

Green, Linda. 1999. *Fear as a Way of Life: Mayan Widows in Rural Guatemala.* New York: Columbia University Press.

———. 1995. "Living in a State of Fear." In *Fieldwork under Fire,* edited by C. Nordstrom and A. C. G. M. Robben, 105–27. Berkeley: University of California Press.

Handelman, Don. 2004. *Nationalism and the Israeli State: Bureaucratic Logic in Public Events.* Oxford: Berg.

Hart, Keith. 1985. "The Social Anthropology of West Africa." *Annual Review of Anthropology* 14: 243–72.

Hayward, Fred M. 1984. "Political Leadership, Power, and the State: Generalizations from the Case of Sierra Leone." *African Studies Review* 27, 11: 19–39.

Higate, Paul. 2004. *Gender and Peacekeeping, Case Studies: The Democratic Republic of the Congo and Sierra Leone,* Institute for Security Studies (South Africa), ISS Monograph Series No. 91. Pretoria, South Africa: Institute for Security Studies.

Hoffer, Carol. 1972. "Mende and Sherbro Women in High Office." *Canadian Journal of African Studies* 6, 2: 151–64.

Hoffman, Danny. 2005. "Violent Events as Narrative Blocs: The Disarmament at Bo, Sierra Leone." *Anthropological Quarterly* 78, 2: 329–54.

———. 2004a. "The Civilian Target in Sierra Leone and Liberia: Political Power, Military Strategy, and Humanitarian Intervention." *African Affairs* 103: 211–26.

———. 2004b. "The Kamajors of Sierra Leone." Ph.D. thesis, Duke University.

———. 2003. "Like Beasts in the Bush." *Postcolonial Studies* 6, 3: 295–308.

Hoffman, Daniel, and Stephen Lubkemann. 2005. "Warscape Ethnography in West Africa and the Anthropology of 'Events.'" *Anthropological Quarterly* 78, 2: 315–27.

Holsoe, Svend E. 1977. "Slavery and Economic Response among the Vai (Liberia and Sierra Leone)." In *Slavery in Africa: Historical and Anthropological Perspectives,* edited by S. Miers and I. Kopytoff, 287–304. Madison: The University of Wisconsin Press.

Honwana, Alcinda. 1997. "Healing for Peace: Traditional Healers and Post-War Reconstruction in Southern Mozambique." *Peace and Conflict: Journal of Peace Psychology* 3, 3: 293–305.

House-Midamba, Bessie, and Felix K. Ekechi, eds. 1995. *African Market Women and Economic Power: The Role of Women in African Economic Development.* Westport, CT: Greenwood Press, 1995.

Hughes, Donna M., and Kathleen Foster. 1996. "War, Nationalism, and Rape: Women Respond by Opening a Centre against Sexual Violence in Belgrade, Serbia." *Women's Studies International Forum* 19, 1–2: 183–84.

Human Rights Watch. 2003. "We'll Kill You If You Cry: Sexual Violence in the Sierra Leone Conflict." New York: Human Rights Watch.

———. 1998. "Sowing Terror: Atrocities against Civilians in Sierra Leone." New York: Human Rights Watch.

Höglund, Anna T. 2001. "Gender and War: A Theological and Ethical Approach." *New Routes, a Journal of Peace Research and Action* 6, 3: 4–9.

Jackson, Jean E. 1990. "Review of Elaine Scarry's *The Body in Pain: The Unmaking of the World.*" *Medical Anthropology Quarterly* 4, 4: 461–63.

Jackson, Michael. 2005. *Existential Anthropology: Events, Exigencies, and Effects.* New York: Berghahn Books.

———. 2004a. *In Sierra Leone.* Durham, NC: Duke University Press.

———. 2004b. "The Prose of Suffering and the Practice of Silence." *Spiritus* 4: 44–59.

———. 1998. *Minima Ethnographica: Intersubjectivity and the Anthropological Project.* Chicago: University of Chicago Press.

———. 1995. *At Home in the World.* Durham, NC: Duke University Press.

———. 1977. *The Kuranko: Dimensions of Social Reality in a West African Society.* London: C. Hurst.

———. 1974. "The Structure and Significance of Kuranko Clanship." *Africa* 44, 4: 397–415.

Jacobs, Susie M., Ruth Jacobson, and Jennifer Marchbank. 2000. *States of Conflict: Gender, Violence and Resistance.* New York: Zed Books.

Kalous, Milan, ed. 1974. *Cannibals and Tongo Players of Sierra Leone.* Auckland: M. Kalous.

Kandeh, Jimmy D. 2002. "Subaltern Terror in Sierra Leone." In *Africa in Crisis: New Challenges and Possibilities,* edited by T. Zack-Williams, D. Frost and A. Thompson, 179–95. London: Pluto Press.

———. 1992. "Politicization of Ethnic Identities in Sierra Leone." *African Studies Review* 35, 1: 81–99.

Kaniki, M. H. Y. 1973. "Attitudes and Reactions towards the Lebanese in Sierra Leone during the Colonial Period." *Canadian Journal of African Studies* 7, 1: 97–113.

Kaplan, Robert D. 1994. "The Coming Anarchy: How Scarcity, Crime, Overpopulation, and Disease Are Rapidly Destroying the Social Fabric of Our Planet." *Atlantic Monthly,* February, 44–76.

Keen, David. 2005. *Conflict and Collusion in Sierra Leone.* Oxford: James Currey.

———. 2000. "War, Crime, and Access to Resources." In *War, Hunger, and Displacement,* edited by E. W. Nafziger, F. Stewart, and R. Väyrynen, vol. 1, 284–304. Oxford: Oxford University Press.

Kelly, Liz. 2000. "Wars against Women: Sexual Violence, Sexual Politics, and the Militarised State." In *States of Conflict: Gender, Violence and Resistance,* edited by S. M. Jacobs, R. Jacobson and J. Marchbank, 45–65. New York: Zed Books.

Kelsall, Tim. 2005. "Truth, Lies, Ritual: Preliminary Reflections on the Truth and Reconciliation Commission in Sierra Leone 2005." *Human Rights Quarterly* 27, 2: 361–91.

Kennedy, Deseriee. 2002. "Decolonizing Culture: The Media, Black Women, and Law." In *Stepping Forward: Black Women in Africa and the Americas,* edited by C. Higgs, B. A. Moss and E. R. Fergusson, 257–70. Athens, Ohio: Ohio University Press.

King, Jamesina. n.d. "Political and Legal Status of Women—A Historical Perspective." Paper presented at the Truth and Reconciliation Commission: The Situation of Women and Girls in the Preconflict, Conflict, and Postconflict Sierra Leone, Freetown, Sierra Leone.

Koeonig, Dorean Marguerite. 1994. "Women and Rape in Ethnic Conflict and War." *Hastings Women's Law Review* 5, 2.

Kopytoff, Igor. 1987. "The Internal African Frontier: The Making of African Political Culture." In *The African Frontier: The Reproduction of Traditional African Societies,* edited by Igor Kopytoff, 3–84. Bloomington: Indiana University Press.

Kup, A. P. 1972. "John Clarkson and the Sierra Leone Company." *International Journal of African Historical Studies* 5, 2: 203–20.

Leach, Melissa. 1994. *Rainforest Relations: Gender and Resource Use among the Mende of Gola, Sierra Leone.* Edinburgh: Edinburgh University Press.

Linden, R. Ruth. 1993. *Making Stories, Making Selves: Feminist Reflections on the Holocaust.* Columbus: Ohio State University.

Lindsey, Charlotte. 2000. "Women and War." *International Review of the Red Cross* 839: 561–79.

Little, Kenneth L. 1975. "Africa's Women—Traditional or Liberated?" *West Africa* (14 July): 799–801.

———. 1973. *African Women in Towns: An Aspect of Africa's Social Revolution.* Cambridge: Cambridge University Press.

———. 1951. *The Mende of Sierra Leone: A West African People in Transition.* London: Routledge and Kegan Paul.

———. 1948. "Social Change and Social Class in the Sierra Leone Protectorate." *American Journal of Sociology* 54, 1: 10–21.

Löfving, Staffan. 2005. "Escaping Vulnerability by Violent Means: Terrorism and State Terror in an Age of Insecurity." Paper presented at the conference, Structures of Vulnerability, Stockholm, January 2005.

———. 2002. "An Unpredictable Past: Guerrillas, Mayas, and the Location of Oblivion in War-Torn Guatemala." Ph.D. thesis, Uppsala University.

MacCormack, Carol P. 1983. "Human Leopards and Crocodiles: Political Meanings of Categorical Ambiguities." In *Ethnography of Cannibalism,* edited by P. Brown and D. Tuzin, 51–60. Washington, DC: Society for Psychological Anthropology.

———. 1977. "Wono: Institutionalized Dependency in Sherbro Descent Groups (Sierra Leone)." In *Slavery in Africa: Historical and Anthropological Perspectives,* edited by S. Miers and I. Kopytoff, 181–204. Madison: University of Wisconsin Press.

———. 1974. "Madam Yoko: Ruler of the Kpa Mende Confederacy." In *Woman, Culture, and Society,* edited by M. Z. Rosaldo and L. Lamphere, 173–87. Stanford: Stanford University Press.

Maček, Ivana. 2000. *War Within: Everyday Life in Sarajevo under Siege.* Vol. 29. Uppsala Studies in Cultural Anthropology. Uppsala: Acta Universitatis Upsaliensis.

Malan, Mark. 2003. "The Challenge of Justice and Reconciliation." In *Sierra Leone: Building the Road to Recovery,* edited by M. Malan, S. Meek, T. Thusi, J. Ginifer and P. Coker, 139–59. Pretoria, South Africa: Institute for Security Studies.

Malkki, Liisa H. 1995. "Refugees and Exile: From 'Refugee Studies' To the National Order of Things." *Annual Review of Anthropology* 24: 495–523.

Mama, Amina. 1997. "Shedding the Masks and Tearing the Veils: Cultural Studies for a Post-Colonial Africa." In *Engendering African Social Sciences,* edited by A. Imam, A. Mama and F. Sow, 61–80. Dakar: CODESRIA.

Mansaray, Binta. 2000. "Women against Weapons: A Leading Role for Women in Disarmament." In *Bound to Cooperate: Conflict, Peace, and People in Sierra Leone,* edited by A. Ayissi and R-E. Poulton, 139–62. Geneva: United Nations Institute for Disarmament Research.

Martin, Sarah. 2005. "Must Boys Be Boys? Ending Sexual Exploitation and Abuse in UN Peacekeeping Missions." Refugees International.

Mattingly, Cheryl. 2000. "Emergent Narratives." In *Narrative and the Cultural Construction of Illness and Healing,* edited by C. Mattingly and L. C. Garro, 181–211. Berkeley: University of California Press.

Mattingly, Cheryl, and Linda C. Garro. 2000. *Narrative and the Cultural Construction of Illness and Healing.* Berkeley: University of California Press.

Mazurana, Dyan, and Khristopher Carlson. 2004. "From Combat to Community: Women and Girls of Sierra Leone." Washington, DC: Women Waging Peace Policy Commission.

Mazurana, Dyan, Susan A. McKay, Khristopher C. Carlson, and Janel C. Kasper. 2002. "Girls in Fighting Forces and Groups: Their Recruitment, Participation, Demobilization, and Reintegration." *Peace and Conflict: Journal of Peace Psychology* 8: 97–123.

Mazurana, Dyan, Angela Raven-Roberts, and Jane Parpart. 2005. *Gender, Conflict, and Peacekeeping.* Oxford: Rowman and Littlefield.

McC. Lewin, Carroll. 1993. "Negotiated Selves in the Holocaust." *Ethos* 21, 3: 295–318.

McKay, Susan. 2007. "Girls as 'Weapons of Terror' in Northern Uganda and Sierra Leonean Fighting Forces." *Studies in Conflict and Terrorism* 28, 5: 385–97.

———. 2004. "Reconstructing Fragile Lives: Girls' Social Reintegration in Northern Uganda and Sierra Leone." *Gender and Development* 12, 3: 19–30.

McKay, Susan, and Dyan Mazurana. 2004. *Where Are the Girls? Girls in Fighting Forces in Northern Uganda, Sierra Leone, and Mozambique: Their Lives during and after War.* Quebec: Rights and Democracy.

Migeod, Frederick William Hugh. 1925. "A View of the Colony of Sierra Leone." *Journal of the Royal African Society* 25, 97: 1–9.

Moore, Henrietta. 1994. *A Passion for Difference.* Oxford: Polity Press.

Moorehead, Caroline. 1995. "Hostage to a Male Agenda: From Somalia to the Balkans, from Rwanda to Colombia, Rape Has Become the Ultimate Weapon in the Dying Century's Wars." *Index on Censorship* 24: 54–69.

Moran, Mary H. 2006. *Liberia: The Violence of Democracy.* Philadelphia: University of Pennsylvania Press.

———. 1995. "Warriors or Soldiers? Masculinity and Ritual Transvestism in the Liberian Civil War." In *Feminism, Nationalism, and Militarism,* edited by C. R. Sutton, 73–88. Arlington, VA: Association for Feminist Anthropology/American Anthropological Association.

Morris, Patricia T. 1993. "Women, Resistance, and the Use of Force in South Africa." In *Women and the Use of Military Force,* edited by R. H. Howes and M. R. Stevenson, 185–206. Boulder, CO: Lynne Rienner.

Moser, Caroline O. N., and Fiona C. Clark, eds. 2001. *Victims, Perpetrators, or Actors? Gender, Armed Conflict and Political Violence.* London: Zed Books.

Mynster Christensen, Maya. 2007. "From Jungle to Jungle: Former Fighters Maneuvering within Landscapes of Instability in Post-War Sierra Leone." M.Phil. thesis, University of Copenhagen, Denmark.

Nenadic, Natalie. 1996. "Femicide: A Framework for Understanding Genocide." In *Radically Speaking: Feminism Reclaimed,* edited by D. Bell and R. Klein, 456–64. Melbourne, Australia: Spinster Press.

Niall, P., A. S. Johnson, and Juergen Mueller. 2002. "Updating the Accounts: Global Mortality of the 1918–1920 "Spanish" Influenza Pandemic." *Bulletin of the History of Medicine* 76: 105–15.

Niarchos, Catherine N. 1995. "Women, War, and Rape: Challenges Facing the International Tribunal for the Former Yugoslavia." *Human Rights Quarterly* 17, 4.

Nordstrom, Carolyn. 2004. *Shadows of War: Violence, Power, and International Profiteering in the Twenty-First Century.* Berkeley: University of California Press.

———. 1997a. *A Different Kind of War Story.* Philadelphia: University of Pennsylvania Press.

———. 1997b. *Girls and Warzones: Troubling Questions.* Uppsala: Life and Peace Institute.

Nyerges, A. Endre. 1992. "The Ecology of Wealth-in-People: Agriculture, Settlement, and Society on the Perpetual Frontier." *American Anthropologist* 94, 4: 860–81.

O'Flaherty, Michael. 2004. "Sierra Leone's Peace Process: The Role of the Human Rights Community." *Human Rights Quarterly* 26: 29–62.

Ojukutu-Macauley, Sylvia. 1997. "Religion, Gender, and Education in Northern Sierra Leone, 1896–1992." In *Islam and Trade in Sierra Leone,* edited by A. Jalloh and D. E. Skinner, 87–117. Trenton, NJ: Africa World Press.

Olujic, Maria B. 1998. "Embodiment of Terror: Gendered Violence in Peacetime and Wartime in Croatia and Bosnia-Herzegovina." *Medical Anthropology Quarterly* 12, 1: 31–50.

Oppong, Christine, ed. 1983. *Female and Male in West Africa.* London: Allen and Unwin.

Orford, Anne. 2003. *Reading Humanitarian Intervention: Human Rights and the Use of Force in International Law.* Cambridge: Cambridge University Press.

Ottenberg, Simon. 1994. "Male and Female Secret Societies among the Bafodea Limba of Northern Sierra Leone." In *Religion in Africa: Experience and Expression,* edited by T. D. Blakely, W.E.A. v. Beek, and D. L. Thomson, 363–87. London: James Currey.

Peace Agreement between the Government of Sierra Leone and the Revolutionary United Front of Sierra Leone ("Lomé Peace Accord"). 1999.

Persson, Mariam. 2005. " 'In Their Eyes We'll Always Be Rebels'—a Minor Field Study of Female Ex-Combatants in Sierra Leone." Uppsala: Uppsala University, Developments Studies.

Peters, Krijn. 2006. "Footpaths to Reintegration: Armed Conflict, Youth, and the Rural Crisis in Sierra Leone." Ph.D. thesis, Wageningen University.

Peters, Krijn, and Paul Richards. 1998a. "Fighting with Open Eyes: Youth Combatants Talking About War in Sierra Leone." In *Rethinking the Trauma of War,* edited by P. Bracken and C. Petty, 76–111. London: Free Association.

———. 1998b. "Why We Fight: Voices of Youth Combatants in Sierra Leone." *Africa* 68: 183–210.

Physicians for Human Rights. 2002. "War-Related Sexual Violence in Sierra Leone: A Population-Based Assessment." Washington, DC: Physicians for Human Rights (PHR).

PRIDE. 2002. "Ex-Combatant Views of the Truth and Reconciliation Commission and the Special Court for Sierra Leone." Freetown, Sierra Leone: PRIDE in collaboration with the International Center for Transitional Justice.

Reno, William. 2000. "Liberia and Sierra Leone: The Competition for Patronage in Resource-Rich Economies." In *War, Hunger, and Displacement: The Origins of Humanitarian Emergencies,* edited by E. W. Nafziger, F. Stewart, and R. Väyrynen, 231–59. Oxford: Oxford University Press.

Reno, William, and M. Alpha Bah. 1997. "Corruption and State Politics in Sierra Leone." *The International Journal of African Historical Studies* 30, 1: 200.

Richards, Paul. 2005a. "Green Book Millenarians? The Sierra Leone War within the Perspective of an Anthropology of Religion." In *Religion and African Civil Wars,* edited by N. Kastfelt, 119–46. London: Hurst.

——. 2005b. "To Fight or to Farm? Agrarian Dimensions of the Mano River Conflicts (Liberia and Sierra Leone)." *African Affairs* 104, 417: 571–90.

——, ed. 2005c. *No Peace, No War: An Anthropology of Contemporary Armed Conflicts.* Oxford: James Currey.

——. 2002. "Youth, Food, and Peace: A Reflection on Some African Security Issues at the Millennium." In *Africa in Crisis: New Challenges and Possibilities,* edited by T. Zack-Williams, D. Frost, and A. Thompson, 29–39. London: Pluto Press.

——. 1996. *Fighting for the Rain Forest: War, Youth, and Resources in Sierra Leone.* Oxford: James Currey.

——. 1995. "Rebellion in Liberia and Sierra Leone: A Crisis of Youth?" In *Conflict in Africa,* edited by O. Furley, 134–70. London: Taurus Academic Studies.

——. 1994. "Videos and Violence on the Periphery." *IDS Bulletin* 25, 2: 88.

Riddell, Barry. 2005. "Sierra Leone: Urban-Elite Bias, Atrocity, and Debt." *Review of African Political Economy* 103: 115–33.

——. 1985a. "Beyond the Geography of Modernization: The State as a Redistributive Mechanism in Independent Sierra Leone." *Canadian Journal of African Studies* 19, 3: 529–45.

——. 1985b. "Internal and External Forces Acting upon Disparities in Sierra Leone." *Journal of Modern African Studies* 23, 3: 389–406.

Rosen, David M. 2005. *Armies of the Young: Child Soldiers in War and Terrorism,* New Brunswick, NJ: Rutgers University Press.

Ross, Fiona. 2005. "Women and the Politics of Identity: Voices in the South African Truth and Reconciliation." In *Violence and Belonging: The Quest for Identity in Post-Colonial Africa,* edited by V. Broch-Due, 214–35. London: Routledge.

——. 2003. *Bearing Witness: Women and the Truth and Reconciliation Commission in South Africa.* London: Pluto Press.

Ruddick, Sara. 1993. "Toward a Feminist Peace Politics." In *Gendering War Talk,* edited by M. Cooke and A. Woollacott, 109–27. Princeton, NJ: Princeton University Press.

——. 1989. *Maternal Thinking: Toward a Politics of Peace.* Boston: Beacon Press.

Sampson, Steven. 2003. "From Reconciliation to Coexistence." *Public Culture* 15, 1: 181–86.

Save the Children. 2005. "Forgotten Casualties of War: Girls in Armed Conflict." London: Save the Children.

Scarry, Elaine. 1985. *The Body in Pain: The Making and Unmaking of the World.* Oxford: Oxford University Press.

Scheper-Hughes, Nancy. 1992. *Death without Weeping: The Violence of Everyday Life in Brazil.* Berkeley: University of California Press.

Schott, Robin May. 1996. "Gender and 'Postmodern War.'" *Hypatia* 11, 4: 19–29.

Schroven, Anita. 2005. "Choosing between Different Realities: Gender Mainstreaming and Self-Images of Women after Armed Conflict in Sierra Leone." M.A. thesis, Georg-August-Universität.

Seifert, Ruth. 1996. "The Second Front: The Logic of Sexual Violence in Wars." *Women's Studies International Forum* 19.

Sered, Susan Starr. 1994. *Priestess, Mother, Sacred Sister: Religions Dominated by Women.* New York: Oxford University Press.

Shaw, Rosalind. 2005. "Rethinking Truth and Reconciliation Commissions: Lessons from Sierra Leone." Washington, DC: United States Institute for Peace.

———. 2002. *Memories of the Slave Trade: Ritual and the Historical Imagination in Sierra Leone.* Chicago: University of Chicago Press.

———. 2001. "Cannibal Transformations: Colonialism and Commodification in the Sierra Leone Hinterland." In *Magical Interpretations, Material Realities: Modernity, Witchcraft, and the Occult in Postcolonial Africa,* edited by H. L. Moore and T. Sanders, 50–70. London: Routledge.

———. 1997. "The Production of Witchcraft/Witchcraft as Production: Memory, Modernity, and the Slave Trade in Sierra Leone." *American Ethnologist* 24, 4: 856–76.

———. 1996. "The Politician and the Diviner: Divination and the Consumption of Power in Sierra Leone." *Journal of Religion in Africa* 26, 1: 30–55.

Shepler, Susan. 2005. "Conflicted Childhoods: Fighting over Child Soldiers in Sierra Leone." Ph.D. thesis, University of California, Berkeley.

———. 2002. "Post-War Trajectories for Girls Associated with the Fighting Forces in Sierra Leone." English language version of "Les Filles-Soldats: Trajectoires d'apres-guerre en Sierra Leone," in *Politique Africaine* 88: 49–62.

Siddle, D. J. 1968. "War Towns in Sierra Leone: A Study in Social Change." *Journal of the International African Institute* 38, 1: 47–56.

Sideris, Tina. 2001. "Rape in War and Peace: Social Context, Gender, Power and Identity." In *The Aftermath: Women in Post-Conflict Transformation,* edited by S. Meintjes, A. Pillay, and M. Turshen, 142–58. London: Zed Books.

Skinner, David E. 1978. "Mande Settlement and the Development of Islamic Institutions in Sierra Leone." *International Journal of African Historical Studies* 11, 1: 32–62.

———. 1976. "Islam and Education in the Colony and Hinterland of Sierra Leone (1750–1914)." *Canadian Journal of African studies* 10, 3: 499–520.

Skinner, Elliot P. 1999. "Child Soldiers in Africa: A Disaster for Future Families." *International Journal on World Peace* 6, 1: 7–17.

Smillie, Ian, Lansana Gberie, and Ralph Hazleton. 2000. "The Heart of the Matter: Sierra Leone, Diamonds, and Human Security." Ottawa: Partnership Africa Canada (PAC).

Sørensen, Birgitte. 1998. "Women and Post-Conflict Reconstruction: Issues and Sources." Geneva: War-torn Societies Project (WSP).

Specht, Irma. 2006. "Experiences of Girl-Combatants in Liberia." Geneva: International Labor Office, Program on Crisis Response and Reconstruction.

Spitzer, Leo. 1974. *The Creoles of Sierra Leone: Responses to Colonialism, 1870–1945.* Madison: University of Wisconsin Press.

———. 1968. "The Mosquito and Segregation in Sierra Leone." *Canadian Journal of African Studies* 2, 1: 49–61.

Spitzer, Leo, and LaRay Denzer. 1973. "I. T. A. Wallace-Johnson and the West African Youth League: The Sierra Leone Period, 1938–1945." *International Journal of African Historical Studies* 6, 4: 565–601.

Squire, Chris. 2000. "Bound to Cooperate: Peacemaking and Power-Sharing in Sierra Leone." In *Bound to Cooperate: Conflict, Peace, and People in Sierra Leone,* edited by

A. Ayissi and R-E. Poulton, 49–66. Geneva: United Nations Institute for Disarmament Research (UNIDIR).

Staunton, Irene, ed. 1990. *Mothers of the Revolution: The War Experiences of Thirty Zimbabwean Women.* London: James Currey.

Stone, Linda. 2006. *Kinship and Gender: An Introduction.* Boulder, CO: Westview Press.

Swiss, S., and J. E. Giller. 1993. "Rape as a Crime of War: A Medical Perspective." *JAMA* 270, 5: 612–15.

Taylor, Christopher C. 1999. "A Gendered Genocide: Tutsi Women and Hutu Extremists in the 1994 Rwanda Genocide." *PoLAR* 22, 1: 42–54.

Tejan-Cole, Abdul O. B. 1998. "Women and Land Law in Sierra Leone." In *Women and Law in West Africa: Situational Analysis of Some Key Issues Affecting Women,* edited by A. Kuenyehia, 230–36. Accra, Ghana: Human Rights Study Center, University of Ghana.

Thomas, V. V., H. Harding, and A. S. Kabbah. 1998. "Inheritance in Sierra Leone." In *Women and Law in West Africa: Situational Analysis of Some Key Issues Affecting Women,* edited by A. Kuenyehia, 169–78. Accra, Ghana: Human Rights Study Center, University of Ghana.

Thompson, Martha. 2006. "Women, Gender, and Conflict: Making the Connections." *Development in Practice* 16, 3–4: 342–53.

Tishkov, Valery. 2004. *Chechnya: Life in a War-Torn Society.* Berkeley: University of California Press.

Trawick, Margaret. 1990. *Notes on Love in a Tamil Family.* Berkeley: University of California Press.

TRC (Sierra Leone Truth and Reconciliation Commission). 2004. "Report of the Sierra Leone Truth and Reconciliation Commission." Freetown, Sierra Leone

Turshen, Meredeth. 2001. "The Political Economy of Rape: An Analysis of Systematic Rape and Sexual Abuse of Women during Armed Conflict in Africa." In *Victims, Perpetrators, or Actors? Gender, Armed Conflict, and Political Violence,* edited by C. O. N. Moser and F. C. Clark, 55–68. London: Zed Books.

Turshen, Meredeth, and Clotilde Twagiramariya, eds. 1998. *What Women Do in War Time: Gender and Conflict in Africa.* London: Zed Books.

UNDP. 2007. "Human Development Report." New York: UNDP/Human Development Report Office.

———. 2005. "Human Development Report." New York: UNDP/Human Development Report Office.

———. 2004. "Liberia Disarmament, Demobilisation and Reintegration Program, Activity Report." New York: UNDP.

UNFPA (United Nations Population Fund). 2005. "State of World Population. The Promise of Equality: Gender Equity, Reproductive Health, and the Millennium Development Goals." New York: UNFPA.

UNHCR/Save the Children UK. 2002. "Sexual Violence and Exploitation: The Experience of Refugee Children in Liberia, Guinea, and Sierra Leone." New York: UNHCR/Save the Children UK.

UNICEF. 2005. "The Impact of Conflict on Women and Girls in West and Central Africa and the UNICEF Response." New York: UNICEF.

———. 2004. "State of the World's Children." New York: UNICEF.

UN Security Council. 2000. "Resolution 1325." New York: UN.

Utas, Mats. 2006. "War, Violence, and Videotapes: Media and Localised Ideoscapes of the Liberian Civil War." In *Violence, Political Culture, and Development in Africa,* edited by P. Kaarsholm, 161–80. Oxford: James Currey.

———. 2005. "Victimcy, Girlfriending, Soldiering: Tactic Agency in a Young Woman's Social Navigation of the Liberian War Zone." *Anthropological Quarterly* 78, 2: 403–30.

———. 2003. "Sweet Battlefields: Youth and the Liberian Civil War." Ph.D. thesis, Uppsala University.

van der Laan, H. L. 1975. *The Lebanese Traders in Sierra Leone.* Paris: Mouton.

West, Harry G. 2000. "Girls with Guns: Narrating the Experience of War of Frelimo's 'Female Detachment.'" *Anthropological Quarterly* 73, 4: 180–94.

White, E. Frances. 1987. *Sierra Leone's Settler Women Traders: Women on the Afro-European Frontier.* Ann Arbor: University of Michigan Press.

———. 1981. "Creole Women Traders in the Nineteenth Century." *International Journal of African Historical Studies* 14, 4: 626–42.

Williams, Paul. 2001. "Fighting for Freetown: British Military Intervention in Sierra Leone." *Contemporary Security Policy* 22, 3: 140–68.

Wilson, Richard A. 2001. "Children and War in Sierra Leone: A West African Diary." *Anthropology Today* 17, 5: 20–23.

Women's Commission for Refugee Women and Children. 2002. "Disarmament, Demobilization, and Reintegration, and Gender-Based Violence in Sierra Leone." New York: Women's Commission for Refugee Women and Children.

Zack-Williams, Alfred. 1995. *Tributors, Supporters, and Merchant Capital: Mining and Underdevelopment in Sierra Leone.* Aldershot, UK: Avebury.

Zack-Williams, Tunde. 2002. "Africa at the Millennium." In *Africa in Crisis: New Challenges and Possibilities,* edited by T. Zack-Williams, D. Frost, and A. Thompson, 1–14. London: Pluto Press.

Zeid al-Hussein, Prince Zied Ra'ad. 2005. "A Comprehensive Strategy to Eliminate Future Sexual Exploitation and Abuse in United Nations Peacekeeping Operations." New York: United Nations.

Index

abduction: of girls, 9, 51, 57, 116–17, 130, 216–17; interviews, 20, 26, 28, 99; narratives of, 17, 19–20, 22–23, 95–100, 103–4, 114–15, 120–23, 128–29, 151, 210

Abdullah, Ibrahim, 37, 41, 42, 43, 47, 100, 126

AFRC. *See* Armed Forces Revolutionary Council

age, 27, 59, 74; at abduction, 96, 115; generational differences, 60–61, 182–86; hierarchies, 42–43, 71–72, 90, 92, 95, 107, 118, 123, 166, 239, 243, 254; at marriage, 83–85

agency, 18, 112, 131, 149–51, 153, 250, 263n15

agriculture, 45, 58, 71, 74–75, 83, 88–89, 105, 186, 187, 197–98; cash crops, 39, 67; during colonialism, 37–38; during the war, 112, 116; role in economy, 38, 65–66, 68; subsistence, 39, 61–62, 65–66; women in, 60, 67, 69, 76, 116–17, 157, 195, 239, 259n16, 262n10

All People's Congress, 44, 45–46

amputations, 6, 22, 31, 51, 54, 109, 120, 143, 145, 148, 150

APC. *See* All People's Congress

Aretxaga, Begoña, 8, 10, 12, 15, 16, 104, 126, 150

Argenti-Pillen, Alex, 18, 25, 56, 149

Armed Forces Revolutionary Council, 48–50, 118, 126, 178, 256n16, 258n34

big men, 35, 43, 72, 79, 107, 159, 202, 238

big women, 72, 202–3, 216, 246

Bledsoe, Caroline, 6, 44, 69, 76, 79, 115, 116, 201–2, 226

bush: and femininity, 218; perceptions of, 14, 101, 152, 214–16; rebel use of, 46, 100, 110

bush marriage, 2, 29, 51, 93, 110–17, 128, 152, 165, 200, 214, 227, 240; formalization of, 2, 219–23, 237

bush wives: ambiguous position of, 57, 216; logistical role, 67, 116–17, 123, 157–58, 179, 239; loyalty to bush husband, 113, 127, 129, 220, 222, 238; rape of, 107, 113–14, 127, 129–30, 147, 240; status, 110–13